Policing Welfare

Policing Welfare

*Punitive Adversarialism
in Public Assistance*

SPENCER HEADWORTH

THE UNIVERSITY OF CHICAGO PRESS   CHICAGO AND LONDON

The University of Chicago Press, Chicago 60637
The University of Chicago Press, Ltd., London
© 2021 by The University of Chicago
All rights reserved. No part of this book may be used or reproduced in any manner
whatsoever without written permission, except in the case of brief quotations in critical
articles and reviews. For more information, contact the University of Chicago Press,
1427 E. 60th St., Chicago, IL 60637.
Published 2021
Printed in the United States of America

30 29 28 27 26 25 24 23 22 21   1 2 3 4 5

ISBN-13: 978-0-226-77922-5 (cloth)
ISBN-13: 978-0-226-77936-2 (paper)
ISBN-13: 978-0-226-77953-9 (e-book)
DOI: https://doi.org/10.7208/chicago/9780226779539.001.0001

Library of Congress Cataloging-in-Publication Data

Names: Headworth, Spencer, author.
Title: Policing welfare : punitive adversarialism in public assistance / Spencer Headworth.
Description: Chicago : The University of Chicago Press, 2021. | Includes bibliographical
    references and index.
Identifiers: LCCN 2020042827 | ISBN 9780226779225 (cloth) | ISBN 9780226779362
    (paperback) | ISBN 9780226779539 (ebook)
Subjects: LCSH: Welfare fraud investigation—United States. | Welfare fraud
    investigation—United States—Case studies. | Welfare fraud—United States. |
    Law enforcement—United States.
Classification: LCC HV95 .H385 2021 | DDC 363.25/963—dc23
LC record available at https://lccn.loc.gov/2020042827

TO BOB NELSON AND LAURA BETH NIELSEN,
WHO GOT ME WHERE I AM

Contents

Abbreviations

ADC	Aid to Dependent Children
ADH	Administrative Disqualification Hearing
AFDC	Aid to Families with Dependent Children
CVU	Central Verification Unit
DA	District Attorney
DMV	Department of Motor Vehicles
EBT	Electronic Benefit Transfer
EITC	Earned Income Tax Credit
FBI	Federal Bureau of Investigation
FNS	USDA Food and Nutrition Service
HEW	Department of Health, Education, and Welfare
HFS	Illinois Department of Healthcare and Family Services
HFSOIG	Illinois Department of Healthcare and Family Services Office of Inspector General
HHS	Health and Human Services
IEVS	Income and Eligibility Verification System
IPV	Intentional Program Violation
IRS	Internal Revenue Service
ISP	Illinois State Police
NPM	New Public Management
OIG	Office of Inspector General (unless otherwise specified, refers to USDA OIG)
OSHA	Occupational Safety and Health Administration
PRWORA	Personal Responsibility and Work Opportunity Reconciliation Act
PTI	Pretrial Intervention
SEC	Securities and Exchange Commission

SLEB	State Law Enforcement Bureau
SNAP	Supplemental Nutrition Assistance Program
SSI	Supplemental Security Income
TANF	Temporary Assistance for Needy Families
UPV	Unintentional Program Violation
USDA	United States Department of Agriculture

The Strings Attached

How much do they get? What are they saying happened? If it's a man in the home [case] . . . , what's going on?[1] Does it look like it really is something? Y'know, does his DMV [Department of Motor Vehicles] address match hers? Does his work address match hers? That's the main thing. If that's the case, "Oh look, we may have something," then let me go investigate a little bit more.

Leslie is a welfare fraud investigator. A White woman in her late thirties, she started her career working in eligibility determination for her state's public assistance agency. Now, after moving to its dedicated fraud control unit, she is responsible for investigating and substantiating clients' rule violations in the Supplemental Nutrition Assistance Program (SNAP) and Temporary Assistance for Needy Families (TANF), the largest federal nutrition and "cash" assistance programs, respectively. She detailed the process of getting a referral from a local welfare office asking her to look into potential fraud: driving by the client's home, talking to neighbors, interviewing the client, and building a case strong enough to file charges. If, after her report is compiled and reviewed, her supervisor declares, "You know what, it's a great report, let's go ahead and file charges," she says, "Yesss!" and heads to the prosecutor's office. Laughing that the prosecutors all know her by name, Leslie described this as her favorite part of her job.

Directing government assistance to needy people is fundamentally a categorization project: determining qualifying characteristics and distinguishing between the eligible and ineligible—those who merit aid and those who do not. Bureaucracies assess household composition and circumstances to determine eligibility and benefit amounts, translating families' characteristics into the state's administrative categories. The validation processes they use to check these categorizations' accuracy have become integral to need-based public assistance programs. The condition of eligibility is substantially structured by delineating legitimate members: separating people with "real" disabilities from "malingerers," people who cannot work from those who "choose idleness," and the "deserving poor" from "scam artists."[2]

Investigators like Leslie are tasked with policing these categories' boundaries. In our conversation above, she described a paradigmatic eligibility fraud case, an "information-provision offense"[3] involving failure to fulfill the duties of transparency and cooperation imposed on clients as conditions of program participation. The modal welfare fraud charge alleges a deliberate misrepresentation or omission intended to skirt eligibility rules, and investigators working in fraud units like Leslie's are responsible for compiling evidence of clients' alleged rule violations. These investigators' jurisdiction and authority are program-specific, and the default punishments for these offenses are administrative: program suspensions and disqualifications, as well as restitution orders for overpayments. As Leslie suggests, however, what begin as administrative investigations can also lead to criminal charges when fraud units refer cases to prosecutors.

Policing Welfare is the first in-depth study of welfare fraud investigation in the United States. Through case studies of five diverse states' fraud units, this book explains how the system works and why it is the way it is. Along the way, I make two central claims. First, I argue that fraud units are legal and bureaucratic responses to basic governance questions regarding the social safety net: who to help, how, and with what conditions. Second, I argue that this response has significant effects, particularly for poor people.

The statutory foundation for fraud units as responses to governance questions is in federal law requiring state-level assistance agencies to maintain these investigative entities.[4] This mandate reflects the idea that eligibility for aid should not derive strictly from material need but should also require diligent rule compliance. In this sense, fraud units resemble other conditions of participation in means-tested public assistance programs, such as work requirements and drug testing. Dedicated fraud units, however, stand out as a particularly punitive response to social safety net administration questions, using investigation and penalization to perform information verification and program oversight functions. Like state-level statutes that specifically criminalize welfare fraud offenses, fraud units are legal and bureaucratic measures that fundamentally treat clients' rule violations as a crime problem, not a public administration problem.[5] This means that fraud workers are trained and socialized to think and act punitively, embracing the criminal legal system's core principles of individual responsibility, deterrence, and just deserts.

Dedicated fraud investigation units demonstrate *punitive adversarialism* within the US welfare system. Punitive adversarialism refers to the institutionalization of surveillance, investigation, formal charging processes, and punishments within bureaucratic structure. The word *adversarial* does double duty here. First, it references the word's jurisprudential meaning, describing a system that uses oppositional contests between parties to adjudicate disputes and assess legal liabilities.[6] As Robert Kagan notes, US welfare programs "tend to rely on detailed rules and rights, enforceable in court."[7] In 1970's *Goldberg v. Kelly*, the US Supreme Court formalized clients' right to a hearing before agencies could terminate their welfare benefits due to ineligibility.[8] Administrative fraud charges are adjudicated in Administrative Disqualification Hearings, and criminal charges are subject to criminal proceedings. Adversarial contests regarding welfare eligibility and rule breaking offer some rights-claiming opportunities; the reliance on rules and rights, however, also pressures officials to pursue comprehensive client oversight and enforce punctilious rule adherence. Dedicated fraud control units constitute specialized instruments for advancing these goals.

The "punitive" qualifier connotes that "adversarial" also carries its colloquial meaning in the concept of punitive adversarialism. That is, punitive adversarialism entails animosity and conflict. Beyond their designated bureaucratic function as tools for launching and substantiating formal rule violation charges, fraud units entrench an antagonistic stance toward program applicants and clients. Friction and enmity often characterize legal processes that qualify as adversarial in the jurisprudential sense;[9] punitive adversarialism, though, describes structures and practices that inherently saturate the relationship between the bureaucracy and its clients with antagonism. Indeed, despite litigation aimed at protecting clients' rights, relative to its international counterparts, the

US system is "more suspicious of fraud and abuse, more demeaning and legalistic, and difficult for recipients to deal with."[10]

Under punitive adversarialism, organizational structures and norms functionally treat administrative problems as crime problems and deviance within bureaucratic systems as crime or crime-adjacent. Punitive adversarialism within welfare bureaucracies tracked with the increased punitiveness of the criminal legal system in the late twentieth and early twenty-first centuries. Like changes in conventional policing, prosecution, and sentencing, legal and administrative interventions that position agencies and clients antagonistically create circumstances conducive to de jure and de facto criminalization of individuals, groups, and statuses, such as poverty.

Policing Welfare's second claim highlights such outcomes, arguing that punitive adversarialism within public assistance carries important consequences for the poor. The suspicion, surveillance, and scrutiny associated with punitive adversarialism shape clients' experiences in ostensibly helping-oriented agencies, producing suspensions, disqualifications, and criminal prosecutions. These measures increase pressure on clients to adopt (or at least profess) normative thinking and behavior.[11] They also exacerbate stigmatization and penalization. Like other forms of law, welfare law "regulates behavior . . . expresses collective versions of the social good, of future goals, of moral values, [and] punishes and marginalizes those who deviate from social norms."[12] As specialized instruments for investigating clients and enabling their punishment, fraud units bring the characteristic principles of the criminal legal system to bear in this generally law-saturated environment.[13]

Thus the title of *Policing Welfare* has multiple meanings. Fundamentally, the title suggests the inquiry's basic subject matter: the policing task that fraud workers fulfill through detecting, investigating, and substantiating clients' alleged rule violations. But it also refers to the way fraud units contribute to the "policing" of welfare in a larger sense. Creating dedicated fraud units as a response to questions about how the social safety net should be administered furthers the proliferation of punitive logics, methods, and actors and generates significant legal, material, and social risks for clients. Such bureaucratic structures and procedures facilitate and further the criminalization of poverty.[14] They also encourage self-policing, intensifying pressure on clients to adopt behaviors and self-presentations that evince "deserving poor" status through demonstrating compliance and personal responsibility.[15]

Substance and Symbolism

Substantively, fraud units provide public assistance agencies with dedicated oversight staff, helping them manage their client populations and enforce program rules. More concretely, they offer a means for denying benefits; "pre-certification" or "front-end" fraud detection efforts help agencies avoid issuing benefits to clients who are determined ineligible, and post-certification fraud charges allow clients to be temporarily suspended or permanently disqualified. Fraud units also help recoup client overpayments. And, through referring cases to prosecutors and providing supporting evidence, administrative fraud control units also create avenues to criminal charges.

From clients' perspective, fraud units' main substantive impact is creating exposure to that host of consequences: denial of benefits, program suspension or disqualification, restitution orders, and criminal prosecution. Like the expanded focus on low-level offenses that characterizes broken windows policing,[16] welfare surveillance and fraud investigations can be described as imposing "a dense mass of petty accountability."[17] Multi-thousand-dollar overpayments sometimes arise. More commonly, the monetary stakes are low. After all, welfare benefits in the United States are relatively meager: in SNAP, where investigators spend most of their time, the average client receives about $126 in nutrition assistance per month.[18] For fraud workers, each investigation is just one out of a large caseload. Individual cases' significance may be blunted for investigators, but investigations' substantive stakes differ depending on where one stands.[19] Despite benefit amounts' modesty, SNAP is crucial to millions of families' subsistence in an era in which "cash" welfare has largely disappeared.[20] In fiscal year 2016, over forty-four million people participated in SNAP in an average month.[21] Material consequences that might seem low stakes or petty to a casual observer take on entirely different significance when understood in the context of poor families' basic survival calculus.

Punitive adversarialism also implicates clients' lives in other ways. Pushing programs further toward surveillance and punishment is likely to influence clients' perceptions of the state and its agencies. Based on fraud workers' accounts, punitive adversarialism can engender defensive and oppositional client behaviors.[22] And fraud investigations' use of snitches, neighborhood informants, and other tactics that turn clients' relationships against them for enforcement purposes threatens to weaken trust, cohesion, and networks of social support in poor neighborhoods where social ties are crucial to survival strategies.[23] Focusing enforcement efforts on such neighborhoods follows from descriptive arguments about fraud as epidemic, particularly in certain locales.

Arguments about welfare fraud's prevalence, however, often treat anecdotes as patterns and the atypical as typical, either implicitly or explicitly.[24] The US social safety net's complex federalist patchwork hinders efforts to calculate national client fraud rates, but the best available data suggest its fiscal impact is small. SNAP's random audit-based quality control system has found an overpayment rate below 3 percent in recent years, only some of which is attributable to intentional client fraud.[25] Based on the SNAP State Activity Report, the Congressional Research Service estimates that, in fiscal year 2016, barely .2 percent of SNAP benefits were lost to fraud, and just over .6 percent were overpaid due to other client errors.[26] Even allowing for the likelihood that some portion of the latter overpayments reflect intentional client fraud that states did not substantiate as such, these numbers trouble narratives that paint fraud as epidemic and high-dollar offenses as common.

Punitive adversarialism in welfare also serves more manifestly *symbolic* purposes. Fraud units' very existence signals a particular type of response to governance problems. To the general public—often framed as taxpayers—fraud enforcement emblematizes exerting control over programs and their clients. SNAP and TANF investigators police the programs most closely associated with the popular idea of "welfare."[27] These are the country's most heavily stigmatized programs, saddled with the racialized and gendered "welfare queen" stereotypes that Ronald Reagan brought to the fore.[28] Fraud units draw motivation from the same ideas about poverty's pathologies and welfare clients' dissolution, and investigators commonly depict rule violators as greedy, malicious, and over-fertile. Thus, beyond functioning as general signals of oversight and accountability, fraud units make specific moral statements[29] about monitoring and sanctioning members of devalued and demonized groups.

Beyond the general public, fraud control measures also send signals to program applicants and clients. These messages manifest from the outset of potential clients' interaction with agencies. Program applications include distinct consent and affirmation stages, detailing the state's expectation that clients will demonstrate transparency and accuracy in

Your Responsibilities

I have told the truth; I understand that I can be held criminally responsible for lying on this application.
I will have to provide papers that show that what I've told the department is true.
I will have to repay any benefits I should not have received, even if it is the department's error.
I will have to tell the department about any changes to the information I provided on my application.
I agree to cooperate with state or federal reviewers for an audit.
I agree to release my information for program needs.
I will use my benefits legally and will not sell, trade, or give away my benefits online or in person.
I have received, reviewed, and agree to the information provided in the Information Booklet.

← By agreeing to this application you are agreeing to these responsibilities

Please refer to your Information Booklet to read a complete description of your rights and responsibilities

FIGURE 1.1. Sample consent and affirmation section

reporting, as figure 1.1 illustrates. Applicants must consent to information verification and to potential agency investigations and agree to cooperate with any such investigations. Applications' consent stages warn of the potential administrative, criminal, and financial consequences of providing incomplete or inaccurate information. To fraud workers, this is a clear communication, demonstrating the state's commitment to uncovering and punishing rule violations and setting out the terms of even asking for—let alone receiving—aid.

Punitive adversarialism's symbolic aspect carries over into its consequences for program clients and other poor people. The fraud investigations suggested in applications' consent stages affect programs' climates, as do database-driven systems of client oversight and evaluation.[30] Such influence may discourage extended participation, or even applying at all, amounting to "administrative exclusion": shaping program participation in ways that dissuade even eligible and interested people from claiming benefits.[31] Among those who persist in participating, knowledge of fraud investigation efforts encourages rule adherence—or at least circumspection in rule breaking. In turn, these prospective deterrent effects are crucial to fraud workers' occupational identities and depictions of their work's importance.

Irregularity

Yet fraud punishments are irregular, lacking the certainty central to ideal-typical deterrence effects. State-level public assistance agencies share a common basic mandate under federal law—maintain units tasked with policing clients[32]—but this dictate leaves substantial leeway for states to design their fraud control interventions as they see fit. Consequently, the on-the-ground realization of fraud control units as responses to social safety net administration questions varies in size and orientation across jurisdictions. This variation is part of why I chose to examine fraud enforcement in five diverse states: this range of sites reveals both nationwide commonalities in this legal and bureaucratic response—such as default suspicion of clients and perceptions of rule breaking as intentional and internally motivated[33]—and significant discrepancies in how investigations are conceptualized and carried out. These variations include comparative degrees of focus on pre- and post-certification investigations, modes of evidence gathering, and relative zeal for pursuing criminal charges.

At the organizational and individual levels, paths to substantiated fraud charges involve multiple stages of discretionary decision-making. Agency leaders and fraud unit managers set fraud control priorities and investigation quotas; investigators select which cases to pursue and what investigative methods to employ; administrative hearing officers decide evidence's probative value; and prosecutors choose which referrals to accept for criminal charges. All these levels of discretionary action beget inter- and intrajurisdictional differences in how and why penalties are applied. With state governments, assistance bureaucracies, and street-level bureaucrats all having appreciable agency in implementation, legal ambiguity[34] and bureaucratic discretion[35] mean that the same behaviors that get one client kicked off benefits or criminally prosecuted may, in another time or place, go unsanctioned.

This irregularity also suffuses punitive adversarialism's consequences for clients. Depending on one's state or county of residence—or even which investigator receives the referral and when—clients have widely varying odds of being administratively or criminally charged. Linda Gordon observes that when clients broke income rules in Aid to Dependent Children (ADC), a precursor to TANF, "luck and skill at dissemblance, not rules, determined who got caught."[36] Chance continues to influence who is caught for fraud and how they are punished for it.

To be sure, although fraud investigations' consequences for clients are irregular, they are not random. Across contexts, investigations' success depends on evidentiary availability. Investigators' likelihoods of taking up referrals, pursuing them aggressively, and substantiating administrative or criminal charges are all positively associated with their access to incriminating information. In general, fraud investigations demonstrate informational exposure as an aspect of living in poverty. Welfare participation entails sacrificing privacy rights,[37] and fraud investigators scrutinize clients' finances and personal lives without the same legal

protections afforded criminal suspects.[38] Because successful fraud investigations rely on evidence, informational exposure shapes fraud punishments' distribution. More thoroughly documented lives are more visible
to investigators. Paper trails with state agencies thus translate into increased vulnerability to fraud charges.

Street-level bureaucrats' discretionary decisions are also susceptible
to biases related to race/ethnicity,[39] presumed criminality,[40] and even
welfare participation.[41] Racial/ethnic stereotypes figure centrally in welfare reform rhetoric, particularly anti-fraud initiatives,[42] and race and
ethnicity affect clients' experiences in means-tested public assistance
programs. Welfare programs' restrictiveness is positively correlated with
states' Black and Latino populations,[43] and Black and Latino TANF clients are more likely than their White counterparts to be sanctioned.[44]
These findings suggest the possibility of similar patterns in fraud workers' discretionary action. While fraud workers asseverate norms of ra-
cial/ethnic neutrality, they also desire to counteract fraud in perceived
"problem areas." These sorts of tendencies may concentrate enforcement on people or situations involving stereotype-confirming markers.[45]

Legacies of Welfare Conditions and Restrictions

Dedicated fraud units represent a recent stage in the long history of assessment and checking in social safety net programs, with much deeper
historical roots in the coevolution of welfare provision and poverty policing. As early as the fourteenth century, English Poor Law involved considerations of counteracting deception in applications for relief.[46] Early
public aid programs also required that claimants—including children—
work.[47] Authorities monitored the poor to prevent drinking and gam-
bling, employing the type of unannounced home inspections that would
become familiar to the poor of later centuries.[48] Over subsequent centuries and into modernity, efforts to separate "idle vagrants" from "honest
beggars" continued to figure centrally in European poverty relief.[49]

The United States followed Europe's efforts to control public assistance populations and closely monitor claims' legitimacy. Nineteenth-
and twentieth-century "outdoor relief" assistance programs entailed
suspicion and surveillance, as caseworkers assessed clients' probity and
deservingness via "suitable home" provisions.[50] Despite official race neutrality, these laws targeted poor Black mothers in practice, demonstrat-

ing how "deservingness" is constructed not just through policymaking but also through action on the ground.[51] With poverty relief programs already gendered and racialized,[52] concerns about ineligible or undeserving people receiving public assistance magnified and intersected with racial animus following post–World War II Black urban migration.[53] Municipal governments in northeastern cities launched investigations into "chiseling" in the 1930s, 1940s, and 1950s, focusing particularly on Black migrants.[54] As rolls expanded and more people of color began to participate in the 1960s and 1970s,[55] popular and political backlash gained further steam.[56] Governmental authorities explicitly invoked welfare fraud and drew direct connections between race, poverty, welfare participation, and crime. President Lyndon B. Johnson's Great Society "enthusiastically blend[ed] social welfare and punitive programs"; perceiving Black poverty as pathological, policymakers and federal funding agencies combined crime control initiatives with social welfare programming to strengthen oversight and control over the Black urban population.[57]

The politics of crime and welfare continued to overlap in the 1970s, congealing into a coordinated effort to "get tough" on poor racial/ethnic minorities.[58] Dedicated welfare fraud control units began to proliferate in this period, increasing investigations, convictions, and restitution orders.[59] In late-1970s Illinois, for instance, at least five different agencies had welfare fraud control assignments.[60] Expanded attention to the issue and bureaucratic initiatives designed to counteract it had appreciable impact; between 1970 and 1979, the annual nationwide number of fraud cases in Aid to Families with Dependent Children (AFDC, ADC's successor) referred to law enforcement increased from 7,500 to over 52,000.[61]

In 1981, Ronald Reagan swept into office on a wave of generally anti-government and specifically anti-welfare rhetoric. Calling on longstanding and deeply held stereotypes, Reagan used "parables" of welfare fraud—particularly racist, sexist images of welfare-participating women as rapacious parasites—as central talking points in his campaigns and gubernatorial and presidential administrations.[62] He built his presidency on a foundation of cutting spending and counteracting "waste, fraud, and abuse" in the public sector, and set about making significant changes to welfare policy immediately upon taking office.[63] The Reagan administration epitomized fraud's mobilization as a welfare reform keyword, as well as the marriage of institutionalized fraud control measures and broader program reorganization and retrenchment. Following a first

Reagan term full of attacks on the purported epidemic of devious, undeserving welfare cheats and corresponding cuts to social service programs, the Food Security Act of 1985 required states to create dedicated
fraud control units within their social service agencies.[64]

Restrictive changes to welfare policy continued into the 1990s. The
Personal Responsibility and Work Opportunity Reconciliation Act of
1996 (PRWORA) is particularly noteworthy. PRWORA dramatically
reshaped the public assistance system, bringing to the fore new rules,
requirements, stipulations, and penalties, and largely succeeding in ful-
filling President Bill Clinton's pledge to "end welfare as we know it."[65]
Transforming AFDC into TANF, PRWORA imposed a five-year life-
time maximum on program participation and added new requirements
to engage in paid work or face sanctions.[66] These work requirements are
specifically oriented toward the formal labor market, prioritizing any
work outside the home over caregiving for children and other unpaid
domestic labor.[67]

Perhaps most consequentially, PRWORA replaced AFDC's matching grant funding with TANF's block grant funding, establishing a set
annual federal contribution of $16.5 billion (unchanged since 1996) and
ending these benefits' "entitlement" status. Demonstrating the welfare
quality control movement's hallmark stringency focus,[68] federal incentives such as "high-performance bonuses" and "caseload reduction credits," coupled with prospective funding cuts, encouraged states to limit
expenditures and reduce client populations.[69] These measures were effective. In 1996, 68 percent of poor families received AFDC; in 2018,
23 percent received TANF.[70] Benefits' real dollar value has also declined, while housing costs and other household expenses have grown.[71]
As "cash" assistance withered, the Earned Income Tax Credit (EITC)
emerged as the largest federal poverty amelioration initiative; such tax
credits, however, are only available to those who work for pay.[72] Work requirements in direct-spending programs reflect similar motivations.[73] Together, these policy changes mean that, even as social safety net spending has actually grown, it is increasingly funneled toward a particular
subset of the poor: namely, formal labor market participants.[74]

As rule enforcement arms of the direct-spending welfare system,
fraud units are outgrowths of desires to closely control the extent of public assistance and the people to whom it is offered. While only one of the
features that make participation in means-tested programs less comfortable and hospitable, welfare fraud units are particularly noteworthy as

bureaucratic formations dedicated to enhancing client control and punishment. This legal and bureaucratic response did not emerge from a vacuum. Rather, it reflects broader developments in welfare and criminal justice, representing the convergence of efforts to "get tough" on socioeconomically marginalized people—especially poor mothers of color—through both systems.[75] Building on the long-standing historical linkage of provision and punishment,[76] paralleling developments in these policy arenas since the 1970s have driven retrenchment, surveillance, and penalization in welfare[77] and broken windows policing;[78] mass incarceration;[79] and mass probation[80] in criminal justice. As specialized mechanisms of control and punishment within public assistance systems, fraud units emblematize a unified approach to governing social marginality, crosscutting ostensibly separate state functions.[81] These uniquely concrete manifestations of the overlap between poverty governance and criminal justice have contributed to the ongoing negotiation—and dissolution—of the boundary between provision and punishment.

The Fraud Control Information Economy

Dedicated fraud control enterprises are bureaucratic instantiations of doubt regarding welfare clients' honesty and deservingness. These enterprises suggest a general assumption that many claimants are simply lazy or criminally inclined and do not really need government assistance. This assumption drives the establishment of units that not only verify eligibility but are explicitly tasked with accumulating incriminating evidence about clients' erroneous attestations and misbehaviors.

Much of today's fraud units' work entails investigating suspected mismatches between clients' "real" circumstances and official records, such that people receive benefits—or benefit amounts—for which they are ineligible. Most commonly, fraud units investigate household composition and unreported income. Household composition refers to claimed dependents who do not live in the home or unreported income-earners who actually do. Enforcement efforts in these cases often comprise attempts to ascertain whether an income-earning significant other who has not been reported as part of the household is, in fact, living there. Other unreported income cases include those in which households are receiving some form of unreported or concealed financial support: on-the-books or under-the-table paid work, for instance, or informal financial support from relatives, friends, lovers, or absent parents.[82]

Like police investigators and prosecutors, fraud control workers are therefore essentially engaged in the pursuit and accumulation of information. Indeed, fraud investigators' role spans functions associated with conventional police and criminal prosecutors. In detecting violations and gathering evidence, they act analogously to police. In presenting evidence to substantiate fraud charges in Administrative Disqualification Hearings, they act analogously to prosecutors. They also act in the vein of police or prosecutorial investigators when providing evidence to prosecutors' offices to support criminal cases.

However, the type of information they seek and its relationship to the suspected offense differ from typical criminal cases. In most conventional criminal investigations, police and prosecutors seek evidence of suspects committing proscribed acts and use circumstantial evidence to support these allegations. Eligibility fraud investigations are different: here investigators primarily seek evidence in the form of otherwise innocuous information about family arrangements and financial circumstances. The actus reus lies in the inaccurate or incomplete attestation of circumstances. To establish mens rea, the hearing officers who arbitrate administrative fraud cases generally accept a signed attestation that conflicts with independently established information—that a signed form's information doesn't match up with what the fraud investigator found. The work of establishing actus reus is therefore in substantiating the conflicting household and individual circumstances. This lends welfare fraud enforcement a distinctly intimate character. Fraud units and investigators are after the most personal details of clients' lives. Some of that information may allow investigators to officially authenticate their suspicions and allegations, such that people lose benefits and risk prosecution.

History shows that surveillance and compromised privacy are nothing new to public assistance participants. Like their predecessors, contemporary fraud investigators draw on assorted resources for information about how people pay their bills, their relationships with their children, and with whom they share their beds and how often. Contact with state agencies increases the informational resources investigators can draw upon: going to lockup, cosigning on a bond, being investigated by Child Protective Services, and having your child evaluated for special needs designation are just a few of many ways that more data about you can become available to investigators. At this juncture, databases and other technological tools play an ever-increasing role in surveillance of all kinds,[83] including welfare program oversight.[84] To varying degrees, fraud workers employ public and private databases, global positioning system tracking software, automated fraud detection systems, and surveillance of clients' online activity. Yet "old-school," embodied investigatory approaches persist. Particularly in certain states, "shoe-leather" evidence-gathering methods—including home inspections, stakeouts, and interviews with clients' friends, associates, and family members[85]— remain central to investigative toolkits.

This study's location at this temporal juncture provides a snapshot of the historical transition toward increasingly technologically sophisticated fraud control methods. Variation between the five case study states—and between investigators within states—demonstrates how punitive adversarialism differs across jurisdictions and between individual street-level bureaucrats. These variations connote significant differences in fraud units' consequences for program applicants and clients. Informational exposure and potential incrimination are universal, but modes of exposure and evidence accumulation vary substantially.

Data and Methods

Considerable scholarly effort has been invested in studies of welfare policies,[86] welfare recipients,[87] and welfare offices,[88] and in linking welfare policies with criminal justice policies.[89] This study builds on this literature, contributing, in particular, to that line of inquiry specifically devoted to welfare fraud and its policing.[90]

Welfare fraud control units tasked with detecting, investigating, and substantiating clients' violations of SNAP and TANF rules[91] generally operate within the state-level agencies responsible for administering these federal programs. There is some national variation in fraud units' jurisdiction and methods, and some units are housed in bureaucracies other than welfare agencies. The national common denominator is that state governments operate fraud control units tasked with investigating and providing evidence of client fraud in TANF and SNAP. Some of these units also oversee other social programs, including subsidized day care services and Medicaid, or enforce child support payment. Throughout this book, the term *welfare fraud units* refers to state-level SNAP and TANF anti-fraud enterprises, bracketing for the time being some of these units' other program integrity objectives, as well as the fact that some conventional criminal justice agencies contain their own welfare-focused units.[92]

Federal and state authorities have designed and implemented various client fraud–focused administrative systems within public assistance. Dedicated fraud control units are the most concrete bureaucratic establishments of such systems. These novel entities are good examples of the welfare state–criminal justice hybrid institutions that characterize neoliberal poverty management.[93] They are noteworthy for their unique bureaucratic situation: they serve a law enforcement function while operating within (or sometimes alongside) agencies nominally organized around the objective of relieving poverty. Their investigative and enforcement work occurs at the intersection of law enforcement and welfare and significantly blends the two, making them a leading case in the ongoing intermixing of poverty management and criminal punishment.

To study these unusual and important organs of social control, I began with a national overview of dedicated fraud control units. I assembled and reviewed publicly available materials about each of the fifty US states' and Washington, DC's fraud control systems,[94] and then followed up with phone and email solicitations for additional unpublished materials and further information from fraud unit representatives. This process produced baseline information about the national picture of fraud control policies and practices.

Based on these initial findings, I selected five case study states. I traveled to each to conduct in-person interviews with fraud unit representatives and gather some additional documentary evidence. I refer to each case study state with a generic one-word identifier indicating its US region: "Eastcoast," "Midatlantic," "Northeast," "Southeast," and "Southwest." Figure 1.2 depicts the geographic spread of the study; one state from each of the regions is included, save the northeasternmost region, which includes both "Northeast" and "Eastcoast." Northeast and Eastcoast are in the same part of the country and share significant cultural and ideological similarities, yet their fraud control enterprises are divergent, allowing for some useful fraud-specific comparisons.

I employ these regional generalizations to anonymize the states, which I selected based on the national variation they provide on three variables with theoretical bearing on fraud enforcement practice: the state's dominant political orientation, the size of its public benefit system,

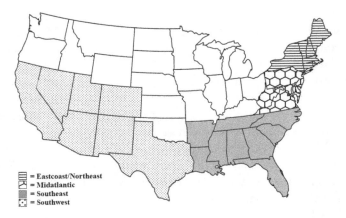

FIGURE 1.2. Case study state regions

and the punitiveness of its conventional criminal justice system, as measured by incarceration rate.[95] Choosing these sites permits me to make
comparisons and draw contrasts across states with different structures
of inequality, criminal justice practices, and public assistance policies,
and thus facilitates insights about the way welfare fraud is conceptualized and addressed in different political, legal, and administrative contexts. Therefore, my sampling strategy provides analytical leverage that
would be lacking if I were to focus on a single state or region. The descriptive overview's findings, along with interviewees' accounts of other
jurisdictions' practices, confirm that the case study states broadly capture the national variation in responses to the federal mandate for state-
level fraud enforcement.

My in-depth, semistructured interviews[96] ranged from forty-five minutes to two and a half hours. They took place in private areas (usually
closed-door offices or meeting rooms) within public assistance agency
buildings. The interviewees represent an array of those involved in welfare fraud control efforts: investigators, data specialists, supervisors,
managers, and agency leaders, including fraud control unit directors and
agency administrators. Each interview covered the same basic range of
topics: the day-to-day work of fraud control, career issues, public assistance in general, the nature of public assistance fraud, the methods and
objectives of fraud control, and connections to broader societal issues
and phenomena. To cultivate rapport and maximize response richness,
I allowed interviewees' responses to determine the order in which I ap-

proached subsequent topics. The time spent on different topics thus varies between interviews. All names are pseudonyms; appendix 1 provides
a table listing each interviewee's pseudonym, anonymized state, occupational position, approximate age, and race/ethnicity.

I recruited volunteer participants via an email message that organizational gatekeepers shared with potential interviewees. Many fraud workers who are agents of state-level fraud control units normally operate
out of local offices in their assigned regions; interviewees in this category traveled to state agency headquarters for interviews.[97] The number
of participants per state ranged from a high of fifteen in Eastcoast to a
low of four in Midatlantic.[98] Even in larger-population states with comparatively robust fraud control enterprises, fraud investigators number
in the dozens, and some states have only a handful of dedicated investigators. Thus the sample size reflects a fairly limited potential population
of interviewees.

To address the question of how rule enforcement policies work in
practice, I use case-based logic rather than the sample-based logic more
appropriate to other types of inquiries (for instance, a study of the numerable outcomes of changes in fraud enforcement policies). Therefore,
my data collection was not based on the goal of representativeness that
motivates the sampling logic best suited for descriptive questions about
populations. I collected interview data with the goal of drawing con-
clusions about the processes through which welfare fraud workers implement law and policy,[99] focusing especially on their interpretations of
their work, perspectives on clients, and the meanings they assign to their
jobs.[100] Interviewees' accounts constitute condensed narratives of experiences and the thinking surrounding them. These narratives reveal their
synthetic understandings of their occupation and their expectations for
future experiences.[101] Informational redundancy[102] across interviews, in
turn, reveals the patterns that ground the book's arguments.

Case study research is most successful when it "look[s] at extremes,
unusual circumstances, and analytically clear examples, all of which are
important not because they are representative but because they show a
process or problem in particularly clear relief."[103] Fraud units provide
an exceptionally clear empirical case for examining how provision and
punishment collide and collude in contemporary US governance. Fraud
workers' accounts offer an opportunity to understand how corresponding social policy responses are realized on the ground.

While fraud workers are positioned to reveal important things about fraud enforcement's conceptualization and realization, there are inherent limitations involved in focusing on this group and not on other parties, such as welfare clients. *Policing Welfare* builds on client-focused work—especially Kaaryn Gustafson's pioneering research[104]—and contributes an enforcement-side perspective on the system. Fraud workers are this setting's agents of formal social control; accordingly, they are best situated to speak to patterns and points of emphasis in enforcement. And they are the workforce responsible for the translation of "law in books" to "law in action,"[105] moving from general policy parameters to specific practices. As legal authorities, fraud workers' interpretations, perceptions, and attitudes hold substantial power, shaping the welfare system's legal-bureaucratic edifice and determining clients' experiences.[106]

This approach requires careful consideration of interviewees' accounts. I cannot simply take responses at face value.[107] Rather, I have set out to understand why things were said—or not said—within context. Without a doubt, self-presentation strategies and social acceptability bias shaped what interviewees chose to report and how they chose to report it. Their recollections and representations are necessarily partial and may privilege some things over others. More dramatic or recent experiences may be more cognitively accessible, and experiential valences can shape recall.[108] Such considerations give cause for caution in interpreting even interviewees' accounts of their own work.[109] Interviewees' accounts, however, are invaluable for pinpointing what respondents find meaningful.[110] Throughout research and writing, I critically analyzed responses to build understandings of both the day-to-day realities of fraud enforcement practice *and* how fraud workers conceptualize, identify with, and present their jobs. All of these aspects of the interview data reveal important things about the social settings under examination. In concert, they yield a synthetic portrait of the welfare fraud control system.

Study Overview and Plan of the Book

This book contributes to existing literatures in law and society, punishment and social control, poverty management, and public policy, not by examining policy creation and change or the quantifiable outcomes of policymaking, but by examining the organizational context within which policies are put into action, or how written policy becomes "real" through application. In so doing, it complements other research examining what Evelyn Brodkin[111] calls the "missing middle" in welfare research: the realm of on-the-ground policy implementation.[112] Previous studies dealing specifically with welfare fraud and rule enforcement have focused primarily on clients' experiences[113] and the integration of mechanisms of control into mainstream public assistance practices.[114] This, then, is the first major study of public assistance systems' dedicated enforcement bodies, documenting their distinct political history, organizational operation, and social impact.

Fraud units' value as a research topic lies in the insights they permit about how provision and punishment commingle in the contemporary United States. Welfare systems and carceral systems evolved together, and they remain tightly linked components of the state's poverty management regime.[115] *Policing Welfare* adds to its theoretical and empirical forebears an examination of a supremely concrete intersection of the welfare and criminal justice systems, revealing not just how the two sides reflect and draw on each other but how they meet, overlap, and cooperate in a unique bureaucratic entity.

Welfare state theorist Gøsta Esping-Andersen cautions that, in liberal welfare states like the United States, "enthusiasm for the needs-tested approach, targeting government aid solely at the genuinely poor, is inherently logical but creates the unanticipated result of social stigma and dualism."[116] In addition to these consequences, this study demonstrates how the means-tested approach generates pressure to establish verification protocols and engage in eligibility category policing. The fraud detection, investigation, and punishment at the core of this study represent the intersection of Esping-Andersen's social stigma and dualism and the impetus for verification and category policing. Dedicated fraud enforcement units result from desires to authoritatively and verifiably populate eligibility categories and police their boundaries. Their place in the contemporary US social welfare system is in part a long-term consequence of the stigma and dualism that result from need-based determinations of eligibility for assistance. More proximally, their recent and current iterations reflect the intersection of these long-standing pressures with increased criminal justice punitiveness and welfare state retrenchment.[117]

This book is fundamentally about what fraud control workers do, why, and how. However, it is also about what fraud units' operations reveal about the social construction of different types of lawbreaking and their perpetrators, the politics and economics of formal social control, and the state of contemporary public welfare programs.

Chapter 2 situates fraud control units as governmental entities and explains political processes' impact on their work. Tracking the development of contemporary fraud units' bureaucratic separation and designated investigatory and punitive function, it shows how welfare programs' changing symbolic valence drove major legal changes and how federalist dynamics influence policy implementation in programs diffused across federal, state, and local levels of government. In chapter 3, I go on to detail what this government response looks like on the ground. This account includes major commonalities in fraud workers' visions of clients and cases and explores the cross-jurisdictional and inter-investigator irregularities that characterize fraud investigation. Chapter 4 focuses on how fraud units intertwine the government functions of provision and punishment. Fraud workers' cooperation and coaction with conventional criminal justice authorities create interagency enforcement "nets" that transcend nominal police/welfare boundaries.

Chapter 5 analyzes the occupational frames that fraud workers draw upon to make sense of their work and navigate their work environments. Occupational frames capture how fraud workers understand and present themselves. In substantive terms, they influence which clients they will pursue; symbolically, they determine what justifies that pursuit. Chapter 6 continues the consideration of symbolism, addressing fraud workers' efforts to perform fraud enforcement in ways that signal effectiveness and efficiency to the public and other government bureaucracies. Money is central to these considerations, and fraud units espouse arguments that fraud investigations "pay for themselves" via cost savings and recoveries; as chapter 6 documents, however, the evidence for welfare fraud investigations' net fiscal benefit is shaky.

Chapters 7 and 8 focus on punitive adversarialism's consequences for clients. First, chapter 7 discusses fraud workers' assignment of blame in the ongoing (re)construction of the welfare rule violator as a social figure. Fraud enforcement invokes—and reinforces—racialized and gendered "welfare queen" stereotypes and understandings of poverty as pathological. And as chapter 8 shows, working knowledge about fraud and its perpetrators shapes fraud workers' discretionary action, and thus fraud control's implementation. Investigators look to catch people who fit their preexisting images and prioritize cases involving people with greater informational visibility and perceived patterns of fraud perpetration; these patterns hold significant implications for reproducing social stratification. In conclusion, chapter 9 highlights some of the book's key takeaway themes, summarizing how bureaucratic and organizational structure shape workers' agency and recounting the core asymmetries that characterize fraud investigation processes. Finally, I suggest some policy changes that would help mitigate punitive adversarialism, ameliorate the potential for between-group disparities in fraud enforcement outcomes, and make program integrity initiatives fairer and more effective overall.

* * *

Building on distinctions between the deserving and undeserving poor, "welfare cheats" have achieved prominence in popular discourse and policymaking. Usually depicted as motivated by greed and not truly needy, people who intentionally break program rules are advanced as representations of undeserving welfare beneficiaries and evidence for the need to "get tough" on clients. As responses to questions of social safety net administration, fraud units foreground the figure of the welfare rule violator as motivation and justification for the further entrenchment of punitive thinking and tactics in public assistance programs.

For clients, punitive adversarialism heightens the surveillance and stigma that accompany welfare participation. Fraud investigations' substantive consequences can be profound, including loss of sorely needed benefits and criminal prosecution. More symbolically, fraud units signal to both clients and the general population how government views poor people in general and poor people who claim welfare benefits in particular. Fraud units also try to signal their investigative capacity and effectiveness, but their interventions are irregular, varying substantially across jurisdictions and individual employees.

Under a common federal mandate, state governments, agency administrators, fraud unit managers, and rank and file data analysts and investigators all play roles in translating law in books into law in action.[118] Ultimately, vague statutory and administrative dictates become real through fraud workers' discretionary decisions, work habits, and rules of thumb.[119] Through these workers' visions of their jobs and their surrounding social context, *Policing Welfare* illuminates fraud control's implementation and explains its portents for poverty governance.

CHAPTER TWO

One Nation, Finding Fraud

Means-tested public assistance programs are among the most charged political issues in the contemporary United States. Dedicated fraud control units within the country's welfare system are noteworthy responses to questions about how government should run these programs and treat their clients. Examining fraud units' political and governmental context helps reveal why this response looks the way it does. The political history of the intensification and bureaucratic separation of client investigation functions, the key underpinnings of today's punitive response to clients' rule breaking, demonstrates the symbolic aspects of this response. Politicians and popular media outlets increasingly disparaged welfare in the later twentieth century, depicting means-tested public programs as corrupt and representative of broader problems in government's handling of poverty. This shift tracked representations of the poor themselves, whose alleged pathologies and parasitism grounded calls to rein in programs designed to help them. Beyond its substantive implications for the climate of program participation and poor people's lives, the nationwide push to more closely monitor clients and punish their rule violations further changed welfare programs' symbolic valence, cementing perceptions of fraud as rampant.

Federal policymakers set the national tone of punitive adversarialism.[1] States, however, have considerable leeway to design and implement their anti-fraud initiatives. Thus, after describing the national shift toward welfare retrenchment and penalization, I shift gears to look at the variation in lower-level government interventions. Comparisons of the five case study states reveal how popular and political salience[2] of the welfare fraud issue influence fraud enforcement. "Background" salience levels that are stable over time at relatively high or low levels underlie some broad state-level enforcement patterns. Sudden shifts in enforcement practices, on the other hand, correspond to shifts in salience, or the relative degree to which welfare fraud is top of mind for the public and policymakers.

As in other public administration contexts,[3] implementing fraud control policy ultimately comes down to the system's frontline workers. Fraud workers' positions as street-level bureaucrats give them significant influence over how federal and state policies manifest on the ground. Their discretionary actions create the local-level fraud control world. Differences between investigators—and between the other state actors who generate many of the case referrals for investigation—mean that these local-level worlds can vary substantially, even under ostensibly uniform state policies, as day-to-day judgment calls shape the variegated translation from law in books to law in action.[4] Creating a fuller picture of fraud enforcement, then, also means assessing individual workers' perceptions of politics and politicians, which reveals disjunctures between the policymaking arena and the people responsible for putting policy into practice.

Federalism, Devolution, and Welfare Fraud Control

The US social safety net is organizationally dispersed. Much of it comprises privately operated benefit systems backed by government funding.[5] SNAP and TANF, for instance, involve the participation of over a quarter of a million authorized and supervised for-profit retailers,[6] along with a host of private firms contracted for an array of services. These public-private hybridizations introduce particular issues of effective oversight, efficient operation, and equitable service provision.

Other issues pertain to programs' administration within government bureaucracies. Federalist dynamics are particularly pivotal. Federal authorities set the basic policies governing SNAP and TANF, including certain baseline fraud control mandates. But the programs are administered at the state level, with local-level offices running day-to-day operations. Between the 1970s and 1990s, federal fraud control mandates expanded significantly. These changes resulted in more muscular enforcement systems overall. They also delegated much of the responsibility for investigating and punishing client fraud to authorities at lower levels of government; the nationwide establishment of state-level fraud control units was a key consequence. Similar processes have unfolded throughout the post–New Deal histories of US social safety net programs, with state governments and local offices implementing national policies, but they have become especially pronounced over recent decades as devolution in welfare state and welfare state–criminal justice hybrid institutions increasingly relocates authority in lower levels of government (and among private actors).[7]

No single policy shift exemplifies this devolution better than the Personal Responsibility and Work Opportunity Reconciliation Act of 1996 (PRWORA). PRWORA not only transformed relationships between welfare authorities and program participants; it also transformed relationships between federal and state authorities in poverty management, increasing states' authority to operate public assistance as they saw fit. Building on prior policy changes that expanded states' ability to specify work requirements and restrict periods of benefit eligibility, this act dramatically shifted control over welfare programs from the federal to the state level.

TANF's block grant funding gives states substantial leeway to choose how to spend their allotments. In ending individual families' entitlement to benefits, PRWORA authorized states to determine categories of TANF eligibility. It permitted states to establish rewards and penalties— described by lawmakers as "carrots" and "sticks"—to incentivize paid work and other preferred behaviors (and disincentivize their alternatives). And, extending devolution into the private sphere, it explicitly authorized states to subcontract with nonstate organizations for benefit administration and service provision. With this newfound autonomy, states substantially shifted their TANF funds away from core benefits and services and toward other purposes.

Welfare devolution also entailed significant and racialized fraud-specific changes. In terms of organizational structure, the biggest of these changes was the establishment of dedicated fraud control units. Various jurisdictions had maintained fraud detection and investigation entities previously, but their modern iterations arose and proliferated between the 1970s and 1990s. The circumstances of their creation echoed broader dynamics of welfare retrenchment and administrative decentralization. Race and racism helped drive these shifts. In the 1960s and 1970s, welfare rights activists advocated for racial/ethnic minorities' social and economic rights,[8] and more Black mothers entered public assistance programs.[9] Popular and political backlash to these developments precipitated disciplinary and punitive alterations to programs' structure and rules.[10]

So one must look back, earlier than PRWORA, to a set of changes to federal law and policy beginning in the 1970s to find how the current fraud control system came to be. Collectively, these changes reflected fraud's increased salience, as well as the motivation and capacity for reactive legislation and regulation. In the mid-1970s, Congress demonstrated significant interest in fraud and abuse within government agencies, resulting in marshaled and aggrandized oversight and investigation capacities. Following multiple congressional hearings and investigations of the Department of Health, Education, and Welfare (HEW), the precursor to Health and Human Services (HHS), 1976 legislation established the HEW Office of Inspector General (OIG).[11] Similar concerns regarding oversight and accountability in federal programs spurred the 1978 Inspector General Act, which created an OIG in the United States Department of Agriculture (USDA), among other agencies.[12]

Perceptions that organizational dispersion was hampering investigative functions' effectiveness drove policymakers to concentrate, consolidate, and better fund these enterprises. Congress also endeavored to increase investigations' independence from other aspects of agencies' work, reasoning that bureaucratically siloed investigatory bodies would have fewer potential conflicts of interest and would better protect investigations' integrity.

Federal interventions designed to tighten controls over welfare clients followed similar logics. These policy changes instituted new oversight and accountability mechanisms, with the bulk of investigative responsibilities devolved to the states. On February 27, 1971, HEW issued regulations requiring state-level administrative agencies to create and maintain procedures to detect, investigate, and punish fraud in AFDC.[13] That same year also marked the establishment of a Quality Control System in the Food Stamp program, followed by the creation of a Quality Control System in AFDC in 1973.[14] Along similar lines, the Food Stamp Act of 1977 required state-level agencies to enact procedures for verifying applicants' income and household circumstances.[15] Notably advancing punitive adversarialism, it also authorized program disqualifications[16] and criminal prosecutions[17] for intentional rule violators, with federal remuneration for 75 percent of states' costs in Food Stamp investigations and prosecutions.[18]

These measures enhanced street-level welfare workers' sanctioning authority and responsibility. Other changes induced the formation of distinct units specifically focused on recipient fraud. The Food Security Act of 1985 required states to create dedicated fraud control units within their systems for administering the Food Stamp Program (now SNAP),[19] leading to the proliferation of such units. Amid the general climate of welfare reform and specific attention to the fraud issue in the 1970s, 1980s, and 1990s, dedicated fraud units' activity in AFDC also grew rapidly.[20]

Nearly all states oversee SNAP and TANF through a single state-level agency,[21] so dedicated fraud control units within these agencies investigate both programs' clients. PRWORA required that states establish and enforce new "standards and procedures to ensure against program fraud and abuse"[22] and specifically required states to use the federal Income and Eligibility Verification System (IEVS) for front-end eligibility fraud detection.[23] But, as with other aspects of their TANF programs, within certain parameters states have broad discretion to design and implement their TANF fraud control systems as they see fit. SNAP, on the other hand, involves both greater investment of federal resources and more federal directives regarding the implementation of devolved enforcement authority.

Vesting enforcement responsibilities in bureaucratically distinct units furthered punitive adversarialism, devolving investigative authority to lower levels of government while adhering to the general principle of separating investigative functions from other aspects of bureaucratic administration. Within the US federalist system, this is a first-order devolution from the federal to the state level, followed by states' second-order devolution of investigative authority to local offices (some almost entirely).[24] The most decentralized fraud control operations are those in a handful of county-administered states where county-level fraud units operate with minimal state-level administration.[25]

In overhauling oversight and investigative functions, federal authorities sought to act as national policy leaders, both suggesting a general policy orientation and encouraging states to pass corresponding legislation. Midatlantic demonstrates state response to this leadership. In the pre-PRWORA 1990s, Midatlantic shifted responsibility for counteracting welfare fraud from its benefit administration agency into a separate executive-branch oversight office in response to federal pushes for independent state-level investigative units. The stated logic was that locating welfare fraud control systems within benefit administration agencies creates a "fox guarding the henhouse" situation. Current representatives of Midatlantic's fraud control regime continue to favor that explanation, arguing that having a distinct investigative division provides them with autonomy, discretion, and freedom.

The bureaucratic separation of Midatlantic's investigative body occurred in two phases. The independent investigatory body that later assumed responsibility for public benefit fraud was originally formed in the 1980s, during the Reagan administration. Reagan's presidency was characterized by a zealous pursuit of accountability in government, often with the goal of reducing the size of government programs. Reagan famously argued that he wanted his agents of oversight and investigation to be as relentless and unsparing as "junkyard dogs" in the effort to identify and eradicate wasteful or ill-advised expenditures.[26] Much of the Reagan administration's criticism and activity focused on assistance programs for the poor, especially TANF and SNAP.[27] That was the backdrop for Midatlantic establishing its own independent oversight and accountability agency. As the welfare reform movement that would culminate in 1996's PRWORA gained steam, this state overhauled its approach to public benefit oversight by decisively disconnecting fraud control from general program administration.

National Consistencies

The federal government directs state-level welfare fraud control enterprises via basic rules and guidelines.[28] Alongside baseline requirements to maintain fraud control operations, these federal policies specify mandatory interventions—such as using an IEVS—and recommend other fraud control steps. These national standards constitute a common structure dictating state fraud units' general orientation.

SNAP and TANF, though, are subject to different levels of attention. SNAP gets the lion's share of fraud units' focus. Fundamentally, SNAP is simply far larger, particularly since the dramatic post-PRWORA drop in TANF-funded program participation. While monthly SNAP participation has averaged around 46 million people in recent years, the average monthly number of TANF recipients in 2014 was only around 3.5 million.[29] Further, since PRWORA, TANF's annual block grant has been frozen at $16.5 billion;[30] in 2013, states supplemented this funding with around $15 billion of their own.[31] Federal contributions to SNAP, by contrast, averaged around $74 billion in fiscal years 2014 and 2015.

States and the federal government split the costs of SNAP administration about equally, and states contributed approximately \$3.7 billion toward the program's \$7.3 billion in administrative costs in fiscal year 2014.[32] Thus, whether measured by participation or budget, SNAP is the bigger fish for fraud investigations.

Benefits distributed through TANF are also more variegated and complex than the nutrition assistance provided through SNAP. Throughout the later twentieth century, about 80 percent of AFDC spending went into "cash" benefits, and two-thirds of all low-income unmarried mothers received direct payments.[33] These rates stayed roughly constant through 1995, just before PRWORA.[34] Now, in addition to sweeping reductions in state caseloads, the share of TANF funds dedicated to such monetary payments has declined precipitously. Only around 25 percent of the total TANF budget goes to direct income assistance; in seven states, this percentage is in the single digits.[35] The remainder is spread across a variety of noncash initiatives, including support for poor families' education and employment preparation, child care, and transportation expenses. Other investments of TANF funds are of more dubious value to the poor. States have, for instance, used TANF resources to fund seminars on marriage, anti-abortion counseling, and scholarships for students with \$250,000 annual household incomes to attend private colleges.[36]

Thus, while states invest more of their own money in TANF than in SNAP, several factors explain the greater focus on SNAP in state-level fraud control enterprises. Although cash assistance through TANF is the most widely criticized type of welfare, each state's population of SNAP recipients is far larger than its TANF caseload, providing a much bigger group of clients to scrutinize. This larger pool of potentially fruitful investigations provides more opportunities for impactful symbolic interventions: identifying and punishing rule-violating clients and making examples out of them. Finally, based on eligibility rules and participation patterns, TANF clients are largely a subset of SNAP's clientele. Investigations initiated in connection with SNAP cases therefore carry over to TANF participation, with evidence gathered regarding SNAP eligibility also pertinent to TANF eligibility.

PRWORA requires states to maintain anti-fraud measures in TANF, yet it largely allows them to design and implement these fraud control systems as they see fit. SNAP is a much larger program, with all of its benefits and half its administration costs federally funded, and the federal government has a correspondingly larger footprint here. This foot-print includes imposing more extensive policy requirements and ongoing engagement and oversight practices. With regard to policy, the USDA Food and Nutrition Service (FNS) is responsible for promulgating and enforcing program regulations through direction and oversight. FNS also determines which retailers are eligible to accept SNAP benefits and takes responsibility for counteracting retailer fraud.

Federal law requires states to have fraud detection units covering ar-eas in which five thousand or more households receive SNAP benefits; however, the personnel who work on fraud detection are not required to work on fraud full-time, nor are they required to work exclusively on SNAP fraud. Indeed, most work in units that cover other benefit pro-grams as well: primarily TANF, but in some cases also child support en-forcement, medical assistance, and other programs.

The FNS requires these investigators to use several specific tools as they attempt to detect eligibility fraud. States, for example, are required to engage in data-matching processes at the time of application and in-termittently throughout the period of benefit to check for overlaps with lists of people who are deceased, incarcerated, or have been disqualified from program participation. Should a given client ask for a replacement card four or more times in a twelve-month period, it must be regarded as possible benefit trafficking (people exchanging their SNAP benefits for cash, goods, or services), and FNS mandates that states track these recipients and pursue administrative and/or criminal action against in-tentional violators. Alongside such dictates, FNS suggests—but does not require—that states use a number of other fraud detection tools, in-cluding various database and data-matching resources. Of course, fed-eral rules and requirements are subject to change, and recent FNS audits have proposed further expanding required fraud prevention and detec-tion steps.[37]

Federal Engagement and Accountability Practices

USDA investigators and analysts are deployed throughout the country, tasked with working collaboratively with state assistance agencies and conventional law enforcement authorities to detect, investigate, and pun-ish benefit violations. Southwest supervisor Carly described the close-ness of the working relationship between these local representatives of the federal agency and the state fraud control unit. Carly is a White woman in her early thirties. With blonde hair pulled back in a ponytail, her no-nonsense attitude and sarcastic sense of humor evoke her military background and the connection she feels with law enforcement, both professionally and personally (her husband is a police officer):

CARLY: The USDA we work with a lot.
INTERVIEWER: On the SNAP cases?
CARLY: Yes. To the point that they might as well just move in here. [. . .] Yeah, they come to like our Christmas parties and things, 'cause they don't have anybody else here [*laughing*]. We work with them *a lot*.

In addition to federal agents working closely with their state counterparts, the USDA has established a robust accountability system to incentivize particular fraud control activities and advance their priorities. This system includes both carrots and sticks: financial incentives for fraud detection and overpayment recovery, as well as penalties imposed on agencies with high error rates in the administration of SNAP benefits. Naturally, these shape state-level priorities and practices. The larger public assistance quality control movement, of which fraud units are a prominent piece, shows a clear preference for limiting errors of spending over errors of stringency.[38] State-level SNAP and TANF fraud units are no exception: they reflect a cost-avoidance mentality and focus on addressing errors of expenditure over unclaimed or underclaimed benefits. This orientation owes to the historical legacies of welfare reform in general—and fraud units in particular. Through incentives and penalties, federal authorities encourage states' investment in certain areas of fraud control practice and implicitly discourage others.

This push manifests most straightforwardly in federal SNAP rules allowing states to retain a share of the federal dollars that they recover via specific fraud enforcement activities. These incentives are limited to cases of client overpayments, with larger incentives for overpayments that are substantiated as arising from intentional fraud. Southeast manager Jack, an easygoing, genial White man in his late forties, told me about his agency's overpayment recovery incentivization account:

JACK: Money in that [account] is to be used for buying equipment, for training, other things related to fraud.
INTERVIEWER: And that fills up based on your recoveries, right? You get to keep a share of recovered funds? What is it, 30 percent?

JACK: We keep 35 percent for [Intentional Program Violations], 20 percent for [unintentional] cases. And if there's an agency error that caused a loss, we don't keep anything [*chuckles*]. We don't get anything for that.

Affecting a stage whisper and looking over the top of his glasses, Jack added in a conspiratorial tone: "'Cause we'd be making money, you know."

Jack is describing how incentive structures emphasize some program integrity activities over others: namely, interventions designed to identify clients subject to suspension or disqualification for Intentional Program Violations (IPVs).[39] He implies that a push to turn program integrity inward would reveal plenty of waste and overspending—that is how they would be "making money" if they kept overpayments that resulted from agency error. However, given the structure of administrative priorities—and particularly monetary incentives—they continue to focus their efforts on clients, the more remunerative targets.

In its broader SNAP quality control program, FNS calculates error rates as the sum of overpayments and underpayments. States are required to review a random sample of their cases for potential errors and report their error rates to FNS.[40] Consistently above-average error rates incur financial penalties. Thus there is some motivation for states to undertake interventions aimed at both types of payment error.

Notably, every state in the country reports substantially higher rates of overpayments than underpayments. Table 2.1 shows a sample of figures for fiscal year 2014, the most recent data available from FNS. States reported overpayment rates averaging over four times greater than underpayment rates. This disparity likely includes some underlying differences in "real" rates of overpayments and underpayments. But it is also likely that federal and state-level authorities' emphasis on identifying errors leading to expenditures affects reviewers' assessments of their assigned cases, driving tendencies to focus on errors of spending and deemphasize errors leading to underpayments.[41] That overpayment focus was even clearer in earlier iterations of the payment error rate calculation, which included *only* summations of overpayments.[42]

Prioritizing client misrepresentation reflects an institutional imperative to cut the public benefit recipient population through suspensions and disqualifications. Punitive policies also have the potential to act as self-fulfilling prophecies: a greater focus on overpayments and intentional fraud means identifying and pursuing those cases, which may in

TABLE 2.1. **Sample SNAP error rates, fiscal year 2014**

State	Overpayment rate	Underpayment rate	Total error rate
Connecticut	4.89	0.95	5.84
Maine	2.24	0.29	2.52
Massachusetts	4.29	0.79	5.09
New Hampshire	3.97	0.85	4.81
New York	4.40	0.83	5.23
Rhode Island	5.17	0.80	5.97
Vermont	2.35	0.41	2.76
Delaware	2.25	0.53	2.78
District of Columbia	6.14	1.24	7.38
Maryland	2.88	0.54	3.41
New Jersey	0.90	0.53	1.43
Pennsylvania	3.34	0.93	4.27
Virginia	4.68	0.05	4.73
Total, all states and territories	2.96	0.69	3.66

Source: Food and Nutrition Service (2015b)

turn influence perceptions of the nature and scope of fraudulent behavior relative to administrative error.

Interstate Variations

The SNAP system is nominally consistent nationwide, but substantial interstate variation has arisen from the combination of a federal mandate for fraud units and a paucity of specific requirements for those units' staffing and operations.[43] Fraud units are most basically distinguished by their size. Large systems employ dozens of investigators, as well as a variety of other staff; among this research's case study states, Eastcoast, Midatlantic, and Southwest all roughly fall under the "large" umbrella. Northeast's small system, on the other hand, comprises a single-digit number of investigators and a handful of support staff. Budgetary allotments drive units' size and investigative capacity: larger budgets permit more staff, as well as greater technological resources and access to proprietary data sources.

The case study states demonstrate how state-level decisions vary within the context of federal mandates, suggestions, incentives, and penalties. Southwest typifies a large fraud control system. Robust and multifaceted, it has a series of offices assigned to counteracting fraud in different programs, as well as specialized staff dedicated to particular tasks, such as SNAP benefit trafficking and liaising with criminal justice authorities. Southwest invests considerable resources in both conventional fieldwork-based investigative techniques and database-driven and other office-based approaches to investigation. Northeast's minimal fraud control enterprise is at the other pole of the size-and-scope continuum. Its relative underdevelopment is marked by fewer dedicated fraud staff with fewer investigative responsibilities. Tabitha, a White investigator in her midforties, explained the small-scale fraud control of Northeast as a consequence of state-level political leaders' priorities, suggesting that welfare fraud has relatively little political salience in her state: "Other states might choose [different] program integrity priorities. Our leadership priorities come from the governor and trickle down through the administration."

ELIGIBILITY DETERMINATION, FRAUD CONTROL, AND THE WELFARE DI-VISION OF LABOR   States also show distinct differences in issues that run alongside matters of fraud control systems' size and sophistication. These issues include the separation of benefit administration and fraud control tasks and fraud units' positions within state bureaucracies.

Southeast, for example, exemplifies a clear demarcation between benefit administration and fraud enforcement. Their program eligibility interviewers are explicitly directed to refrain from questioning applicants' attestations or engaging in any front-end verification processes. The fraud unit is responsible for any and all detection and investigation of potential misrepresentations. This wasn't always the case; it is a change spurred by a broader reorientation of Southeast's eligibility determination protocol, in which the state has moved away from traditional face-to-face interviews with applicants and toward a web- and phone-based system. Under this system, applicants are evenly distributed to eligibility technicians scattered around the state, rather than discussing their applications in person with a staffer at a local office. The web- and phone-based approach allows eligibility technicians to work from home, and many of the people doing this work are now employed on a part-time or ad hoc basis. The state saves money by lowering office overhead costs and reducing expenditures on full-time employees' fringe benefits.

Eastcoast, meanwhile, has moved in the opposite direction. While Southeast's recent actions have separated application processing and eligibility verification as widely as possible, Eastcoast has become a national leader in front-end prevention and detection measures. Its benefit agency continues to enhance assessment and verification at the time of benefit application, to the degree that it recently conceptualized, designed, and implemented an automated information verification protocol inbuilt to the eligibility review process. TANF and SNAP applicants in Eastcoast report income, asset, and household composition information to eligibility workers, who record that information in a computer program. As the information is entered, an automated process checks it against more than twenty different federal, state, and private sector databases, assessing the correspondence between the applicant's attestations of finances and household circumstances and documentation of these variables elsewhere. The system generates pop-up messages if conflicts are detected as the interview proceeds. Initially, these appear as reminders, indicating that a discrepancy is present, generating a link to the data source that contradicts the client's attestation, and instructing the worker to resolve it. Eligibility interviewers are trained to review any potential conflicts with clients and resolve disparities before continuing with interviews. The interviewer does have the option to temporarily ignore contradictions between clients' statements and the various databases the system queries. However, bypassed conflicts are logged, and at the conclusion of the interview, the interviewer will face a final eligibility determination page listing any outstanding contradictions. Interviewers can elect to proceed with benefit approval despite conflicts but will later have to answer to their supervisors for any applications approved under such circumstances.

Generally speaking, the implementation and expansion of dedicated fraud control units demonstrates a growing separation between "sides of the shop." Front-end review initiatives push back toward the coexistence of benefit administration and verification functions within the same bureaucratic structures and actors. Eastcoast's automated verification system provides an example, albeit one in which initial checking and assessment work occurs without active input from the eligibility worker. Front-end verification protocols do not, however, necessarily imply bureaucratic unification of the agency's explicit provision and rule enforcement objectives. Dedicated fraud control units can and do host strengthened front-end review processes.

Midatlantic provides an excellent example of bureaucratically separated front-end detection efforts. Like its counterparts in Eastcoast, Midatlantic has designed a fraud control enterprise that tilts heavily toward front-end detection. Its preventive fraud control system is several times larger than its reactive system. Midatlantic also draws on databases for information about applicants' financial and residential situations, but the investigative feel of their front-end detection system is decidedly more old-school. In contrast to many states, the large majority of dedicated welfare fraud investigation staff in Midatlantic are assigned to front-end investigations. When eligibility workers deem a case suspicious, they refer it to this front-end investigative workforce, which uses the turnaround time between application and benefit issuance to validate—or invalidate—applicants' declarations. Their investigations focus primarily on the areas of suspicion raised by the referring staffer and involve both database-driven and conventional fieldwork investigative techniques.

This approach means that eligibility staff play a pivotal role in the fraud control enterprise (and wide disparities in fraud referral frequencies suggest some eligibility workers adopt that role more avidly than others). However, the actual verification work is bureaucratically separated from application eligibility processing—unusually separated, in fact. Midatlantic is an outlier, both nationally and within this research's case study states, in that its welfare fraud control enterprise is located entirely outside of the state agency that administers TANF and SNAP. This intentional and physical separation is a prominent instance of the interstate differences that characterize fraud control enterprises.

EXPLAINING INTERJURISDICTIONAL DIFFERENCES   Like other contexts involving enforcement crosscutting federal, state, and local levels, the TANF and SNAP fraud control landscape is a "multijurisdictional patchwork of enforcement policies and practices."[44] Policies that appear relatively standardized in federal legislation are variegated in state-level interpretation and implementation. And state-level policies are themselves realized disparately across local contexts.

Welfare fraud is especially salient in particular times and places.[45] Differences in fraud's salience help explain differences in how states construct their fraud control enterprises. Talking to fraud workers underscores the relationship between public and political attention and state-level action with regard to welfare and welfare fraud. Among my interviewees, fraud workers from Southeast and Southwest depicted welfare fraud as a consistent focus of popular and political reproach. They readily recalled various incidents that kept fraud in headlines and atop legislative agendas.

Overhauls to state-level fraud policies illustrate how policymakers

can whip up and then use outrage about alleged fraud to advance political priorities. Ronald Reagan's role as a fraud salience pioneer began
when he was governor of California. During his terms in the late 1960s
and early 1970s, Reagan foregrounded fraud, spearheading multiple policies designed to detect and punish social service clients' intentional
rule violations. These more stringent fraud control measures included
the creation of dedicated fraud control units within both the public assistance system and the state's criminal justice bureaucracy.[46] Hawaii
presents another bellwether case. In his 1974 gubernatorial campaign,
Governor George Ryoichi Ariyoshi promised to crack down on welfare
defrauders. Upon inauguration, Ariyoshi made good on that promise,
making Hawaii an early adopter by creating a dedicated fraud unit for
his state in 1975.[47]

In more recent history, Eastcoast offers a strong example of the ways
that changes in welfare fraud's salience shape state-level fraud control
policy. Over the mid-2010s, Eastcoast's fraud control system grew by
leaps and bounds; a fairly minimal operation transformed into a large,
technologically sophisticated system regarded as a national leader in
front-end fraud prevention efforts. Administrator George O'Connor
outlined the recent changes in his unit:

> I really can't bitch too much, because you gotta remember, when I came in
> here I had no [dedicated data staff]. I now have a director and I have two peo-
> ple doing [this], two analysts. My investigators force has [grown several times
> over, and my other subunits have also grown significantly]. . . . So I mean,
> my dedicated [resources] to my projects has been crazy. I mean, to the point
> where field directors and field reps would say, "Oh, Jesus, I'm so sick of hear-
> ing about O'Connor and his next project." But I steal them all the time. I re-
> ally have to say, I'd be a real whiner if I said, "Geez, I don't like the way things
> have been going." I've had everything sort of given to me that I needed to fix
> it, I mean, and I fixed it. But it took a lot. It took money. It took resources. It
> took staff. So we sort of got to the point where no news is good news.

Scandal drove these changes, with local media drawing attention to a series of client fraud incidents and providing the political impetus to rev-
olutionize the state's fraud control system. Fraud workers told me that
media outlets misreported and the public misunderstood these stories,
yet their sensationalism gave them traction and staying power. These accounts offered the media and politicians the chance to construct narra-

tives with clear-cut villains and victims: malicious chiselers stealing from hardworking taxpayers, abetted by lazy or negligent welfare employees. Politicians used Eastcoast's public assistance program as an example of governmental failure, presenting the (over)simplified accounts of fraud as emblematic of problems in state government that should be addressed through changes in political leadership.

This is hardly the only sociolegal context in which such constructions—or exaggerations—of social problems have had outsize influence. US tort reform discourse presents a compelling example, with atypical anecdotal cases (or misrepresentations of those cases) and cherry-picked or dubious statistics advanced as evidence of a systematic "crisis" in the civil legal system.[48] Tort reform rhetoric parallels welfare reform rhetoric: stressing individual responsibility; moralization, especially through invoking identifiable "victims"; and emphasizing the sensational over the typical.[49] Anecdotes and narrative characterizations are similarly powerful in driving welfare policy changes, even when they differ from—or directly contravene—more systematic evidence.[50] In both contexts, rhetoric uses "extraordinary occurrences [to] symbolize ordinary outcomes."[51]

Sensationalist media coverage notably elevated fraud's salience in Eastcoast. In this environment, agency administration moved to enhance fraud control, bringing in George O'Connor to helm their revitalized fraud control enterprise and disburse newly allocated funds. A veteran of Eastcoast's welfare fraud control system and other bureaucratic investigative work, George returned to public assistance primed for major impact: he had wide-ranging experience and policy enforcement expertise and the closest thing to a blank check any public administration official is likely to get. He had immense discretion in reconfiguring the fraud control enterprise according to his vision and, perhaps more significantly, the budgetary resources necessary to reinvent and expand Eastcoast's program integrity system.

George's comments to me suggested his influence as a bureaucratic entrepreneur. With a mandate from state political leaders to overhaul fraud control measures and significant resource allocation, he substantially strengthened Eastcoast's fraud control enterprise. In so doing, he and other key actors demonstrated commitment to cost-benefit thinking and facility with the logic and language of evidence-based policy. Their emphasis on front-end detection and data-driven methods are the most notable features of this "new wave" of fraud control in Eastcoast.

Evidence-Based Policy and the "New Wave" in Welfare Fraud Control
Late twentieth-century and early twenty-first-century public administration have foregrounded evidentiary justification in social welfare policy.[52] Eastcoast's reinvigorated fraud control activities exemplify this
mentality in state-level welfare fraud enterprises. Commitments to efficiency and return on investment are paramount in this approach to policy design and implementation, the "New Public Management" (NPM)
that imports business approaches to management and evaluation into
public sector organizations.[53] In fraud control systems (as in other areas
of government) these principles manifest in the embrace of language and
ideas traditionally more closely associated with MBA than with MPA or
MSW programs. Hiring staff with business backgrounds—as Eastcoast
has eagerly done—suggests their embrace of this approach.

Generally, fraud workers' experience is based in law enforcement
and public assistance. That is, as chapter 5 discusses in greater detail,
many people enter welfare fraud control after working elsewhere in their
state's public assistance system or in criminal justice agencies. Eastcoast's recent expansion of its program oversight workforce, however,
demonstrates significant commitment to recruiting staff members with
different backgrounds, including business education and private sector work experience. This tendency tracks with the evolving emphasis
of fraud control and public administration: when attempting to build a
fraud control system that adheres to the business world's conventional
objectives of efficiency and return on investment, it is logical to employ
individuals with relevant training and experience.

Eastcoast's pursuit of these goals involves developing and deploy-
ing database-driven and automated methods of detection and investigation. Such measures require technological competencies not conventionally associated with public assistance work—another reason the state has
sought out employees with atypical credentials and job histories. New-
comers on their staff include an individual with years of experience in
private investigation and Las Vegas casino security and another who
worked in subscriber database management for a national periodical.
Alongside these private sector transplants, Eastcoast has hired younger
people with business and technology training directly out of college.

These staffing decisions point to the way that Eastcoast's revitalized
fraud control system focuses on more thoroughly integrating program
integrity objectives into benefit administration itself. Earlier in his ca-

reer, George was a member of a robust fraud investigation staff. Under relatively low-salience conditions, the number of investigators on his team dwindled, reaching its nadir around the turn of the millennium. In revitalizing the fraud unit, he is not trying to re-create that old investigatory team, which specialized in traditional investigative techniques and was separated from the benefit administration side of the shop. Instead, George has funneled his abundant resources into front-end fraud prevention and detection and investigation techniques based on database matching. Staff hires have followed suit, bringing risk-assessment and data-mining skills into the investigative team.

Over the long term, George's aspirations include expanding his unit's bureaucratic territory and reclaiming some of the now-attenuated conventional investigatory workforce's jurisdiction. But those are just aspirations; he thinks such expansion is unlikely because of the dominance of cost-benefit analysis and return-on-investment thinking in the push for tighter program controls. Eastcoast's state government has demonstrated substantial willingness to invest resources in strengthening their fraud detection and enforcement apparatus. However, they emphasize a rationalist approach, and prioritize those fraud control policies and practices that they judge most cost-effective. In Weberian terms, Eastcoast is advancing toward ideal-typical bureaucracy, as instrumentally rational action pushes aside remnants of value-rational or traditional organizational action.[54]

Eastcoast's fraud control workers are not alone in the perception that the most fiscally efficient approach to controlling fraud is to catch it before erroneous benefits are issued. Front-end detection reduces erroneous benefit issuance and departs from the disparaged "pay-and-chase" model. Once overpayments are issued, agencies struggle to recoup them from underresourced clients. But among the case study states, it is Eastcoast that has most fully embraced the goal of front-end detection and designed its interventions accordingly.

Eastcoast's business-style approach to fraud control also emphasizes big data resources as efficient and effective tools for policing public assistance. This is true in the state's extensive front-end detection system, which integrates automated database checks into the eligibility determination process. It is also true of the state's efforts to detect ongoing fraud, which rely heavily on various database searches and matches. This development reflects Eastcoast's role in disseminating NPM ideas in the fraud enforcement context and their contribution to the transition from NPM to "digital-era governance."[55]

Local-Level Variation   As federal programs administered at the state level and run out of local-level offices, SNAP and TANF are affected by discretionary actions at multiple stages and by multiple actors. Local-level actors' discretion within the public assistance system[56] produces noteworthy intrastate variations in the practice of punitive adversarialism, despite common bases in shared state-level policies.

Local office characteristics have significant implications for irregularity and arbitrariness in the realization of fraud control policies. Administratively, differences in caseload and staffing affect capacities to pursue fraud claims. Further, it's important not only how many staff members are in any given office but also who those staffers are. Some caseworkers are much more likely than others to refer clients for investigation, increasing the odds that clients who work with them will find themselves charged with fraud. Similarly, fraud workers note disparities in caseworkers' referrals: some referrals come to the fraud office with much more elaboration and supporting evidence than others. Outcome-oriented fraud workers prefer more detailed referrals, which are more likely to generate full investigations.

Midatlantic manager Hank referred to local office caseworkers as one leg of a tripod of effective fraud enforcement. The others are the fraud unit and criminal prosecutors. Hank argued that each leg is necessary and that offices that generate fewer referrals for fraud unit investigation and possible prosecution are not free from fraud but are deprioritizing detecting and reporting violations: "It's not that [fraud's] not happening, they're just not getting the referrals. You need the initial caseworker guy to find something wrong; trying to review all the cases is like looking for a needle in a haystack. You need the caseworkers to make referrals."

And, with fraud investigators generally assigned to work particular regions within their states, location determines who will investigate a case. Investigators diverge in their approaches to their jobs, exhibiting differences in investigatory priorities, willingness to "settle" for Unintentional Program Violations (UPVs), and desire to push for criminal charges. As such, any given referral's outcome can hinge substantially on the investigator assigned to work it. Southeast investigator Danielle, a White woman in her late forties with long brown hair and a gregarious disposition, described her locally embedded role and her major departures from her predecessor:

> DANIELLE: Being in a local office I'm able to even nip things in the bud, because I've worked in all these local offices. The analysts know me, so they can come to my office and go "I just interviewed this person and their situation sounds a little iffy," because the analysts have good instincts. So I'm like, "Okay, well, let's check it out." I'll do my little checks and I can stop it from becoming a fraud case that'll get referred to me six months in the future, because I'll give the person a call and say, "Hey, I'm the fraud investigator and your case was just referred to me and I'd like to review a few things." A lot of times, I can help them realize that it doesn't pay. This is like maybe one a month out of the hundreds of interviews people do, but I can talk to them and say, "Hey, this is what's going to happen if you continue in this line, but I've started looking at you and I notice that your husband has the same address as you on your driver's license. I noticed this and this and this, and would you like to tell me what's really going on in your house?" They'll usually say, "I just want to withdraw my application." It's like, "Well, thank you. Okay, let's get that done, but in the future you have to make sure—" and I go over the rights and responsibilities with them again [laughs]. I can do that because I'm in the [local] office and it's few and far between.
>
> INTERVIEWER: Do you think there are other investigators who are in local offices who do sort of similar proactive fraud intervention before the issuance of benefits? Or is that kind of a unique thing for you?
>
> DANIELLE: I don't know. I know the woman before me didn't, because I didn't even know she existed [laughs].

Danielle and other fraud investigators confirm that street-level discretion shapes fraud control practice. As she depicts it, Danielle's approach to the job contrasts sharply with her predecessor's. A fraud referral's outcome could differ starkly depending on whether it landed on her desk or in the inbox of the investigator before her.

State-Level Politics and Fraud Enforcement Practices   As cross-party support for federal-level welfare retrenchment and punitiveness suggests, state-level differences in welfare fraud control policies do not always break neatly along conventional party lines. However, patterns do appear to correspond with states' general ideological orientations.

Among this study's small sample, Southwest and Southeast, the two most reliably "red" of the case study states, are also places where fraud workers describe fraud as highly salient and where fraud control policies follow suit. Both fieldwork investigative techniques and the pursuit of criminal charges are more common in these more conservative states, a fact that tracks with research demonstrating that local-level political climates affect SNAP enrollment rates, regardless of comparative administrative (de)centralization.[57]

Northeast and Eastcoast, on the other hand, have fraud control systems less oriented around field investigations and formal criminal charges, as one might expect given these states' status as among the country's more reliably "blue." In particular, Northeast's minimal fraud control system suggests a less punitive orientation. Northeast investigator Tabitha, her boss Veronica (an experienced administrator in the state's public benefit system), and others in their agency all perceived a connection between this tendency and the state's Democratic leanings. Tabitha said that "the commitment to poverty is there" in the state legislature and that political attention to issues of fraud in public assistance "breaks along party lines."

Eastcoast's expanded fraud control efforts and vigorous front-end fraud detection regime may appear somewhat anomalous for a left-wing state. Its efforts follow a neoliberal, business-style approach to social policy, and doubtless make things harder on many poor people. Yet their fraud control efforts lack some of the teeth we see from their red-state counterparts. Eastcoast's approach bears the hallmarks of the dispassionate and the technocratic. Some Eastcoast fraud workers wish their state would more fully embrace the field investigative techniques championed in the two Southern states—these frontline workers believe that such tactics have psychological impact and deterrent effects on would-be fraudsters. Eastcoast, however, programmatically eschews this approach. At least partially, this derives from cost-benefit analysis. The punitive criminal sanctions vigorously pursued elsewhere are downplayed in favor of approaches deemed more pragmatic and fiscally sound.

Like "tough on crime" criminal justice policies, welfare fraud control interventions have proven popular across a variety of political traditions and situations. It is not always Republicans who are responsible for tightening fraud control or Democrats for loosening it. There are numerous examples of state-level Democratic politicians pushing for stricter anti-fraud measures. It thus makes sense to look at the proximate pressures that engender political salience and push politicians, regardless of party affiliation, to espouse the cause of welfare fraud control and particular pieces of policy.

Fraud Workers' Perceptions of Politicians

Fraud workers' accounts of why politicians do what they do reveal an important aspect of the translation of law in books to law in action,[58] showing how local-level actors understand the reasons behind the imperatives their superiors pass down. Fraud workers do not typically give politicians a lot of credit on the issues of public assistance and public assistance fraud. When asked to reflect on the way political actors understand, discuss, and create policy on these issues in their states, fraud investigators' criticisms key in on two bases of undesirable action from politicians: misunderstanding and intentional self-interest.

Misunderstanding

Fraud workers are not universally critical of politicians' actions on welfare fraud. Unequivocal enthusiasm for politicians' work on the matter may be rare, but some workers expressed general feelings of support for the political leadership under which they operated or gave the sense that politicians do a reasonably good job dealing with a complex and fraught issue. Relatedly, some suggested that politicians generally operate with good intentions (varied, of course, by these workers' own opinions about the best overall course for welfare policy) but fail to fully understand the issues. Put simply, even if politicians mean well, ignorance sabotages their decision-making. Eastcoast administrator Robert discussed this problem in our interview:

> INTERVIEWER: You mentioned that sometimes it's a particular politician, and I think you used the phrase "who wants to make things right." How often, in your view, is the intent of the politician actually about making things right in a true sense, versus they want to play to the popular opinion that's out there? How often do you think it's their motivations are pure?
> ROBERT: I think they want to make things right, but I think they generally misunderstand things. [. . .] I think, lots of times, (a) If they knew what we were doing, and (b) If they knew that the SNAP program, for example, is

largely federally mandated, and (c) That lots of times we are hamstrung by our own regulations or by federal regulations, if they knew the complexities of what we deal with, they would realize that there are lots of right in the beginning. But if I may say so, I think their outlets are largely, they're good intentions, but I think they don't understand the level of complexity and why things likely are the way they are. And, not that we're perfect, because God knows we're not.

Failure to grasp the regulatory structures within which benefit agencies operate—particularly the role of federal rules and regulations—was a common theme in fraud workers' criticisms of politicians. Some also noted that political actors may be ignorant of social realities or circumstances in clients' lives that affect policy implementation. Southeast supervisor Antoine, a tall, dapper, avuncular Black man in his midfifties, lamented the unintended consequences that can come with ill-informed policy: "It looks good on paper. And I've always said that, someone telling you that they have a new mousetrap, and they can catch more mice and all of that, is fine until you look at the one that you have."

Policy changes, in effect, may seem more desirable in their abstracted form than when they are applied by frontline workers in a complex and dynamic social world. Later in our interview, I asked Antoine about the unique characteristics of his state. He replied,

It's just a state that is unique, as every state is unique. The overall makeup of the state changes [with geography, and] there are differences throughout, which has bearing on the type of cases we're gonna get, the type of people who wanna go in and apply for benefits, and sometimes the overall length of time that they're gonna stay on the benefits. It's not something that you can actually pigeonhole, which I think a lot of politicians try to do: "Let's just make this one encompassing thing."

Here again, Antoine suggests that abstract policies can create problems when they come up against a real population's variable characteristics. (This is, of course, an issue with substantial generalizability to considerations of government well beyond the context of US public assistance programs.[59])

Intentional Self-Interest

Other fraud workers pointed directly to politicians' attempts to protect or advance their personal fortunes. I asked Eastcoast investigator Patricia, a tall, trim White woman in her midfifties, what politicians in her state say about public benefits and public benefit fraud. She responded, "They're grandstanding. They're just talking to their public. They know what their constituents want to hear." Her colleague Stephen, an engaging Black manager in his midforties, works in Eastcoast's data-driven fraud control enterprise. He went into further detail as he described the way a particular political figure in their state mobilized concern over welfare fraud to gain office:

> STEPHEN: That was used to get him elected . . . [and] then he gets here, then he's got nothing. Had a big whole welfare reform plan, then it must have been an illusion that was there. Because there was a huge screen of public deception that was negative about welfare, was that he's gonna fix these things that are out there that are wrong. But most of these things about welfare reform and most of these things that he's gonna change over the next couple of years were already fixed. So the general public didn't know and understand that. [. . .]
>
> INTERVIEWER: You think he was aware, that this was kind of a cynical thing, that the positions stated didn't reflect the real picture? Do you think that he was aware of that, or do you think that he was genuinely misinformed about the state of affairs?
>
> STEPHEN: I think he was aware, because he's a pretty bright guy. But I think he was aware of what triggers to pull in order to manipulate the public perception in a beneficial way.

Like many fraud workers I spoke with, Stephen sees a distance between welfare fraud's popular and political salience and the realities of the social world and policy implementation. There is a perception that significant political capital can arise from mobilizing concerns over welfare fraud—in this case, at least, drawing centrally on calculated misrepresentations—even in a liberal state like Eastcoast.

Hailing from an area of the country with a much different dominant political ideology, Southeast investigator Danielle nonetheless shared similar experiences with politicians and misinformation:

INTERVIEWER: Do you hear politicians talk about public assistance, public assistance fraud, very much?

DANIELLE: Now and then. And that's all wrong. [. . .] I yell at the radio in my car. . . . That's so frustrating, when they try to stir up the uninformed public over something without giving them all the facts. So yeah, I yell at the radio.

She spoke with levity, but Danielle clearly has strong reactions to what she sees as the deliberate propagation of misinformation. She connected political misinformation, proliferated through the media, with the general public's misunderstandings of public assistance and how those misunderstandings affect her as an agency employee:

I try to tell people. When they say, "What do you think about that?" I'm like, "Okay, let me let you know, and tell other people that this is not right." I don't know how far that gets [laughs]. That's frustrating. . . . And it's the "Oh, they can go to the strip club and get cash on their food stamp card." No, no, and no [laughs]. Let me tell you why what you just said is all wrong. But that's what they say on the radio. They'll have these debates on the radio and these idiots will call in and go, "Yeah, that's not right!" I'm like, oh, I want to call in. I can't disguise my voice enough [laughs].

Even Southeast supervisor Antoine, who assigned blame for many problems to politicians' lack of knowledge, joined other fraud workers in arguing that politicians often intentionally misrepresent information or mislead the public in pursuit of self-advancement:

ANTOINE: You hear them talk about public assistance fraud when they feel there's something they can get some press on. Not that, I don't think that it's a *big* talking point for them, but it's something they can get some press on. Or if something happens, and we, "They didn't do this for this group, and not for this group," or whatever, it becomes a soapbox for them to stand on sometimes.

INTERVIEWER: You think that when they do talk about it, they're usually accurate, inaccurate, fair, unfair?

ANTOINE: Usually they're inaccurate, because usually the information that they're trying to say, they try to skew one way or the other. And that's just *across* the board.

Responses to Circumstances and Political Climates

Sources of political capital are subject to change, and fraud workers suggest that politicians usually prioritize their electoral prospects over dogged adherence to any given policy or platform. Over time, local political currents and incentives shift as politicians move through offices and election seasons. In the eyes of the more cynical, politicians' opinions and positions on public assistance and public assistance fraud vary freely with the political winds and their own perceived self-interest. Antoine described receiving pressure from political figures: "Sometimes, depending on what time of year it is, if it's election time and the local DA [district attorney] is running for reelection, so they wanna get those, wanna have this big 'round up' and their face on TV, you know: 'We're pursuing this.'"

Antoine's colleague, Southeast supervisor Rosemary, felt similarly. A slightly harried White woman in her early fifties, she gave the example of a prominent public assistance scandal and how it was depicted first in the media and then in the political sphere:

> ROSEMARY: Oh God, that was just, oh my God, the flurry that caused. And you know: "How?" and "What is the government doing about it?" And so then all the legislators go, "Rah-rah-rah!" and beat their drums, and "I'm going to push this law, and change this law," and, you know.
>
> INTERVIEWER: . . . Generally, what is your sense of how [politicians] react to benefit fraud? Do you think it's mostly the same sort of thing, when there's like a spectacular case or some sort of scandalous case that they pay attention to it? Do you think that they give it the attention that it deserves? Do you think they're fair, accurate, informed?
>
> ROSEMARY: I don't think they give it the attention it deserves; I think they live by polls. And so, if it's a sensational story and everybody is up in arms, "So now I need to get involved and I'm going to do something." But on the other hand, when someone who really does care and does try to do something about it like having drug tests or IDs, oh my God. They're vilified: "How can you treat the poor like this?" and "You hate the poor." And so when someone actually really does try to get at the core of the problem and do something that would actually help, no, that can't be, you know. So then they're just going to back off because they want to be reelected.

INTERVIEWER: So the incentives are different for politicians, and maybe conflicting.

ROSEMARY: Incentives are way different, you know, and they'll be all for helping welfare fraud when they're [campaigning], but as soon as they get elected, then they won't sign on anything, because then once you get up there, then the reality is then you're going to be the one on the news that hates poor people. But when you're trying to get elected, you're going out to the working people who see their money, their tax money, being wasted, so, "Yeah, I'm going to do something about this." But I don't think they care.

Denunciations of the undeserving poor can provide political capital.[60] In her comments on the malleability of politicians' positions on these issues, Rosemary acknowledges how concern over fraud can be mobilized such that politicians responding to scandals or stumping for votes can use crackdown rhetoric successfully. But Rosemary also sees the perception cutting the other way; in her view, politicians fear damaging reputational effects if they are seen as being too hard on the poor.

These comments suggest the ambivalence and contradictions of poverty relief in the United States. The history of US assistance programs includes the ideal of helping needy people but also pronounced efforts to closely control that help and those who receive it. Fraud workers' experiences at the intersection of provision and punishment feel fraught because they are. Fluctuations in political and popular salience echo through the administrative units charged with carrying out enforcement within an assistance-oriented field, concentrating in the frontline workers responsible for investigating clients and enabling their punishment.

In both relatively stable and more fluid salience environments, political positions related to welfare fraud often favor the symbolic over the substantive.[61] Such symbolic steps of questionable validity or fiscal value include recurrent debates over policies requiring program participants to undergo drug testing or the inclusion of client photos on Electronic Benefit Transfer (EBT) cards. Across states, many fraud workers share the view that political responses to public benefit and benefit fraud are at least as much about signaling a particular perspective or position to the electorate as they are about pursuing any type of meaningful social impact. And, of course, political rhetoric and policy changes affect public opinion, contributing to an evolving, dynamic interplay between political and popular salience.[62]

Claiming Objectivity

Encapsulating fraud workers' ambivalence about politicians' intentions, words, and actions, Eastcoast administrator Zosia said: "Some are accurate. Some have agendas. . . . They often don't know the facts and regulations, and they can mislead the public."

Amid all this, fraud workers face pressure to toe the line and minimize critiques of political leaders. Ken, a bespectacled White man in his late forties, is a Northeast administrator who works as a liaison to state government. He shares the frustration many feel with political actors they often perceive as "just interested in making a splash." Still, given the nature of his position, Ken must maintain at least the appearance of neutrality, even more than his colleagues doing work specific to fraud control or program integrity. "Rarely do we oppose things," Ken explained. "The last governor said not to use the word *no*." When the agency feels it must push back against rhetoric being used in the political arena, "We have to handle it delicately. We can't say, 'this is stupid.' We have to be diplomatic."

Fraud workers emphasize their commitment to neutrality in multiple contexts. With regard to politicians and the political context surrounding fraud enforcement, this manifests in self-presentations as objective: dispassionate, disinterested, or even mechanistic functionaries applying the rules passed down to them without evaluation or assessment.[63] The world of politics and politicians is, this view implies, irrelevant to the work of fraud control and beyond the fraud control investigator's or manager's bailiwick.

Most people working in the fraud world were willing to proffer at least some opinions about politics and politicians, but others demonstrated their dedication to objectivity through noncommittal statements, indicating that policies and politicians simply "are what they are." For such workers, spending time thinking about the political factors driving punitive adversarialism is, for one, outside their job description and, more pragmatically, pointless. Eastcoast manager Vincent took this perspective.

VINCENT: Yeah, I mean, you know, you're limited sometimes by the rules of the program, or sometimes you're limited by what we do. But I think that's why I don't try, I don't get that bogged down in it. I don't take it personal. You know, maybe ten years ago I did because you're younger and you don't have a lot of hours, but once you get that experience and start dealing with individuals, you know, I couldn't change this even if I wanted to. Why take up that cause? You gotta work within these parameters and that's what we do. I mean, this is a changing business, you know, especially when you get . . . a political change in climate with a new governor. That will change the [agency leadership]. . . . But the work itself is the same. Some of the other ideology or the, you know, ideas on . . . how we're going to go. But *basically* the same fundamental programs and eligibility requirements. Those aren't changing. So you continue to keep those wheels turning.

INTERVIEWER: So you kind of try to keep out of the ideological stuff and just keep your head down, do your job?

VINCENT: Yeah. That kind of stuff doesn't affect what I do. Sometimes, you know, it comes into play, minimal, at least as far as I'm concerned. You know, we matched, identified potential dead people. We're not going to pay out dead people. We match people who are in prison because they can't receive benefits while they're in prison. People who have warrants can't entitle themselves to cash benefits . . . if they have an outstanding warrant. So that's my job, to make sure these people aren't getting it. That, I mean, it shouldn't change, based on ideology. I don't think anybody wants to be in an agency where you're not paying the correct people. So we just keep those wheels turning and everything else works out.

Vincent explicitly grounds his *que sera, sera* attitude toward politics in pragmatism. With experience, he explained, he learned not to invest too much in politics or political changes outside of his control. And a prescriptive position about the way fraud control work should be done parallels Vincent's descriptive argument for pragmatic apoliticism. According to this prescription, the job of fraud control is simply to "keep those wheels turning" to enforce rules and protect the validity of organizational operations—a perspective that fits neatly with the Weberian description of bureaucracy as the zenith of the rational and impersonal in human organization.[64]

Emotions and affect are inevitably significant in organizational contexts.[65] However, depictions like Vincent's demonstrate the pervasive notion that the skilled bureaucratic worker is a disinterested operator. Southwest investigator Dusty also said he approaches his work apolitically. A former police officer, Dusty is a White man in his late twenties with a stubble beard. Currently assigned to undercover fraud investigation work, he wore jeans and a hooded sweatshirt on the day of our interview. Like Vincent, Dusty tries to cultivate serenity regarding political rhetoric about welfare fraud that is outside of his control:

> DUSTY: I try to stay out of it, yeah. I try to stay out of all the politics . . . whether it's state, whether it's national. I'm not the type of person that's going to kiss ass, I guess you could say. . . . Sorry [*laughs*].
>
> INTERVIEWER: No skin off my nose. When you hear politicians talk about it, you stay out of it, but do you think that they're usually fair? Usually right? . . .
>
> DUSTY: I'd say they're usually fair. You know sometimes, sometimes there's disagreements there. But then again, it's at a much higher level than I can even throw my two cents in. I don't know, I guess I've got to just kind of roll with it.

Bureaucratic organization tends to create oligarchies and concentrate power in the hands of a small elite.[66] Given that Dusty is a relatively low-ranking member of the organizational hierarchy, one might expect him to feel distanced from the political and administrative decision-making process. But higher-ranking people within public assistance agencies expressed similar commitments to the Weberian formulation of the ideal bureaucratic official, distant from the political process of rulemaking.

A leading Eastcoast administrator, fifty-something Edward has a high-level bureaucrat's typical trappings: a corner office and a crowded schedule. He mulled over the political impact of perceived fraud scandals in his state:

> It grabs headlines. Of course, every drug dealer has fifteen EBT cards in his pocket, and that looks just great. Then we had the overpayment issue with USDA. I think there was a feeling among some that that agency is just giving benefits to anybody and there's all kinds of fraud. I don't know if that's what led to the legislation, but I would imagine that was in there somewhere. That's what led to a lot of change in this agency.

Edward is a gubernatorial appointee, with direct connections to the state's political power structure and wide-ranging authority and influence within the agency itself. Yet he too claimed neutrality and positioned himself as a simple applier of rules: "We start talking in that vein, and folks are saying, 'You guys are different. This is different than it used to be.' We've got a set of rules, and we always have. We're just playing it straight. There are eligibility criteria, and we're going to stick to them."

Even as he describes changes in the agency's enforcement practices, Edward espouses the Weberian ideal and places ultimate responsibility for benefits provision and denial in disembodied, abstract rules, stripped of personal and political context. This emphasis on the ostensibly objective and neutral character of rule enforcement demonstrates the continuing strength of the rhetoric put forward by the national welfare quality control movement. Strengthened and bureaucratically liberated fraud systems augment control over the public assistance system and its clients. They also send signals about government's capacity to effectively oversee itself and ensure compliance with formalized rules.

Conclusion

Fraud is a lightning rod, a "condensation symbol."[67] The term *welfare fraud* compiles, distills, and attaches to a single concept a group of opinions and sentiments about the poor.[68] Arguments about fraud provide a focal point that attracts and condenses a wider set of political, economic, and cultural orientations and opinions. Welfare fraud is thus a quintessential vehicle for "symbolic vilification: the process wherein less powerful actors are discursively deemed as less worthy, problematic, or in some regard dangerous."[69]

Amid broader pushes for government accountability and oversight, the establishment of state-level welfare fraud units represents a particular type of response—a punitive reaction to perceived abuses in public assistance programs for the poor. The state-level entities that emerged from these policy movements share common ground today, established and guided by federal rules and regulations, including incentive structures that encourage detecting and substantiating clients' intentional rule violations. In brief, bureaucratically separating enforcement functions creates a strictly enforcement-focused labor force. At the same time, jurisdictions demonstrate substantial variation in going about the business of fraud control. Political and popular salience influence state-level tendencies, such that consistently aggressive fraud control systems reflect elevated baseline salience of the fraud issue and significant shifts in fraud control intensity correspond to significant shifts in salience.

Even within ostensibly uniform state policy environments, local-level differences produce variations in implementation. Some caseworkers are more inclined than others to refer clients for investigation, and some of their referrals are more likely than others to lead to substantiated charges. Between-investigator differences further contribute to local-level variation in when and how clients are investigated and potentially punished. Like between-state variations in enforcement, these inter-investigator differences have both substantive and symbolic implications, shaping concrete outcomes for program applicants and clients as well as the meanings attached to public assistance programs and their participants.

Welfare fraud control is undeniably political. Individual fraud workers are ultimately responsible for implementing the program rules and enforcement policies that political processes produce. Many say they try to function apolitically, depicting politics as a black box. Describing their work in this way could mean adopting only the responsibility to enact politically produced rules, rather than evaluations of their production system. Yet fraud workers tend to share critiques: they feel that politicians' understandings of programs' rules and day-to-day operations are partial at best, that electoral considerations are often at the forefront of both political rhetoric and policy priorities, and that the disconnect between policymaking and implementation frustrates them as street-level implementers of law and policy. Frontline welfare bureaucrats cannot control what regulations say on paper and have little influence on the processes by which rules are made. They are the ones, though, who have to look someone in the eye, talk to her about her reasons for requesting help, and formulate the government response to her case. In fraud control units, such conversations support a single core mission: catching clients for breaking rules.

CHAPTER THREE

The Mill and the Grist

Welfare fraud investigation units across the country share some fundamental traits. Each is part of a punitive response to program management questions, begetting institutionalized suspicion about clients' rule compliance as a national common denominator. And, as the bureaucratic entities assigned to investigate clients and enable their punishment, fraud units seek to obtain client suspensions and disqualifications through substantiated IPVs. The push for establishing deliberate fraud cases reinforces the punitive thinking that accompanies work in an enforcement-specific setting.

Working in such settings shapes fraud workers' opinions on program policies. For instance, despite recognizing the appeal of streamlined eligibility determination processes for general administrative efficiency, fraud workers overwhelmingly believe such processes come with fraud-enabling consequences. Fraud workers, distinct from the "catch-all bureaucrats"[1] employed elsewhere in welfare agencies, are specifically "catch-fraud" bureaucrats. Given their incentives to maximize successful IPV charges, they prize valid and useful damning information and those who can provide it: they value good sources of case referrals and struggle with those they see as less dependable (including, sometimes, members of the public who report suspected fraud).[2]

Within the national pattern of fraud units foregrounding punishment and prioritizing promising cases, there are also irregularities in investigatory methods and evidence evaluation across jurisdictions. These differences connote variation in the translation of general fraud control mandates into concrete fraud enforcement practices and consequences for clients. States diverge in their comparative degrees of focus on retroactive fraud investigation and front-end fraud detection and in their comparative use of fieldwork-based and database-driven investigative techniques.

Individual investigators, too, vary in the extent to which they use "shoe-leather" tactics versus computers and databases. At the same time, they are united by their pursuit of good evidence and solid cases. They cultivate relationships with key actors that help them access the former and construct the latter. Their ongoing associations with the hearing officers who oversee Administrative Disqualification Hearings (ADHs) are particularly pivotal in driving fraud control outcomes. These court-analogous proceedings are where the fraud control mill[3] produces its most directly consequential output: substantiated charges.

Ultimately, fraud control is an exercise in bureaucratic objectification: reducing individual and family biographies into legible cases amenable to assessment and categorization.[4] Because fraud control units' version of "people processing"[5] is characterized by punitive adversarialism, in this context bureaucratic objectification involves the institutionalization of surveillance, suspicion, and formal charging processes. To fraud workers, these institutionalized oversight and punishment mechanisms are routine. For clients, bureaucratic objectification's stakes are much higher. What is to the investigator essentially a single iteration in an ongoing cycle—another instance of this type of case or that type of case—is to a fraud suspect potentially the difference between her children eating or going hungry next month.

Defining the Fraud Issue

State-level fraud units have substantial independence in designing their fraud control enterprises but share the same basic mandate of client-directed policing and codification of the main types of welfare fraud offenses. Fundamentally, most means-tested assistance fraud cases allege deliberate misrepresentation of the household characteristics assessed in eligibility determinations. Prototypical fraud charges in this category involve misrepresentation of finances—usually concealing on- or off-the-books employment, income, or support. Eastcoast investigator Tiffany classified such allegations as "normal, didn't report her income" cases. Other cases in this category involve misrepresentation of household composition—usually denying the presence of a wage-earning adult, or sometimes claiming the presence of absent dependents.

Unapproved uses of benefit resources are the second major category of welfare fraud. Using SNAP benefits to purchase things other than eligible food items—such as food that is served hot, food to be eaten in-store, alcohol, tobacco, or any other nonfood items—constitutes misuse,[6] as does using TANF "cash" benefits at ineligible businesses such as casinos, liquor stores, or strip clubs. This category also includes SNAP trafficking: clients exchanging SNAP funds for cash, goods, or services. These exchanges can occur between individuals or between clients and businesses. Retailers who engage in trafficking violate program policies by offering cash or noneligible items in exchange for EBT cards containing SNAP funds. Fraud investigators cite a typical return of fifty cents cash per dollar of SNAP benefit value in trafficking transactions and frequently attribute the behavior to clients' desire for cash to spend on drugs or alcohol.

Fraud units' caseloads can also involve activities like enforcing mandated child support payments, but eligibility misrepresentation and benefit misuse constitute the bulk of their work. These units are specifically founded upon and organized around the objective of policing participants in public assistance programs.[7] Other civil and criminal enforcement bodies oversee other pieces of the system, including public sector agencies and subcontractors. These efforts are more governmentally centralized than client-focused enforcement, operating primarily at the federal level. Fraud perpetrated by businesses and professionals nearly always involves larger sums than client-perpetrated fraud. By all accounts, the costliest fraud in the US social safety net is committed by health care organizations and medical service providers in publicly supported health care programs.[8] These organizationally based fraud schemes routinely run into the millions of dollars. The federal government polices fraud in health care programs through the Health and Human Services Office of Inspector General and fifty state-level Medicaid Fraud Control Units. In SNAP, the USDA Office of Inspector General attends to retailer trafficking, where transaction volume enables larger-dollar-value fraud. To varying degrees, state-level agencies coordinate on these efforts and carry out their own initiatives aimed at these forms of fraud, with some undertaking substantial efforts.

Client-perpetrated fraud, however, attracts attention and institutional investment that belies its comparatively small-dollar status. Its disproportionately high profile has resulted in dedicated fraud units, the most concrete bureaucratic product of client fraud's pronounced symbolic stakes.

Charges, Investigations, and Evidence

"It's not what you know, it's what you can prove." — Denzel Washington as Alonzo Harris in *Training Day*

As they are put into practice, rules require interpretation. The study of legal institutions in action is fundamentally the study of such interpretation and implementation processes.[9] The exercise of legal authority in welfare fraud enforcement involves significant discretion exercised by multiple actors at multiple points as they interpret and implement policy.

Fraud workers' discretion in choosing which cases to pursue and how to pursue them is particularly notable. Like other rank and file bureaucratic offices,[10] fraud units have a workload of assigned tasks that far outpaces their resources, including worker-hours. Chapter 6 addresses the organizational and administrative implications of the disjuncture between capacity and demands in more detail, but for the moment, the key point is that fraud units receive far more case referrals than they can thoroughly investigate. That means deciding how much energy to devote to different referrals. This process varies across states, with differing administrative structures and amounts of discretion allotted to investigators, supervisors, and managers. Nationwide, however, investigators substantially control where and how they invest their time hunting down fraud.

Investigators generally concur about which types of cases most merit prioritization. First, they want cases that they believe they can substantiate. No one is eager to pursue dead-end investigations. They also prefer to spend their limited time on higher-dollar cases, though this is not a universal orientation. Eastcoast investigator Tiffany commented,

> Every investigator does things a little bit differently, too. Small-dollar for me is not a factor; I'll go after a client even if there is a zero-dollar overpayment. . . . What I look for is whether they lied on documents: that to me is intentional, regardless of the overpayment amount.
>
>   . . . There definitely is a lot of discretion, absolutely. I mean, we all pretty

much have the main basis, but some people, like some people will go after something if there is no overpayment, which, those are really rare. Most of the time if you're having anything that's being lied on you're going to have an overpayment. . . . But some people don't want to go after something with a low dollar amount. But it really is a preference for certain investigators. I have no problem going after someone for a couple hundred dollars if they lied on something. But yeah, there is definitely a lot of discretion with our cases.

Tiffany's comments communicate the variation in how different investigators use their discretion while confirming the powerful uniting theme of seeking out cases with evidence of fraudulent intent. All the structural forces that apply to their work funnel fraud workers' discretion toward maximizing successful charges. "Good" cases, valuable cases, desirable cases are cases that lead to sanctioned IPVs.

IPVs and the Road to Disqualification

Fraud control activity is organized around the goal of substantiating fraud charges. In turn, establishing IPVs allows agencies to remove people from assistance programs, temporarily or permanently. Clients cannot legally be suspended or disqualified for violations that are not substantiated as intentional. The basic IPV sanction structure follows a "three strikes" model. First and second offenses result in suspensions of one and two years, respectively (PRWORA doubled these penalties from their previous levels of six months and one year). Third offenses result in permanent program disqualification.

Some states are deeply invested in adding criminal charges to these administrative sanctions, but fraud units across the country share a fundamental commitment to IPVs. This commitment orients fraud enforcement toward the ultimate objective of removing people from SNAP and TANF. Tiffany put it succinctly: "Our goal is actually to get, you know, someone disqualified from the program, and get the overpayment."

Tiffany is no outlier. In my interviews, investigators, managers, and administrators universally highlighted the importance of establishing IPVs rather than settling for unintentional violations. If an overpayment is identified but intent is not substantiated, agencies can move to recover funds but cannot suspend or disqualify clients. Thus investigators disdain cases where they cannot show intent; to many of them, as to their managers and administrators, anything that does not move an individual or family toward disqualification for rule violations is a failure. Unintentional violations also lack IPVs' symbolic heft; censuring clients for actions formally labeled as deliberate and applying the associated sanctions sends notably different signals about enforcement than does identifying and correcting mistakes. Fraud workers note this discrepancy. In addition to highlighting IPVs' importance to their individual performance evaluations and unit-wide assessments, they describe substantiated IPVs as crucial to the messages their work sends to both client populations and the broader public.

Investigators' attributions of intentionality, so pivotal to fraud enforcement, become legally consequential when they allege deliberate fraud. Intent is inherently private, making its invocation in legal processes necessarily complicated and often contentious. Even when authorities indisputably demonstrate that rules were broken, interpretations can vary. Fraud investigators and clients may hold and present differing understandings of the character and motivations of the actions in question.

Efforts to overcome these factors and evince intent structure fraud investigation practices. Administrators and managers emphasize this most productive category of evidence, and investigators seek it out. Documentation is crucial here. In the paradigmatic eligibility misrepresentation case, documentation constitutes authoritative evidence that a client knew she was making a false attestation of circumstances. In practice, investigators need documentation of two things to pursue these cases: client indication of a particular material condition conducive to eligibility and evidence of that indication's untruth. So, for instance, if a person claims unemployment on a SNAP application but an investigator finds Department of Labor records showing that the person was employed at the time of application, the person's signature on that application constitutes evidence of an IPV.

In client-focused research, many clients admit violating program rules through behaviors such as earning unreported income or selling SNAP benefits. Facing significant gaps between available resources and basic household expenses, many poor people who participate in public assistance programs feel that they have no choice but to "work" the system, whether that means selling food stamps, earning unreported income, or covertly receiving personal assistance from their social networks.[11] Such rule violations are intentional in the most basic sense: clients are aware that these strategies constitute rule violations, fear detection and punishment, and prefer work-arounds they think are least likely to draw welfare authorities' attention.[12] Yet, unable to meet their households' financial needs through strictly "by the book" program participation, clients feel impelled to bend or break rules. When they acknowledge rule-violating behaviors, clients tend to cite their situational constraints and exigencies, not internal dispositions toward fraud. Indeed, clients—even those who admit breaking rules themselves—denounce rule violations they believe arise from greed or sloth, rather than true need.[13]

Clients also recount unintentional or unwitting rule violations. Program rules are complex, and clients experience information overload and encounter bureaucratic impediments to information access.[14] Accordingly, most clients—even the best informed—have limited and flawed knowledge of the specific conditions that pertain to their program participation and information-reporting obligations.[15] Poor people's lives are typically precarious and unstable; ensuring total compliance with program stipulations and requirements may not be a top priority and can get lost in the shuffle.[16] This is especially true for the most severely marginalized clients, whose day-to-day struggles for survival impede meaningful engagement with bureaucratic systems.[17]

By contrast, fraud workers depict rule violations as overwhelmingly intentional and dispositionally (rather than situationally) motivated.[18] Investigators are steadfast that they pursue cases as IPVs only when they believe that violations are truly deliberate.[19] Fraud units' general approach, though, is not particularly hospitable to the notion of rule violations resulting from errors, oversights, or situational constraints. Investigators tend to see intent like the digital and physical paperwork they use to substantiate it: in black and white. Barring complicating conditions, information contradicting a signed attestation of circumstances constitutes evidence of an IPV worth pursuing. Accountings of behavior foregrounding intentionality and internal motivation are predictable consequences of being embedded within units dedicated to counteracting deliberate fraud. These accounts, in turn, justify client punishments.[20] Constructions of intentionality as default—if not universal—also suggest self-fulfilling prophecy effects.[21] Investigators approach cases believing clients purposely break rules; indeed, given their assigned tasks and occupational incentives, they *need* clients to have purposely broken rules. It is unsurprising that they report consonant findings—and that many investigators suggest there is a group of incorrigible rule breakers who can only be prevented from committing fraud through being removed from the program.

The push for suspensions and disqualifications, to be sure, comes from higher-ups. State and federal administrators stress disqualifications as the goal of fraud control activity and use IPV numbers as both a primary measure of fraud unit performance and evidence of fraud's prevalence. And, as chapter 2 described, federal authorities provide financial incentives for establishing client IPVs. The strategic loosening of federal purse strings via these overpayment recovery retention systems pulls state-level agencies in particular directions. In total, prioritization and incentive systems show how agency activity is orchestrated to advance broader goals, especially shrinking the client population. Suspensions and disqualifications advance this objective. So does the punitive adversarialism that renders program climates suspicious and antagonistic, imposing hostile and burdensome conditions that discourage participation and contribute to client attrition.[22] Fraud workers acknowledge that their work involves not only pursuing individual cases but also acting as a countervailing force against a general experience of program participation that they see as too easy, too comfortable, and too often taken for granted.

The mandate of client control and punishment filters through governmental and bureaucratic hierarchies. Federal authorities have devolved authority to states but also instituted protocols to shape state-level decision-making in preferred punitive directions. In turn, street-level actors respond to pressures to make programs less permissive and hospitable. Individual fraud workers' mindsets and activities demonstrate how creating specialized enforcement units engenders punitive thinking and corresponding results.

*   *   *

Officially establishing IPVs is not always as simple as the binary conceptualization of intent suggests. First, investigators or their supervisors may decide not to pursue intentional fraud charges in some cases, for various reasons. Factors that can discourage charging clients with IPVs include advanced age, mental disability, or mental illness—markers conventionally associated with the "deserving poor."[23] Even in cases where they have established what they consider airtight documentation of violations, investigators sometimes question intentionality. These situations may involve misunderstanding of rules or requirements, perhaps related to cognitive impairment. For most fraud workers, they are the exception, not the rule.

Second, there is the basic matter of staffing. As in any organization, labor resources affect fraud units' work capacity and their ability to pursue particular objectives. Specifically, labor shortages impede their ability to pursue as many IPVs as they would like. Establishing intent to violate program rules in a hearing is a significantly higher threshold than establishing an Inadvertent Household Error (IHE) or Unintentional Program Violation (UPV). A substantiated UPV demonstrates a rule violation but does not require convincing a hearing officer that the client acted deliberately. When they lack the resources to do the additional work of establishing IPVs, fraud units may settle for UPVs, even if they believe clients have purposely broken rules.

Eastcoast administrator George is a large—and largely unfiltered— White man in his early sixties. In his thick regional accent, he spoke frankly about the shortcomings he sees in public assistance and program integrity efforts. George shared bar charts of his unit's UPV and IPV numbers in 2012, 2013, and 2014. In 2012, the unit established about five times as many UPVs as IPVs; by 2014, the figures for the two types of charges had nearly equalized. George explained this abrupt ratio change:

> I added a ton of investigators. So I think maybe, you know, you're looking at the case differently. You have an investigator doing it that's really, you know, saying, "Let's make this into an IPV, because it is an IPV." . . . We had found some of our investigators were going to the hearing stage and, right before the hearing would start, saying, "Let's make this a UPV." We're not playing that game. So I said to [a manager], "Get them in here and find out what the hell's going on and get back to me." And he said . . . they were new employees, and they realized as they came along and the cases were waiting to go to hearing [that] maybe [they] didn't have what they needed to make it an IPV. So I said to him, "Now, no more backing out. If you call it an IPV going in there—I'll train well enough now—if you call it an IPV going in, you're going to the hearing as an IPV. If we lose it, go with God. You lost it."

George's explanation foregrounds staffing's importance for establishing IPVs (and thus producing client suspensions and disqualifications). The combination of a hiring surge and directives from unit leadership to avoid settling for UPVs produced a fivefold increase in the share of referrals that resulted in substantiated IPVs. There may have been a shift in the real-world incidence of fraud during this time, yet the vast majority of the change clearly resulted from staffing changes that supported a greater managerial emphasis on IPVs versus UPVs.

Patricia, an investigator who worked in George's unit before and after his arrival—and the arrival of his no-nonsense attitude about pursuing IPVs—confirmed the change in investigatory strategy. She made a clear link between investigator staffing and the move toward harder-to-prove IPV charges:

> PATRICIA: I can tell you offhand that there is a lot of cases that we could pursue as a disqualification [IPV], but we go for just the overpayment [UPV], and a lot of times that's a time thing. If we also went for the [IPV], not only would we get an increased amount of repayment per month, but we would be—I forget the wording of where you're reducing what you're giving out because of the disqualification—
>
> INTERVIEWER: Cost avoidance?
>
> PATRICIA: Right. So if we had more people, even with the same number of cases that came to our desk, we would IPV more of them.

Front-End Detection and Back-End Investigation

Problem-oriented state interventions not only require a working definition of the issue at hand. They also depend on a theory of operations, a foundational idea of what is to be done to address the problem as delineated. Sometimes agencies' authorizing legislation denotes basic theories of operations, but more commonly they arise from traditions that develop over time and gradually solidify into a status quo.[24]

Welfare fraud control units exemplify this general trend. They operate under vague legislative dictates and draw their guiding theories substantially from sources other than specific legal rules. Historical practices of assessment and verification in public benefit programs and strategies conventionally associated with law enforcement agencies combine to influence their usual course of action.

In conceptualizing their theories of operation, all fraud units engage with a basic distinction between approaches to the eligibility cases that constitute most of their workload: "back-end" versus "front-end" fraud control. Back-end investigation entails efforts directed at the existing client population: people who are receiving or have received program benefits. In a back-end investigation case, the fraud unit receives a referral about a client's suspected violation. Fraud unit representatives assess that referral and, if they decide to pursue it, attempt to accumulate evidence retroactively substantiating the allegation.

Front-end detection differs fundamentally. Instead of surveilling and scrutinizing program participants, front-end detection looks at *potential* program participants: those who have applied but have not yet been declared eligible for benefits. Rather than look for irregularities in client populations, front-end detection concentrates on shaping—and winnowing—the group of people approved as clients in the first place. Though fraud workers ascribe back-end investigations some preventive value, as chapter 8's discussion of the informal criminology of welfare fraud describes, back-end work better represents the derided "pay-and-chase" system. Front-end detection, on the other hand, parallels predictive policing in aiming to head off violations before they occur.

To some extent, these vigorous attempts to avoid assisting clients who do not legitimately fall into official eligibility categories are the logical conclusion of long-used verification practices. Front-end methods demonstrate commitment to preauthorization control over benefit resources and managing risks of fraud perpetration. Back-end measures attempt oversight of resources after their release and over the course of their administration. Decisions about which of the two deserves greater emphasis in a given fraud unit can be reduced to decisions between Ronald Reagan's adopted Russian adage, "trust, but verify," and an alternative formulation, "verify before trusting."

Front-End and Back-End Investigative Methods

Front-end detection and back-end investigation both use database-driven and fieldwork-based methods of evidence gathering, though under differing time constraints. Federal regulations require that eligible clients be granted SNAP benefits within thirty days of application (those in extreme need can get "expedited service" and gain approval within seven days), limiting the time available for fieldwork-based investigations of claimed circumstances before benefit disbursement. Thus policy creates a push toward front-end detection via database searches and matches. Database-driven front-end checks are quicker and can be automated, even built into the eligibility determination process. These less laborious interventions make it easier to scrutinize a wide subset of applicants, or even all applicants. After investing time and resources into conceiving, designing, and implementing these database systems, fraud units can use them indefinitely with relatively little investigative investment.

Nevertheless, some jurisdictions use field investigations in front-end detection. Like back-end investigation, front-end detection using dedicated investigative labor and fieldwork relies on case referrals, focusing on cases flagged as suspicious, usually by eligibility reviewers; there are just too many applications and too few fraud control resources to conduct labor-intensive investigations of all applications. Midatlantic is exemplary here, employing substantially more front-end than back-end investigative staff. In this unit, a considerable number of investigators receives referrals from eligibility workers and visits homes, neighborhoods, schools, workplaces, and day care centers to gather information aimed at discrediting clients' statements.

Trends and Variations in Preventive and Reactive Approaches

In the occupational lexicon, front-end detection's goal is to obviate the need for the "pay-and-chase" model. These efforts are meant to prevent ineligible applicants from receiving benefits in the first place, in a way that corresponds to a broader preference for "police patrol" over "fire alarm" approaches to government oversight.[25] Many states supplement federally required front-end eligibility verification procedures with additional data-matching, referred case investigation, or both, and many fraud workers see preventive detection as the wave of the future.

Eastcoast's front-end detection regime is among the most sophisticated in the country. Their push toward seamless integration within the eligibility determination process is the centerpiece of this fraud unit's recent reinvention. Their automated protocol overlays a fraud control function onto the foundational work of benefit administration: the system creates a rule enforcement process that runs in the background, scrutinizing each piece of applicant-supplied information and juxtaposing it with information from other sources. This system results from localized discretion regarding the specifics of fraud control operations and demonstrates the potential for fraud-dedicated units' work to feed back into broader agency operations and profoundly shape program implementation.

This protocol also represents an intersection between the work of public assistance agencies and the data-driven surveillance and prediction methods used in twenty-first-century law enforcement. Large police departments use statistics, algorithms, and mapping tools to attempt to predict where crimes will occur and identify people likely to be involved in them, as either perpetrators or victims.[26] Eastcoast's robust front-end fraud detection staff brings similar tools to bear in the public assistance context. At the same time, because their data-matching system is largely automated and integrated into the eligibility determination workflow, its ongoing demands on the time and resources of dedicated program oversight staff are minimal. This system's creators and developers come from both the private and the public sectors, and leaders from both sides are eager to promote it. They make concerted efforts to advance it as the cutting edge of fraud prevention, including a live demonstration for at least one inquiring social scientist. Eastcoast manager Vincent explained the fraud unit's vision for the system:

> So what [the new front-end fraud detection system] did was it forced these matches to be addressed during that period of eligibility [determination]. Now, there are issues that would . . . because of a certain specific situation, [allow us] to override that [conflict]. . . . Because some matches are not verified upon receipt and require [our] agency to reach out to other agencies, which is not always, you know, the response time isn't always there [*chuckles*]. So we built in some of these fail-safes so we are not dragging out, and we're making our timely first payments as required. So this is just a way for people to see it. To be able to not allow them to move forward without some supervisory input, if they want to. And the idea would be to not pay out and have to chase it, to be a little more proactive for initial approvals.

I summed up his comments in response: "Move away from the pay-and-chase." Vincent, usually loquacious, repeated the phrase back to me, then, shaking his head, added a laconic "Which, you know, goes nowhere."

STREAMLINED APPLICATION PROCESSES   In Northeast, a combination of currently low fraud salience and limited fraud control resources have curtailed front-end verification work. These efforts were also central targets for past criticisms that fraud control efforts were hindering over-

all agency efficiency and failing to satisfy the desired cost-benefit calculus. For the time being, fraud control measures have taken a backseat to
other priorities.

Similarly—and to its fraud workers' chagrin—Southeast is a noteworthy counterexample to the trend toward front-end detection. Recent
policy changes have streamlined their application process, transitioning to a heavily phone- and web-based eligibility determination protocol in which a central dispatching unit distributes applications evenly
across regional offices. Under the new system, eligibility determination
happens primarily online, without face-to-face interviews, or via phone,
with eligibility workers asking applicants the questions from the online
form and entering their responses. Because applications are assigned to
local offices on a rotating basis, applicants may live hundreds of miles
from the eligibility workers reviewing their applications.

The expressed logic for this move is cutting overhead and speed-
ing the application process for both clients and the agency. Some fraud
unit representatives confirmed that rationale, saying that the move was
meant to increase efficiency and responsiveness, to decrease overhead,
and to more equitably distribute work across local offices. But others argued that the agency's new eligibility process is actually aimed at growing the client population. They suggested the move may be intended to
qualify the state for greater federal funding or as a way for politicians to
appeal to specific voting blocs.

Under Southeast's reconfigured system, eligibility workers are in-
structed to simply input information rather than inquiring about any
statements they find suspicious. This setup epitomizes the separation of
benefit administration labor from fraud control. Fraud units' very existence is the biggest initial step down this road, as the bureaucratic instantiation of the idea that information verification and rule enforcement
functions should be the purview of a dedicated workforce. Southeast
has gone further by consciously removing verification and enforcement
functions from eligibility determination and concentrating them entirely
in their dedicated fraud unit.

Fraud workers decry this policy change. They generally question
clients' reliability as sources of information and believe this policy increases the likelihood of fraud (sometimes with the tongue-in-cheek
concession that they like the new system's implications for their own job
security). Many feel that it is easier for applicants to lie over the phone or

when completing an online form than in a face-to-face interview. Southeast supervisor Antoine highlighted how this back-end-only approach contradicts enforcement folk wisdom:

> ANTOINE: When you can get on your laptop, and . . . fill out an application, and put down your contact information, and someone's gonna call you, and they're gonna interview you over the phone. They've never seen you before; they have no idea who you are. You can tell us you're Jimmy Carter. And we ask, "Can you send us some verification of your identity?" and you scan it to us or fax it to us . . .
>
> So we go ahead, and your case is certified. You could be in Tahiti on the beach someplace. The system does not cross-match addresses or any irregularities that pop, say, "Wait a minute, . . . this doesn't match." Or, one even better: if your mailing address and your residential address that you've given are thirty miles apart, well, no one [is alerted]. Those are things that I see all the time. And a lot of times we look at cases with out-of-state transactions, where this person is certified in Southeast, but all the transactions have been done in St. Louis, or California, or something like that. That's because that person didn't have to come in. And I think sometimes it's hard to convince individuals who never did the [eligibility determination] work that this needs to be done. When someone who's never did this work is tellin' you, "Well, this is an easy way to do it . . ." [chortles]. It is an easy way to do it, but you're forgetting the fact that you're dealing with people. You're not dealing with things that don't talk back to you, or you don't have to get information from that entity to get your job done.
>
> INTERVIEWER: You need that interactive process.
>
> ANTOINE: Exactly. I mean, it may be there's a way that you don't have to see that person every six months . . . but you wanna put some eyes on that individual and you wanna be able to verify that information. Also one of the things that I've had to tell many supervisors in offices is that we live in this technological age, that you have to be able to look at things. You have to look at situations, look at documents very closely . . .
>
> My grandfather always told me . . . "Before you put the horse in, you check the back fence." You don't put the horse in [if there's a break in the fence, or] the horse will get out. Then you're concerned about you got a hole in the back fence. And my point I've said is that you want to make sure that everything is where it's supposed to be at, and if there is a ten-

dency, if there's something in your system that's not right, fix it. Don't kick the can down the road or assume that it's gonna fix itself. 'Cause it's not. It's not.

Beyond the loss of face-to-face interaction, Southeast interviewees point to the loss of local knowledge associated with distributing applications across regional offices. They see value in balancing different offices' workloads but note that eligibility workers, especially those in rural and sparsely populated areas, may have valuable, grounded knowledge about the people who live in their regions. Supervisor Helen is a Black woman in her early forties. After years of experience working in different roles in social services, she has arrived at a tough love perspective on clients and their behavior with regard to program rules. Here, she described some of the fraud-related drawbacks she associates with the dispersed applicant system, which she calls "round robin":

> The thing that the state started is they are doing applications across the state. Which means you can be anywhere in Southeast and have a caseworker [somewhere else]. If the [caseworker] is not in a local area, you really don't know what is going on. And prior to that it was better, because we used to get a lot of referrals from local offices, because it was one of those situations where most of those caseworkers are in the community and they can see it. If you can't see it, you really can't say, "Oh yeah, it's going on." I dislike round robin for the simple fact that you're just so used to getting cases from people that you know. And then when you get this case you'll be like, wow, it takes somebody [from somewhere else so long] to figure out this is what's going on, where somebody here could have just done it much faster. So I just don't care for round robin at all.

Like Helen, Antoine values personal knowledge of one's jurisdiction. He shared an anecdote to demonstrate how knowledge of the local population and their circumstances can help resolve informational errors and minimize the unnecessary investment of fraud control resources:

> Sometimes you get a case, and you think that it's a good, prosecutable case until you realize that this information was available to the agency but no one took action on it, or that the circumstances involved here are wrong. An example, one recently, where it was the wrong Social Security number that got

entered into the system somewhere and showed up under this person's number, this person's name, but that person never worked for that company. And we discovered that as part of the investigation. [...]

Some employer somewhere down the line keyed in the wrong [Social Security] number for someone, but it was actually this person's number. And that happens a lot. [...]

It just happened that the person, when their name came across my desk, and I was talking to my investigator down in [that city], she told me about the case, and I said, "That's the same person I know. [*Very matter-of-factly:*] He did not work for this company. He did not make thirty-seven thousand dollars in a quarter." . . . Fortunately, there, because I worked in that area for a very long period of time, there are names I remember, there are people I know.

At another point, Antoine described an experience supervising disaster-related SNAP sites:

So I was bouncing around, 'cause I had staff in several different sites. And I walked into that site one morning, and a state trooper's standing by the door. So I go, "What happened?" And he said, "This should be fun." I said, "What do you mean?" He said, "It's quiet in here. Nobody's saying nothing. Nobody's even lookin' up." I said, "Okay."

So I went and spoke to [my investigator] and spoke to the site manager and a few things. And [the investigator] said, "Things [are] quiet in here." And the site manager went, "Because people know him. He lives here. They know him. Some of them are now questioning their decision to come in." And I walked out.

Well, before I got to my next destination, my investigator called me, and she said . . . "When you walked out, this lady walked up to me and wanted to know who I was. And I told her I was an investigator, and she asked me how did I know you. And I said, 'Well, he's my supervisor.' 'Supervisor of what?' So I told her, and she went and told some people and the whole little group just walked out the door."

[*Antoine chuckles.*] I said, "Yeah, I know her. She had a red vest on? Yeah, she's a cousin." [*Antoine continues laughing.*] But it happened a couple other places. Because I worked in the [region] for over twenty years . . . I know a lot of people. A lot of people know me. And I just walked in and I saw some people. "Good morning, hi, how you doin'?" And [when] I looked around again, they were gone. Because they no way met the income limit for the program.

Antoine's comments suggest the problems he sees with reducing embodied knowledge's role in rule enforcement processes. Southeast supervisor Peter, a big White man in his late fifties, told me in his deliberate southern drawl that he shared Antoine's distaste for the new system. Peter thinks contacting the agency is now akin to calling overseas user support: "You can have somebody in the north part of the state one time and somebody in the south part of the state another time, and the person lives in another part of the state. Contacting, you know—it's just short of talking to Andy from India [for technical support]."

Southeast fraud workers believe that the move away from face-to-face interviews has increased illegitimate benefit receipt, producing more fraud to detect and investigate later. Several also depicted the new work-from-home, decentralized eligibility worker role as encouraging minimal engagement and high turnover. These weren't, they implied, committed employees invested in social service careers; investigator Danielle said, "they're more like temps."

The Value of Face Time

To different extents, other states have also reduced or eliminated requirements that clients show up in person. But fraud workers link face-to-face interaction to better informational outcomes. They believe clients are more likely to tell the truth, and the whole truth, in person rather than over the phone or in writing, in keeping with the idea that "it's harder to lie to someone's face."

Concentrating enforcement functions in specific agency units creates internal constituencies inclined to resist these sorts of changes. Investigators consider phone or online applications lowered barriers to entry, and they lament losing opportunities to identify suspicious cases and preliminarily observe evidence of possible fraud. They note, for instance, that a client arriving at an in-person interview in an expensive car could be a red flag and recount raising their eyebrows at Cadillacs, Mercedes-Benzes, and Bentleys. (Southeast investigator Danielle mentioned that she occasionally trolls for suspects by taking down license plate numbers on luxury cars she observes parked in the agency's lot.)

Many workers repeated the idea that in-person appearances generate leads and provide preliminary, even preventive evidence of fraud. Like many of her colleagues, Southwest investigator Ashley used to work in benefit administration. Now in her midthirties, Ashley recalled referring

a "man in the home" case for investigation based on contextual information revealed through an office visit. As grounds for suspicion, Ashley noted that a man accompanied the applicant to the office and held
her baby during the interview, that the applicant was "acting funny,"
and that the applicant left in a luxury vehicle. Ashley, who was sometimes reticent in our interview, built momentum and effervescence as
she spoke about these matters:

> Probably our biggest problem [in the entire agency] is that—I think that, like,
> a lot of times they do . . . interviews by phone. . . . The local offices are *so
> full*. There's hundreds of people there, like six o'clock in the morning, seven
> o'clock in the morning. It's so busy. I think when I was a interviewer, it was
> they all had to come to the office. . . . And I think you learn a lot about a per-
> son. They're looking at you . . . they're shaking, they're just, you know. . . . I
> don't think over the phone is a good thing. [. . .]
>
> I think that is our biggest thing is, is that I think it should be face to face. I
> think you can catch more. And [in one case], at the time I wasn't an investiga-
> tor, but at least I can be like, "Oh, I'm gonna write up a [fraud investigation]
> request now" because she was acting funny at the interview. She . . . a *man*
> dropped her off at the office, you know, [and] he was holding the baby in the
> lobby. . . . I saw her take off in an Escalade. You know, stuff like that.

Ashley's comments demonstrate the particularities of fraud units' priorities and motivations. Eligibility streamlining aims to better serve clients
and ease demands on local offices, an issue that Ashley herself recognizes as significant in describing overcrowding. Fraud workers, though,
overwhelmingly bemoan such changes due to perceived implications for
their bailiwick. Indeed, Ashley identified the move away from face-to-
face interviews in response to a question about the *single biggest* problem facing her state's public assistance agency. Of course, fraud workers are disproportionately likely to key in on fraud-related issues when
considering their agency's problems, especially in the context of a fraud-
focused interview. Nonetheless, her direct juxtaposition of eligibility
streamlining and hopelessly overcrowded local offices is noteworthy.
Many of these offices' eligibility workers doubtless welcome changes designed to ease their workload. But, looking to their own inboxes, most
fraud workers agree with Ashley.

Ashley's comments also show visibility's importance in fraud control practice. Fraud workers trust and value information subject to direct observation and documentation and accentuate scandalous symbols like high-end cars. A key part of welfare queen rhetoric from the beginning, instances of clients riding in expensive vehicles still stand out to some fraud workers as representative of fraud problems. These rare, superficial stand-ins for clients' parasitism and greed continue to have an outsize role in understandings of welfare fraud as a phenomenon and take on noteworthy substantive significance when treated as sources of suspicion by fraud investigators.

Investigators and their organizational superiors decry policies and regulations that limit their ability to form suspicions and accumulate evidence via direct interactions with clients. Hank, a Midatlantic manager, described his agency's move away from face-to-face eligibility interviews as something his unit has "had to overcome." He linked this change specifically to greater difficulties in establishing intent, the *sine qua non* of substantiated IPVs. In-person applications establish eligibility workers and other employees as repositories of key evidentiary knowledge who can offer testimony backed by legal-bureaucratic authority. Decision-makers in Administrative Disqualification Hearings and criminal prosecutions can then call upon these witnesses for attestation that clients understood the application process and grasped the rights and responsibilities of program participation. These witnesses can also testify that clients affirmed statements about household status and means, fully apprised of the expectations of transparency and consequences of misrepresentation.

In the absence of these authoritative statements, there is more "wiggle room," as Hank put it. When application materials are completed online or over the phone, clients can more cogently argue that they did not fully understand the application process, the rules of program participation, or the consequences of rule violation. Accused clients can also claim that they did not personally complete applications at all, as suggested in Ashley's statement that "it might not even be that person," and Antoine's joke, "you can tell us you're Jimmy Carter."[27]

From the enforcement perspective, the lack of authoritative identity verification and confirmation of clients' comprehension is crucial. That deficit weakens fraud workers' position in arguing for the fraud unit's version of events in formal adjudication settings, creating potential weaknesses in their cases. This can create room for competing constructions of the situation, potentially fostering doubts in the minds of hearing officers, judges, or juries.

Referrals and Evidence: The Sources and Substance of Rule Violation Knowledge

Retroactive investigations—and some front-end investigations—begin with case referrals. Fraud units receive most of their referrals from three sources: assistance agency workers outside the fraud unit, other government agencies, and public informants sending or calling in fraud tips. The most common referral sources are local office staff and members of the public (including other clients).

Differential Referral Valuation

Fraud workers see some referral sources as more useful than others. They are more dubious of public informant reports than of referrals from caseworkers or police officers. Public informant reports are the most grassroots form of fraud referrals and are prima facie attractive to enforcement authorities as intelligence sources. Just as police officers often feel that local residents are likely to know more about what is happening in an area than the police assigned to work it,[28] investigators note that informants are likely to have insider access to information about their friends, family, and neighbors.[29] Information that caseworkers or fraud investigators would need to invest considerable effort to find may be immediately apparent to personal acquaintances, particularly family members or other close ties. Substantiating household composition in a "man in the home" case, for instance, can take several days of investigative work triangulating information from multiple sources, perhaps including database searches, stakeouts to document comings and goings, home inspections, and soliciting statements at workplaces, schools, or day care centers. To a friend or family member, on the other hand, the man's place of residence may be common knowledge.

Thus fraud units solicit tips from voluntary reporters and actively seek out incriminating information from people acquainted with fraud suspects.[30] Exploiting clients' relationships in this way provides an adjunct labor force to advance enforcement efforts. This resource is useful to investigators. However, despite informants' comparative advantages of informational access, fraud workers express some reservations about these reports.

REASONS FOR DOUBTING HOTLINE REFERRALS   To some extent, fraud investigators' ambivalence about informant reports reflects a general tendency to partially or wholly discredit information from members of stigmatized populations.[31] Many public reports of suspected welfare fraud come from other clients or people from similar socioeconomic strata. Poor people and welfare clients are subject to a wide range of negative stereotypes and stigmatizations, which demonstrate interacting effects of class, race, and gender discrimination.[32] Agency employees are not immune to stereotypes and stigma, and some subscribe to dominant and disparaging narratives regarding welfare and welfare reform.[33]

Beyond their reluctance to invest time and energy pursuing referrals from unreliable sources, fraud workers say hotline referrals have characteristics that give them pause. Fraud workers are primarily interested in successful case substantiation and believe public tips are less conducive to this outcome than referrals from other channels. In part, this disparity may result from a self-fulfilling prophecy, wherein investigators take publicly referred cases less seriously from the outset and therefore invest less energy in investigating them. The specific reasons investigators provided for doubting public reports stem from a mixture of personal experience and information circulating within welfare agencies, especially within fraud units.

First, fraud workers invoke informants' ulterior motives as a reason for doubting the veracity of their reports. Fraud workers see envy, malice, or desired leverage as spurring most public fraud tips, rendering them inherently suspect compared to the relatively "clean" referral channels: state agents acting in their official capacities.[34]

Second, although acknowledging that friends, family members, and neighbors have informational access advantages, investigators describe problems with the quality and utility of the evidence they provide. Misunderstandings of program rules and enforcement policies and practices commonly cause such shortfalls. Eastcoast investigator Patricia offered an illustration:

> The [informant] is sending pictures of them together, and pictures of their boat, and [*interviewer laughs*], yeah, and pictures of the house. And we

already knew that he was in the home! One of the very lax regulations is that there is no legal reason you have to have somebody in your household on your benefits. The question is "Do you purchase and prepare your food together or not." I wish they would do away with that because that's a ridiculous reg[ulation]—I'm getting a little off [track] here, but all you have to do is say "no." So she had said "no."

Here Patricia illustrates how asymmetry in the policy knowledge held by agency insiders and outsiders shapes the information fraud units receive. Fraud suspicions often involve some prominent valuable asset—a home, or a car, or a boat. However, these types of nonliquid property do not generally affect eligibility determinations.[35] Further, most states use broad-based categorical eligibility policies, in which households that qualify for a TANF-funded or maintenance-of-effort-funded benefit automatically qualify for SNAP, without an asset test requirement. Eligibility for the TANF-funded or maintenance-of-effort-funded benefit usually does not include an asset limit.[36] Thus tips about expensive property provide, at most, circumstantial evidence of unreported income. At their worst, they reify negative ideas and stereotypes omnipresent in welfare reform discourse. They also reveal how fraud leads skew toward the highly visible, even when there is substantial mismatch between what is visible and what constitutes a rule violation.

REFERRALS FROM LOCAL WELFARE OFFICES AND POLICE OFFICERS   Referrals from local welfare offices, police departments, and other bureaucratic sources can also contain errors. Like public reports, referrals from non-welfare agencies sometimes reflect misunderstandings of program rules. As Southwest supervisor Carly puts it, police officers are not "program people," and their knowledge of rules and regulations is often limited or flawed. This can precipitate reports of things that do not constitute violations or are difficult to substantiate as violations. "Bad" referrals from within assistance agencies do not usually reflect misunderstandings of general program rules. But they can reflect misunderstandings of the information-gathering capacities, authoritative limitations, and evidentiary requirements that pertain to fraud enforcement processes.

Fraud workers invoke their specialized knowledge to claim their bureaucratic territory: they possess knowledge of their rule-bound operating environment that generalist law enforcement actors do not, *and* they possess knowledge of the specifics of enforcement within that environment that generalist public assistance actors do not. Police officers' referrals can reflect their limited knowledge and experience regarding public assistance, and caseworkers' referrals can reflect their limited knowledge and experience regarding law enforcement. Fraud units straddle the boundary between the bureaucratic domains of welfare and criminal justice, acting on leads and evidence from both sides. In processing case referrals, they look for each source's typical weaknesses, attempting to weed out less-promising referrals and focus attention on those most likely to lead to successful charges.

Fraud units also watch for more idiosyncratic and less structurally driven causes of variation in referral quality. Benefit administration workers and police officers differ in their zeal for referring cases and in their investment of effort and prowess in their referrals. That means some referrals arrive at the fraud unit already substantially advanced toward completion, with thorough allegation description and documentation, while others arrive as only brief statements of suspected violations. As they build cooperative relationships with other state actors over time, fraud investigators learn which individuals and offices tend to supply strong referrals and which tend to produce weak ones. These reputations influence how fraud workers view and prioritize referrals. A shaky referral from an otherwise reputable source is more likely to get the benefit of the doubt.

Put differently, referral sources' histories of reliability shape their standing with fraud units. Via the "Matthew effect" or cumulative advantage processes,[37] initially small advantages in the usefulness of referrals from a particular source increase the likelihood that investigators will take that source's future referrals seriously and pursue those cases aggressively. And the reverse is true: notoriety as a source of bad referrals can damage future referrals' prospects, further lowering the source's reputation.

Visibility and Legibility in Fraud Evidence

Visibility to agencies structures fraud investigation. This parallels other oversight and enforcement contexts. For instance, organizations that never file with the Internal Revenue Service (IRS) often fly below regu-

latory agencies' radar,[38] and "bust-out" credit card frauds based on fabricated identities are difficult to control because there is no immediate
victim to alert authorities about illegitimate transactions.[39]

Welfare fraud control authorities similarly rely on informational resources that are accessible and seen as valid. Often this reduces to written documentation or contentions supported by reliable witness testimony. This results in stark disparities, for example, between how fraud
units handle different types of unreported income allegations: investigators prioritize cases involving officially documented income because
proving under-the-table earning is much harder.

Off-the-books work is common in the United States. The total value
of this underground economy is difficult to ascertain exactly, but it is
appreciable; recent studies estimate that $2 trillion in income goes un-
reported to the IRS annually[40] and that members of more than half of
US households participate in informal work,[41] which is particularly commonplace among the poor.[42] However, the lack of authoritative evidence
in such cases makes them less attractive to outcome-oriented fraud control authorities. Substantiating informal income requires investing significant investigatory time and energy without strong sanctioning prospects. Comparatively, evidence availability for unreported but otherwise
documented income makes these cases fraud control mainstays.

Eastcoast investigator Diego explained the difficulties inherent in establishing under-the-table income. A conscientious and insightful Latino man in his late thirties with a shaved head and a neat goatee, Diego's prior experience as an investigator for a prosecutor's office gives
him unique perspective on evidence gathering and case substantiation:

> DIEGO: *Extremely* difficult cases. . . . Those cases are almost nonexistent,
> unless you know someone. That's a good point [the question raises]. . . .
> I've had cases where, you know, you have someone doing someone's lawn.
> It's not necessarily a landscaping company; the person's been doing it for
> several months. Someone in the community sees it, decides to report it,
> 'cause somehow they know the person's on benefits. And you get it, and
> you're just kinda like, "Oh, let me look into this," and you kinda see, "Oh,
> he is working. Eh, he was gettin' paid." You contact maybe the home-
> owner that's paying, and they're willing to [help you]: "Oh, I'll give you
> the pay stub, the paychecks that I paid him with." So now you can develop
> [a charge]. But unless you know a firsthand source it's a difficult case to

prove. When jobs are worked under the table, unless someone reports, you don't have a money trail to follow.

INTERVIEWER: Right, no paper trail.

DIEGO: And not only that, you just don't *know* about it. That's really the challenge.

Hand-to-hand EBT card sales between individuals are similarly tricky to document. Southwest has taken a hard line on such benefit trafficking, using undercover work and surveillance to catch more of these often-obscure violations. But without such zealous measures, investigators are usually hard-pressed to find strong evidence and may be less likely to pursue such cases.

SNAP trafficking evidence is more accessible when retailers are involved (particularly in rare cases like those described by Midatlantic and Southeast managers, who found businesses had kept detailed records evincing their trafficking involvement and implicating clients). Federal FNS agents with primary jurisdiction over retailer trafficking share evidence with state-level fraud authorities, who take the lead on investigating clients alleged to be involved. State Law Enforcement Bureau (SLEB) agreements facilitate such cooperative enforcement. These arrangements permit administrative authorities to deputize law enforcement officers to investigate program-specific charges normally outside of police jurisdiction, advancing punitive adversarialism through police–welfare coordination across the federal, state, and local levels (see chapter 4 for further details).

Even when federal authorities provide investigative leads, state-level investigators sometimes find evidence of clients' alleged SNAP trafficking elusive. Veteran Eastcoast investigator Patricia said,

We could easily have, at minimum, one person who their only job is doing trafficking cases. And instead it's just like tacked on to everything else. When we get information from USDA regarding a store that's been disqualified, it always comes to us with pages of case numbers that they have identified that they believe were trafficking with the store. They go after the store; we go after the clients. And there's pages of people that we could potentially pursue. And we can't. We don't even dent it. It's like a needle in a haystack. We just go after however many we can, which is not very many. So there's probably plenty of that going on. One part of trafficking that I find really hard to prove is customer to customer. It's like, there's just not a lot of evidence out there. But I think that happens more times than not, and the ones that traffic with the store, with the mom-and-pop store, it's still very hard to prove; you're putting together a lot of circumstantial evidence, but I can do that much easier than customer to customers. I think there's a lot of that going on. And I can't tell you the number of caseworkers, just caseworkers, who have mentioned to me . . . [that] they have been approached by some stranger saying, "Do you wanna buy my benefits?"

Patricia's comments demonstrate enforcement attention's irregular—but nonrandom—distribution across the population of potential rule breakers. Authorities disproportionately see people whose actions are exposed and whose affairs are documented and legible. Clients who go "on record" by selling their benefits to businesses, for instance, are more vulnerable to trafficking charges than those who stick to hand-to-hand deals, which often fly under the enforcement radar. Although Patricia's account of caseworkers solicited to buy benefits might be apocryphal, it foregrounds the limitations she sees on agencies' ability to control such off-the-books activity.

Fieldwork and Databases in Fraud Control Practice

Fieldwork

Fraud workers qualify as street-level bureaucrats,[43] but their connections to "the street" vary according to fraud units' differences regarding fieldwork. The five case study states exemplify the national range of heterogeneity in fieldwork policies. At one pole are Southwest and Midatlantic, where fieldwork is heavily utilized in fraud control efforts. Investigators in these states engage in an array of different investigatory actions outside the office, including visiting suspects' residences to conduct field interviews and home inspections. Northeast is at the opposite pole, with no provision for fieldwork in the fraud investigator position.

Southeast and Eastcoast lay between these poles. Like their relatively close neighbor's in Northeast, Eastcoast's policies de-emphasize fieldwork. Fraud investigation work in this state is primarily office-based and relies especially on database-driven fraud detection and investigation techniques. At the time of data collection, Eastcoast's investigators reported sometimes traveling to local offices to review paper case files.

But, in keeping with their technologically driven approach, they were in the process of scanning these materials into their computer system to allow investigators to gather this information without physical travel.

Southeast uses fieldwork more heavily, manager Jack explained:

> Whenever we hire people, I want to make sure that they're, one, that they're self-starters, and two, that they're not afraid to get out in the field. Because I like to see people out in the field. . . . Even to the point where when I was an investigator, I would just go around, I would go talk to people, go talk in the field. I didn't mind knocking on a door and saying, "Hello," you know, "I'm looking at your neighbor, I'm trying to find out who lives in that home over there." And of course they would tell me, they would ask, "Who are you?" and "What did they do?" And because of confidentiality rules and such, I couldn't say, "Well, those people over there are committing food stamp fraud." But I *could* say, "I investigate food stamp fraud, and I'm just talking, I'm trying to find information about those people over there." I leave it up to them to put one and one together.

Jack values investigative fieldwork, linking it to more reliable fraud evidence and what he sees as stronger deterrent effects. Unlike Southwest and Midatlantic, though, Southeast investigators do not go directly to suspects' residences (they describe this as a safety issue, in line with how investigators in home-visit states report personal safety as a concern). In framing the policy as a source of strength, Southeast fraud workers describe maintaining agency offices as the site of contact with suspects as an advantage in interviews and interrogations. Evoking police officers' use of spartan interrogation rooms,[44] these investigators argue that interactions outside of clients' comfort zones are more conducive to valid and useful responses. This depiction evinces how state-level discretionary policy choices shape fraud units' ongoing creation of punitive adversarialism in practice.

Inter-investigator Variation

Investigators also have substantial discretion when it comes to their modi operandi. There are differences between those working in the same agencies, the same units, and even the same offices. Some investigators working in fieldwork-oriented states fully embrace "shoe-leather" investigative work such as field interviews and surveillance, while others

prefer to operate from their desks as much as possible. These stylistic departures may in part reflect differences in comfort and facility with information technology, which some fraud workers depict as generational.

These differences demonstrate the relationship between assessments
of informational utility and discretionary action. Investigators have to
manage their investment of time and energy. Perceptions of evidentiary
accessibility and reliability influence investigators' assessments of cases'
promise and thus their decisions about which cases to prioritize. Accordingly, individual investigators make judgment calls about how to evalu-
ate labor-intensive fieldwork evidence relative to other, more immediate
informational resources, especially computer-driven research.

Beyond its capacity to produce reliable evidence, pro-fieldwork investigators report that it can provide contextual information and investigative leads. Interviews and informal conversations in neighborhoods
can be an excellent avenue to general familiarization with a situation.
These interactions can also reveal potential violations and introduce
new sources of evidence. Like Jack, many investigators value getting out
in the field and "just talking."[45]

Even in states without robust fieldwork systems, some fraud workers
prize fieldwork-derived information. Eastcoast administrator George is
interested in expanding his investigators' fieldwork role. In the mean-
time, he creatively deploys his available resources to compensate for
his unit's paucity of field-based evidence gathering. Here, he described
how he uses local offices' program oversight staff—whom he called "his
stormtroopers"—to carry out the sorts of fieldwork assignments that investigators in his office do not take on:

> Those are the guys who will go out when the shit hits the fan somewhere. I'll
> say, "Okay, I'll send out [my stormtroopers]." We'll check this. We'll check
> that. We'll check this. We'll do research. We'll go out and see what's going on
> with this. . . . If I get a whim that I wanna check, [I'll say], "You know, some-
> thing doesn't smell right with the Social Security numbers. Let's do a check
> and see how many names come up. Let's try and do a check of how many
> names come up against the appropriate Social Security number."
>
> How many workers are maybe just pushing it through without disposi-
> tioning correctly? Even when they received information it may be incorrect.
> And that's when I use a division like them. Because they'll go out, and no
> one seems to know what the hell they're doing. They're out there and they're
> looking for cases. They're doing this. They're doing that. Then they were

brought back to me and I'd go to the [agency leadership] and say, "We got a shit show. We got a problem here. We gotta fix this."

George points out the enduring appeal of in-person information gathering for some types of rule enforcement practice, even in a state that has embraced database matches and other technologically advanced methods of detection and investigation. These IT-based techniques play an ever-expanding role in welfare fraud control.[46]

Databases

Relying on database information involves placing a fair amount of trust in other actors. It means having faith that information was entered accurately, categorized correctly, and updated appropriately. Fraud workers—even those who place the most stock in database information—recognize these inherent characteristics and describe instances where quality standards were not met.[47] Those who favor the primary-source knowledge obtained through fieldwork are particularly likely to note database information's associated assumptions and instances of failure. In contrast, those who highly value these tools point to benefits that they say outweigh their costs.

This fieldwork-database continuum roughly maps onto a "quality vs. quantity" debate in building fraud control knowledge. Some fraud workers argue that time investments in traditional fieldwork pay off with more comprehensive and viable information. Others stress the facility of database work for rapidly aggregating multiple pieces of information to build IPV cases. Indeed, a major benefit of tech-assisted investigation techniques is the relative speed of obtaining information by querying government and private sector databases (such as those maintained by Thomson Reuters and LexisNexis), as well as using other data-driven tools like geographic information system mapping of clients' benefit use patterns.

Fraud workers also think database-driven work can break information silos. George called creating new pathways of intragovernmental communication that make client information more transparent one of the most important accomplishments of his eventful term. Elsewhere—and to some extent still in Eastcoast—fraud workers bemoaned longstanding informational barriers between agencies, saying restricted information flow impedes fraud control efficacy. Numerous bureaucratic entities are implicated: the myriad agencies of the patchwork social safety net; various criminal justice organizations; and a host of others not explicitly connected to either welfare or law enforcement, including departments of motor vehicles, departments of labor, and school systems. Many fraud workers feel that they generally have the tools and freedom to do their jobs effectively but said information silos hinder their work. Some of this siloing is an intentional product of regulations designed to protect individual privacy. Other information-sharing problems result from weak connections, rivalries, disagreements between agencies, and discrepancies between databases.

Simple human communication failures add their own complications. This especially characterizes information requests from agencies in other states, which are physically, organizationally, and psychologically distant. This cumulative distance weakens incentives for cooperation and disincentives for noncooperation. Some investigators maintain cooperative relationships with specific colleagues in other states, a practice that offers mutual access advantages; losing such a contact can be quite problematic, especially if it was in a state commonly implicated in duplicate benefit cases. Fraud investigators cherish relationships with those who can help them break down barriers and access the broadest possible range of information.

Hearings and Hearing Officers

As they pursue IPVs, fraud workers ultimately attempt to assemble evidence that administrative hearing officers, judges, or juries will deem valid and sufficient. Accuracy is a first-order concern. In his characteristic deliberative manner, Eastcoast investigator Diego described his attention allocation process:

> DIEGO: I put emphasis on having an accurate case. Making sure that, if I'm gonna bring forward an Intentional Program Violation, all my documentation's there. That the client knew, that the client signed their application, [that] I have those applications. I have the data matches showing, hypothetically, let's say it was employment or unemployment, or any source of income, I have those matches. I verify from the first-party source, their employer, the [labor department]. I've calculated the numbers, I've had a secondary calculation done by our calculation unit, and then a re-review

and an ultimate peer review, and then the supervisor to sign off. And then a case like that is good, you know, to go forward with a hearing.

INTERVIEWER: Mm-hmm. So the peer review—is that just another investigator?

DIEGO: Investigators and senior staff. You know, as many eyes as you can get to [say], "Hey, you missed this" or "[This] is my opinion on it, this is what I think" or "What about using this to bolster it a little bit more?" or "Maybe that's a UPV." You know.

INTERVIEWER: But you feel like you get to do at least a minimal review of all your referrals, or are there some that you've got to say, "I can't even look at this because I've got too many things to do?"

DIEGO: I would say we get to look at all of them. It's just not all of 'em are going to go on.

Diego's comments illustrate the conscientiousness and circumspection he brings to his job, as well as the administrative structures that contextualize the validation process. In describing the multiple steps involved in producing a "good" case, he demonstrates the factors that weigh into fraud units' version of "creaming" clients. In other social service and welfare–criminal justice hybrid contexts, "creaming"[48] or "filtering"[49] clients refers to electing to provide services to those deemed more likely to succeed. This practice aims at improving agency outcomes and thus defending reputation and legitimacy. In the welfare fraud context, the analogous process is prioritizing referrals deemed most likely to produce substantiated charges. As Diego put it, "not all of 'em are going to go on." Substantiating IPVs requires investment. When IPV cases reach the latter stages of the process but do not succeed, these sunk costs are lost. Investigators are therefore motivated to choose carefully which cases go on.

IPV charges are adjudicated in ADHs. The US Supreme Court ruled in 1970's *Goldberg v. Kelly* that the Fourteenth Amendment prohibits termination of welfare benefits without due process.[50] Prevailing jurisprudence dictates that necessary due process in these cases includes providing clients with a notice of charges and a fair hearing, but not other protections required in criminal proceedings, such as the right to an attorney.[51] Unless clients waive their right to a hearing, investigators pursuing IPVs present their evidence to third-party hearing officers in ADHs. As administrative congeners to criminal courts, ADHs satisfy the fair hearing standard established in *Goldberg*. These hearings—and the preferences and proclivities of the officers who oversee them—are pivotal. Their characteristics bear out in the ways investigators and supervisors assess the referrals they receive, make judgments about which to pursue, and go about the acquisition and compilation of evidence. Punitive adversarialism reaches its climax in the ADH. This is where the state officially determines wrongdoing and opens avenues to program sanctions and criminal prosecutions.

Navigating the Hearing System

In the conventional criminal justice system, police officers learn what prosecutors look for in cases and how to write reports and statements to maximize the chances of a successful prosecution. These localized requirements and preferences are more specific than the foundational constitutional rules applying to reasonable suspicion and probable cause, and they vary between prosecutors and across prosecutorial settings.[52] Welfare fraud investigators similarly learn how to write reports to maximize their chances of success in ADHs and criminal prosecutions and how to tailor their writing to local contexts. Eastcoast investigator Tiffany spoke about how the characteristics of hearing processes and hearing officers shape the day-to-day business of fraud investigation:

> Something that definitely has an effect on each of our investigators [is] the hearing officer. Some hearing officers . . . will have certain views about certain types of fraud, so if you know you have that hearing officer often, sometimes that can really affect your cases too.

Tiffany will pursue IPVs even in low-dollar-value cases. As she pointed out, though, success with these smaller cases—or any cases—depends on working with a hearing officer who is willing to find against these clients. This indicates how investigators consider norms and patterns in hearing processes when assessing cases' prospects. As Tiffany suggested, investigators accumulate knowledge about hearing officers and their orientations and preferences, which they can use in deciding which cases to pursue as IPVs. Personal hearing experiences and shared knowledge about hearing officers inform judgments about the types of cases particular officers favor or disfavor and what kinds of evidence they might require to demonstrate intentional rule breaking.

Hearing officers are officially neutral arbiters, and fraud workers generally attest that the neutrality standard is upheld. Some investigators even contend that some hearing officers are biased in favor of clients, despite their status as state officials. Certainly, though, familiarity with the charge adjudication process is a comparative advantage separating investigators from clients. Structural positions and ongoing working relationships with hearing officers allow investigators to cultivate valuable knowledge that helps them secure IPV rulings. Clients lack such resources. Here, Tiffany described some of the variation in hearing officers and their approaches to the hearing setting and the presentation of evidence:

> It is stressful. Because sometimes you just don't know what to expect when the client shows up. Or if they don't show up, you know, you just present your documents. But if the client shows up, sometimes obviously they're upset. So . . . it can be stressful because of that, the atmosphere. I mean, basically what the setting is, you're in a fairly small office, in the [local] office usually, and it'll be me, the hearing officer, and the client. So you have a small room with these three people, and I'm sitting there accusing them of something. I mean, it's uncomfortable for me, it's uncomfortable I'm sure for the client who's obviously upset, so with that environment too it doesn't make for a good setting either. So yeah, it can be stressful. . . . I mean . . . that's like the biggest part of my job, is the outcome of these hearings. [. . .]
>
> Personally, that's probably the hardest part of my job. Because everything else I'm off doing on my own. I don't feel stress in that. The stress is when you actually have to bring it all together and present it. And some hearing officers too will question you about very specific things of a case. And when you're putting together so many cases . . . and you're recorded during these hearings, to be put on that spot and to possibly not know the answer to something is what causes me stress. Which is why I come in two hours prior to the hearing and [look over] every single thing so that if I'm asked something during a hearing I can answer it correctly. And because, obviously, everyone's case can be completely different from each other. So that for me is definitely the most stressful part of the job. Just because of that—you're put on the spot and you have to be questioned about certain things that you're presenting.

Later, Tiffany elaborated on the significance of the hearing officer's approach for not only determining the outcome of her case but setting the

entire tenor of the hearing, a high-stakes and high-stress environment
for both the accused client and the accusing investigator:

> Once I present the evidence, some hearing officers will actually kinda take
> over, and then they start the communication fully with the client, which
> makes it really easy for me because basically I just have to present what I
> have and the hearing officer and the client would go back and forth regarding
> what I presented. Which is actually a good day for me. But if I have a hear-
> ing officer that kinda sits back and doesn't really say much, then I'm the one
> who actually has to be the [one to] communicate back and forth with the cli-
> ent. And that can obviously escalate the client's anger. Because obviously . . .
> I'm not the neutral party, I'm the one saying . . . "These are the allegations.
> We believe you're committing fraud." Whereas when the conversation goes
> between the hearing officer and the client, it's more neutral because that is
> the neutral party. So that when I have to go back and forth with the client
> to make my point or to dispute what they're saying, that is stressful to me.
> Because it's almost like confrontation back and forth—he said, she said. Be-
> cause, you know, I'm presenting documents, but then the client's saying this,
> and that can just be stressful and repetitive. It can be very repetitive some-
> times. I had one hearing that lasted over two hours. And it wasn't anything. It
> was just a normal "didn't report her income." Like, it wasn't anything crazy.
> And, I mean, that's a long time to sit there and argue with someone about
> documents you have.

Investigators can tailor their report writing and approaches to hearings
according to their learned knowledge about hearing officers' tendencies.
But the implications of investigators' ongoing associations with hearing
officers do not stop with familiarity and consequent tailoring of work
processes and products. These sustained relationships also create opportunities for investigators to provide feedback to hearing officers and vice
versa, potentially influencing future hearings.

Patricia, another Eastcoast investigator, has substantial experience
with her regular hearing officers. They have a good working relationship
with which she is generally satisfied. Nonetheless, she argued that not all
hearing officers are similarly competent or willing to adhere closely to
the letter of the law in adjudicating fraud charges:

> I generally work with two specific officers [in my region] and they're terrific.
> And I know that they know what they're doing, and I agree with their hearing

decisions. There is one issue with one of them, which I think is in process of being worked out, but there is some nightmare issues with some of the other officers that I personally don't have much contact with . . .

For example, I just saw, because of my new position now, clerical sent these like five or six hearing decisions to the investigator. They were all written by the same hearing officer . . . and the clerical staff was alerting the investigator to the fact that the hearing officer decided it wasn't intentional—yes, there's an overpayment, but it wasn't intentional. And I think maybe all of them were basically the same thing, where the client didn't put something in writing during the period of fraud.

And the hearing officer would say, "Yes, this should've been reported, and yes, the client signed off agreeing to do that, but it doesn't [qualify as an IPV]." Even in some cases the client didn't even come to the hearing. [The officer was] just assuming for the client, who wasn't even here saying this, that it wasn't intentional. Regardless of the fact, ignoring the fact that they signed paperwork saying that if you don't report [changes], you know, that it is considered intentional. And just by that fact alone it's an IPV. Here was just a very recent example of five or six hearing decisions where the hearing officer made that decision: half of them the client had come in [for the hearing], and half [the client] didn't come in. If those hearing officers that do that were ones I had to deal with personally, I would be going nuts. I'd be really pissed and upset.

With their signatures, clients affirm the veracity of reported household circumstances and promise to report changes in their financial situations. When investigators provide solid evidence of circumstances that differ from the attestations in agency files, these client signatures are typically considered probative of deliberate fraud. Patricia described a hearing officer who fails to abide by this standard, instead setting a higher bar for the substantiation of intentionality, and predicted how she would react to such decisions in her cases.

Clients, of course, might also disagree with hearing officers' decisions; however, as "one-shotters" coming from outside the agency, they are in a less advantageous position to impactfully raise those concerns than are "repeat players" from inside the agency.[53] Patricia exemplifies the advantages of repeat players, who have opportunities to learn about claim adjudication settings and potentially influence their outcomes. Each time she presents evidence in an ADH, she learns more about how to investigate and present her evidence. And, unlike the clients who cycle through

ADHs, Patricia is able—and willing—to let hearing officers know if she is upset with a decision and suggest a different approach.

Conclusion

Fraud units attempt to advance a core welfare reform objective: shrinking public benefit programs' size. They do so directly through establishing IPVs, which permit client suspensions and disqualifications, and through front-end detection measures, which prevent people from accessing programs in the first place.

As a particular type of response to welfare administration questions, fraud units enhance surveillance and penalization in assistance programs. Fraud workers' objectives involve getting clients excluded from programs, not facilitating program access.[54] Accordingly, fraud workers are not particularly sanguine about policies that facilitate client participation, such as streamlined eligibility determination. Despite their potential to help advance agencies' provision objectives, enforcement authorities decry their implications for fraud prevention and detection. When viewed from the enforcement wing, changes that ease clients' informational exposure requirements are inherently undesirable.

Fraud control efforts run on information. Busy fraud workers value informational transparency, deprioritize information of dubious validity or utility, and applaud information-sharing provisions. They also strive to build good working relationships with informational sources, law enforcement figures, and ADH officers, all of whom help them access evidence and convert it into officially validated cases. These substantiated IPVs are the central currency of fraud control success and the key instrument through which fraud units fulfill their assignment of catching clients who break rules.

CHAPTER FOUR

The Welfare Police

Welfare reform expanded conventional welfare workers' purview and discretion[1] and also enlarged and formalized the workforce tasked specifically with detecting, investigating, and punishing rule violations.[2] Today's fraud units occupy a designated enforcement role carved into the public assistance system.[3] As a class of bureaucratic actors, dedicated fraud investigators embody the clear demarcation between enforcement and the agency's benefit administration function. Their administrative separation and specialization create space for punitive adversarialism within public assistance systems.

Welfare fraud enforcement exemplifies how government activities reflect "multiple and contradictory logics."[4] Fraud control units compellingly demonstrate the artificiality of the division between state functions of provision and punishment. Blurring this boundary involves formal information sharing and organizational coaction between criminal justice and public assistance agencies. Informal, individual ties cutting across bureaucracies further facilitate cooperative enforcement strategies. Sanctions are also crucial in tying provision and punishment. In some jurisdictions, administrative enforcement units are especially eager to work with police and criminal prosecutors to pursue criminal charges for welfare rule violations, a dramatic outcome of punitive adversarialism. Incarceration and other harsh criminal consequences are more likely when people are accused of large-dollar offenses or when welfare fraud charges can be added to other criminal proceedings. Though rarer than fraud cases leading to administrative sanctions, criminally charged cases have disproportionately high profiles—and disproportionate impact on the ongoing symbolic construction of welfare fraud as a pressing political and social issue.

Intertwining Provision and Punishment

Oversight and punishment functions in systems nominally dedicated to assisting the needy are nothing new. As Kaaryn Gustafson puts it, "[The] dual purposes of providing for the sympathetic deserving poor and policing and surveilling families at the margins have held steady through American aid programs, both private and public."[5] Government assistance in the United States has long-since involved mechanisms of control, surveillance, and sanction, often justified with paternalist arguments about "improving" poor people—especially poor people of color—through counteracting their pathologies.[6] Indeed, invasiveness and punitiveness in means-tested assistance programs have continually outpaced parallel efforts to counteract similar types of "paper crimes," including other government-specific offenses like tax fraud.[7] This has especially been the case in the most heavily gendered, racialized, and stigmatized public assistance programs, including ADC/AFDC/TANF and Food Stamps/SNAP.[8]

In every state, welfare fraud units' operations evidence the intertwining of social provision and social control. As chapter 3 discussed, however, there are significant differences in how fraud units operate across jurisdictions. The variegation of methods and motivations results in an uneven application of state functions between "pure" public assistance and law enforcement orientations.

Sanction preferences combine with differences in investigative techniques to drive this variation. Welfare fraud enforcement consistently focuses on establishing Intentional Program Violations (IPVs)—the administrative offenses that permit legal client suspensions and disqualifications—but states part ways in their zeal for actively pursuing criminal charges. My five case study states differ substantially, giving a good sense of the national variation: Southeast, Southwest, and Midatlantic are much more inclined toward criminal charges than are fraud enforcement authorities in Eastcoast and Northeast. Accordingly, the former states' fraud units hew more closely than the latter's to criminal justice agencies and the broader governmental function of punishment.

Because fraud units' enforcement assignment is specific to nominally assistance-oriented programs' clientele, even comparatively punitive units are formally associated with the state's provision function. This overlap is not just a matter of abstract social theorizing. It is realized in the concrete experiences of welfare clients who encounter these hybrid government agents. Southwest investigator Ashley describes how her boundary-blurring, legally ambiguous status as a welfare fraud investigator facilitates her effectiveness in the field. In particular, she notes that her quasi-police status helps her gain compliance from clients who might not understand exactly who she is, what agency she represents, the extent of her authority, or their own rights in the situation. Ashley told me about going out on home inspections:

> ASHLEY: When I've gone to these houses, they [say], "Who are you? Where are you from?" They're just so surprised. Which I guess I think is good in a way for my position at that time because, you know, the biggest thing is getting them when they're not aware that we're around.
>
> INTERVIEWER: So when you show up and you identify yourself: you have like a badge, an ID of some kind, do you just verbally announce who you are?
>
> ASHLEY: I do, when we go, I say, "I'm Investigator Baxter," and I do have a badge, and it has my ID in it also. And that's how I usually identify myself—I'll just say, "I'm with the [fraud] unit."
>
> INTERVIEWER: What's the most common immediate reaction when you show up?
>
> ASHLEY: Mmm. . . . A lot of times, they're like—they usually get afraid, just because they think I'm a cop, for whatever reason?
>
> INTERVIEWER: Right. I mean, if you show 'em a badge . . .
>
> ASHLEY: Right, they just automatically assumed I'm a police officer.

Ashley seemed in no rush to disabuse clients who assumed she was with the police. That assumption is useful to her. Without a search warrant, Ashley lacks the authority to require clients to grant her access to their homes.[9] Her comments reveal, though, how investigators can leverage their quasi-police status and official signifiers—including badges—to gain cooperation and consent. Partially, this a product of clients being caught off guard, their uncertainty about the rules that pertain to the situation, and their fear of losing needed assistance. Like police, welfare fraud workers can capitalize on uncertainty and trepidation and use intimidation to pursue investigative agendas.[10] They can also capitalize directly on their novel, boundary-blurring status. "Welfare fraud investigator" is a relatively unusual social category, with distinctive ties to two different worlds. This allows investigators to self-present strategically, foregrounding either their assistance agency association or their enforcement role depending on what they believe will best advance their objectives.[11] Together, these circumstances and tactics prove effective for investigators' purposes, with refusals relatively rare exceptions to the norm of receiving consent to search.

Southwest's and Southeast's emphasis on field investigations and criminal sanctions bears out in their fraud investigators' stronger identification with conventional police. Eastcoast and Northeast, on the other hand, are less closely aligned with criminal justice agencies' methods and motivations. In response to a question about his unit's methods and the types of cases they pursue, Eastcoast administrator George spoke of his state's move away from fieldwork techniques:

> Eastcoast [in the past] had an extremely successful [field investigation division]. We had our own unmarked cars. We went out. We did all the investigations. We'd go out to the neighborhoods and everything else before [people] got on aid. Workers loved it because, you know. So I reached out. The problem is it costs a lot of money, it's dangerous, [there are] a lot of different pieces in that. I was reaching out to different states. I was reaching out to [a major city]. They ended up having a lot of ex-cops, retired cops, go out and do some of these investigations. So it's a ton of information you can have if you go out.

George describes an earlier iteration of the Eastcoast fraud control enterprise with a fraud investigator role closer to that of a police officer. He also explicitly connects that investigative style with police agencies, suggesting that former police officers may have the skills and training best suited to that type of work; such skills and training diverge notably from the software knowledge and data analysis background many of his own recent hires possess.

Interagency Connections

Predictably, George was not the only person I interviewed to make a connection between policing experience and qualifications relevant to fraud enforcement, particularly in high-fieldwork states. It is not uncommon in these states for fraud investigators to come into the job from conventional policing. This is especially apparent in Southwest, which has both frontline investigators and unit management figures hailing from law enforcement backgrounds and sworn peace officers working in its fraud unit.[12]

Beyond a partially shared labor market, there are multiple formal connections between anti-fraud enterprises and federal, state, and local law enforcement agencies, including collaborative investigation and enforcement projects and cooperation on task forces. Over the past few decades, police and other criminal justice actors have become increasingly active in spaces previously closed to them.[13] Welfare offices are an important example of that trend.[14]

State Law Enforcement Bureau (SLEB) agreements constitute one notable area of activity in formally connecting welfare agencies and police agencies. The USDA FNS instituted this policy in 1989 and recruited thirty-two participating states by 1994.[15] Today, all fifty states, the District of Columbia, and the US territories that administer SNAP are included in the SLEB program.[16] SLEB partnerships formally tie welfare and police agencies through allowing assistance agency fraud control units to enlist local law enforcement agencies to help gather information related to suspected SNAP fraud. Information flows the other way, too, in partnerships between fraud units and law enforcement agencies, when criminal legal authorities call on administrative welfare fraud authorities regarding particular suspects or cases. As Southeast supervisor Peter indicated, fraud unit representatives strive for responsiveness and effectiveness in addressing law enforcement requests: "Most of our times we've been helpful. I've been able to help them find the guy they're looking for. For whatever it is they're [doing]—they don't always tell us what they are doing." It is good practice for fraud investigation teams to work with the police so that, should they need information and help in return, the police reciprocate.

When fraud units recommend criminal charges, investigators also work closely with prosecutors' offices, supplying evidence to support criminal convictions. Prosecutors' interest in pursuing criminal charges for welfare rule violations varies, but members of the Southeast fraud unit reported a particularly strong working relationship with prosecutors' offices, which they find willing to seek criminal convictions in cases the fraud unit brings them. Southeast manager Jack enthused,

> They will prosecute everything that we take to 'em. . . . We're hardly ever, we're never turned down, I don't think, on cases. . . . The [prosecutors] know

what kind of work we do here, the quality of work we put out. And so they're willing to take our cases. You know, [prosecutors'] offices have their own investigative staff that will look at cases, but they . . . never assign investigators to work our case or anything. They pretty much go with what we provide 'em.

Jack takes pride in his unit's reputation for sound investigative work. Indeed, fraud units' specialized expertise supports prosecutors' trust in their evidence: dedicated welfare fraud investigators have program-specific knowledge and experience relevant to substantiating rule violation charges. This makes them essential intermediaries between social service agencies and criminal justice agencies, as Southeast supervisor Antoine explained:

> ANTOINE: I think we're always in the middle. Because the relationship, the way we deal with law enforcement, is completely opposite of the way we deal with the [assistance] agency. We deal with the agency because we're dealing with the policies, the regulations and the rules of the program. Law enforcement, we're dealing with the criminal aspect of what happens. So you pretty much stay in the middle, because [police] don't understand this side.
>
> INTERVIEWER: And they don't understand each other a lot?
>
> ANTOINE: They don't, they don't. And [police's] perception of this side is skewed.

Antoine described fraud units as middlemen between governmental departments formally dedicated to poverty management and crime control. In this role, they translate between the native tongues of the bureaucracies on either side and, like a set of locks, facilitate the transfer of cases between different administrative bodies of water.

Interpersonal Ties

Social ties between fraud unit staff and members of other agencies support both formal interagency collaborations and informal cooperative functions. Interpersonal ties and unofficial partnerships with conventional law enforcement officers vary from investigator to investigator, influenced by personal histories, investigative styles, and social networks. Investigators who have lived and worked in particular areas for long periods tend to especially highlight their off-the-books relationships with law enforcement agents.

These relationships are based in personal affinities and mutual benefit. They are treasured investigatory resources for fraud workers, who endeavor to maintain these ties and lament their loss. Southeast investigator Danielle detailed her ongoing cooperation with law enforcement, particularly her close working relationship with a state trooper named Burt:

DANIELLE: [Police agencies] do my arrests for me . . . print my DMV photos for me and all. When they're looking for somebody, and local law enforcement too, they'll all call me, and they're like, "We can't find this guy. What address do you have for him in your system?" and I'll help them out that way. They can't look at Department of Labor stuff. They're like, "Can you tell me when he last worked at all?" I'll look that stuff up for them and pass that information on. It's usually on the phone. Burt's like, "I'm at this place and we're trying to get this lady. We're doing a murder investigation and she's here with these two kids and these kids are just in diapers and they're filthy, and she said her food stamp card ran out last month and she doesn't have any food for them. What can you do about that?" I'm like, "I can't do anything about that! What do you mean? Let me look her up." I'll look her up and be like, "No, she let her case close, so there's nothing she can do. She needs to reapply. Do you want me to talk to her?" So he'll put the woman on the phone. He said, "Because she said if we could help her with her food stamps, she'll tell us who did the murder." He'll call me with these weird situations and I'm like, "Where are you?!" [*Laughs*] It's kinda fun, but I'm able to help him out. And she came in and I said, "Do you have a computer?" She went on a computer and Burt helped her reapply. He's like, "That helped out good. We all put up some money and we went to the grocery store." Because he said the kids had nothing to eat. I'm so glad I don't have his job. I like my law enforcement lite [*laughs*].

INTERVIEWER: . . . So [you have] a lot of personal relationships with police, particular police officers that you use, and you exchange information that way.

DANIELLE: A few around, yeah.

INTERVIEWER: Are there rules about what you can tell them, confidentiality stuff or—?

DANIELLE: I don't give them printouts of anything, but I confirm over the phone. I can give him an updated address, I can give him an updated

phone number and stuff because they're law enforcement. Or, "Look, it
looks like he worked here at the last—" But we don't give them any printouts. I don't think I'm supposed to give them any printouts or anything,
but he doesn't need any printouts. It's usually over the phone, [what] he
needs. "What do you have? Okay, we're going to look there." [. . .]

   They love it when they get my reports. The detectives, they're like,
"The work is already done!" I mean, the work's done, I've done all of the
footwork, just go get them. They all read through my reports and they'll
call me [saying], "Well, I got a question about this," and I can explain it,
"okay, okay, okay." Because there's a couple of things that might not make
sense. Now that I'm working with the same [officers]—except for [local
county], I'm getting a new detective—they understand the programs. A lot
of the times they didn't understand the programs and they're like, "Why
is this wrong?" and I'd explain to them, but they're pretty familiar with it
now. Although the state troopers want to tack on: "Oh, I can probably get
them on computer fraud, because she used a computer to submit this application." I'm like, "Don't get too hyper about it." [*Laughs*] This is [al-
ready] felony theft! He wants to tack on a hunk anyway. I'm like, "I don't
know what you're talking about!" He's gotta get out his book.

INTERVIEWER: [*Pantomiming a trooper looking through a book for additional charges.*] "Well, let's see what else we can do here."

DANIELLE: I'm like [*hands up, pantomiming "whoa"*], "No, it's okay, Burt."
[*Laughs*] "Calm down."

Danielle's account illustrates how administrative fraud investigations
connect to other systems of formal social control. Her comments are
worth quoting at length for the numerous details they provide about how
welfare fraud investigators and police can help each other and share information through informal partnerships.

Federal law explicitly authorizes some formal information exchange
between fraud units and police. The Food Stamp and Commodity Distribution Amendments of 1981, for instance, permitted welfare agencies
to share information from their administrative investigations and information from clients' case files with police for purposes of enforcing federal regulations.[17] These law enforcement information-sharing provisions, as elaborated further in PRWORA and elsewhere, apply not only
to clients but also to their past and current household members.[18] Fraud
units help get information about clients officially on the record, facilitat-

ing its subsequent admissibility in criminal proceedings. Interpersonal ties bolster these officially sanctioned provisions while also creating informal informational access opportunities. Each effect contributes to a multisited net of surveillance and social control.

Entanglements between social services and law enforcement have pronounced consequences for socioeconomically disadvantaged Americans, increasing their exposure to the state's coercive, controlling "second face."[19] Social service employees who perform an express social control function and work with conventional police encourage generalized distrust of the state on the part of people who interact with welfare bureaucracies.[20] Overlaps between ostensibly provision-oriented and ostensibly punishment-oriented agencies are unlikely to strengthen relationships between clients and agencies. Indeed, "system avoidance" effects[21] are likely, resulting from personal experiences with enforcement authorities or from knowledge of coordination and information sharing between law enforcement and public assistance. Within the "custodial citizenship" model,[22] these effects may present as efforts to minimize contact with state agencies. Alternatively, they may manifest in avoidance of other "surveilling institutions," such as the formal labor market.[23] In the welfare fraud context, clients who know that one can be burned via documentation of on-the-books work may avoid such entanglements. Most concretely, coordination and cooperation between designated welfare enforcement authorities and criminal justice agents produces new and expanded legal risks and injurious legal outcomes for poor people.

Criminal Charges

A range of formal responses, different from the choices available to police, prosecutors, and other social control agents located squarely within the criminal justice system, are available to fraud workers who pursue punishments for rule violations. Generally, conventional criminal justice actors can choose between different criminal charges or choose not to pursue criminal charges.[24] Welfare fraud control units—like other fundamentally noncriminal social control agencies such as the Securities and Exchange Commission (SEC)[25]—have a wider array of formal social control mechanisms at hand, including administrative penalties, civil proceedings, and referring cases for criminal prosecution. (The

Food Stamp Act Amendments of 1980 explicitly gave states the options of administrative, civil, or criminal proceedings as responses to fraud allegations.)[26]

A study of public benefit fraud is therefore not a study of crime. Or, more precisely, it is not a study of officially designated "crimes" alone. Delineating between rule breaking, lawbreaking, and crime are key activities in welfare fraud control. Individuals are criminalized when the state labels their actions or statuses as crimes.[27] Like police[28] and prosecutors,[29] fraud control agents exercise considerable discretion in dictating who is formally criminalized.

For most types of lawbreaking, police are criminal legal processes' primary gatekeepers. Through organizational and individual practices with regard to patrol strategies, investigative techniques, and arrest and charging decisions, police forces are central to constructing crime as a social problem. These practices also drive the determination of individuals and offenses deemed constitutive of that problem.

For conventional paper crimes, law enforcement agencies are again typically the primary gatekeepers to criminal cases. When this type of lawbreaking is suspected within a specific policy-bound environment, however, noncriminal justice agencies are more likely to play this role; the SEC's jurisdiction over investment fraud is one example. Welfare fraud units are not as high status or high profile as the SEC, but their specialized knowledge and authority with regard to the system they police make them analogous. Both the SEC and welfare fraud units demonstrate how the conventional criminal justice system does not monopolize social control and punishment. While police, courts, jails, and prisons remain the centerpieces of the state's formal social control efforts, these entities increasingly share space with noncriminal state organs, including regulatory, civil, and administrative justice systems.[30] Dedicated units tasked with counteracting public assistance fraud are a leading example. They use two tracks of enforcement: they apply their own noncriminal sanctions and act as feeder organizations for the conventional criminal justice system. Actions in both tracks contribute to the intersection and overlap of criminal justice and poverty management.[31] The SEC has specialized jurisdiction in financial markets that in some ways parallels welfare fraud units' authority in public assistance programs; yet comparing the rarity of high-level financial fraud prosecutions to the ongoing practice of criminalizing welfare fraud demonstrates the socioeconomic polarization of formal social control in the United States.[32]

For a detailed model exemplifying the multiple levels of discretion in welfare fraud sanction choice and criminalization, it is useful to turn briefly to a state outside of the five case study states.[33] Illinois' state welfare fraud unit is the Department of Healthcare and Family Services Office of Inspector General (HFSOIG). The office's Central Verification Unit (CVU) serves the fraud unit's initial gatekeeping function. All external fraud referrals, from citizen tips to reports from local Healthcare and Family Services (HFS) offices and other local, state, and federal agencies (including law enforcement agencies) pass through this body. The CVU then performs the pivotal function of following up on referrals via wide-ranging access to HFS data and information from a host of other sources, including the Illinois Secretary of State and the Illinois State Police (ISP).[34] The CVU's decisions on which referrals to follow up and how to pursue them set the foundation for the official sanctioning of alleged violations.

HFSOIG's expressed central logic for referring clients to a state's attorney or US attorney for criminal prosecution is the size of losses, with cases involving particularly costly fraud referred for prosecution or to the Bureau of Collections at the Illinois Department of Human Services for civil litigation.[35] These cases can include receiving benefits under multiple or false identities, unreported income, sustained fraud concerning the client's personal and financial situation, and other situations involving large overpayments.[36]

Still, even HFSOIG allegations of sizable overpayment do not guarantee that law enforcement agencies will pursue these cases criminally. For instance, in 2002, the ISP declined a case involving a child care contractor suspected of defrauding HFS of more than $100,000. When the ISP refused the case, HFSOIG's own Bureau of Internal Affairs investigated, presenting its evidence directly to the US Attorney's Office for federal criminal prosecution.[37] Rebuffed by a state law enforcement agency, the organization mobilized its internal investigative body and then approached a federal prosecutor with the evidence produced. Strategic and organizational flexibility, operational latitude, and discretionary actions like these are shared by other jurisdictions' fraud units and reflect the possibilities engendered by their organizational and institutional hybridity. With a wide range of formal social control options available to them, fraud units have multiple points of influence on cases' ultimate dispositions.

ASSESSING CRIMINAL LIABILITY IN THE WELFARE FRAUD CONTEXT   In legal philosophy, two basic principles are commonly advanced to delineate criminalizable behaviors. The "harm principle" focuses on the harm (or offense) resulting from action and the prevention thereof.[38] The "legal moralist" approach, on the other hand, focuses on actions deemed inherently wrong.[39] Under the logic of the harm principle, which rose to predominance in the United States during the Reagan years,[40] some paper offenses inflict evident harm on identifiable victims. Embezzlement and directly victimizing forms of fraud like Ponzi schemes fall into this category. For many forms of lawbreaking mediated through organizational contexts, though, harm implications are cloudier. It is unclear, for instance, how to calculate harm in cases of insider trading or forms of stock manipulation that affect publicly traded companies' share prices. These actions certainly have effects, often broadly dispersed ones; ironically, however, this very characteristic complicates efforts to specify the harm caused. It may be easier in such cases to identify ill-gotten gains than to identify unjustified harms, absent a theory of harm that effectively weighs factors such as imposition of risk or injury spread across a diffuse collective like "stakeholders" or "the market." Identifying harm in these cases may require construing the idea more broadly, with the "victim" category stretched beyond the referent of the specific natural person. Offenses that victimize the government or the public at large share these characteristics while, in a more immediate sense, they do not victimize anyone in particular.

Potentially illegal or criminal activities in this realm tend to be characterized by much larger "gray areas" between the immoral and the illegal[41] and between administrative, civil, and criminal legal liability.[42] The national common denominator is for welfare fraud offenses to be handled administratively, punished with sanctions internal to the programs in which they occur, and paired with restitution requirements whenever possible. But fraud units can and do refer cases for criminal prosecution (among the five case study states, the practice is particularly popular in Southwest, Southeast, and Midatlantic).[43] The transfer of cases from the administrative enforcement system to the criminal legal system evinces fraud units' contribution to the criminalization of poverty, calcifying the connection between the bureaucratic concentration of enforcement functions and formalized punishment within the public assistance system.

ELECTING CRIMINAL CHARGES   Civil and administrative cases' characteristics can make them more practical options than criminal charges for authorities hoping to curtail welfare fraud. First, criminal charges are not necessary to move toward recovering funds through restitution orders; authorities can obtain these orders via administrative actions that are simpler than criminal actions. Additionally, the prosecutorial burdens of showing criminal intent and substantiating charges beyond a reasonable doubt impose evidentiary requirements that can be daunting to overtaxed investigative workforces.[44] Essentially, it is easier to default to pursuing noncriminal sanctions.

In some ways, the structural and statutory interpenetration of criminal justice and welfare authorities has shifted this balance, facilitating the use of criminal sanctions in fraud cases.[45] In my interviews, though, even strong law-and-order types noted that administrative sanctions can be the more pragmatic choice. Southwest manager Oscar, a mustachioed, white-haired White man in his early sixties with an extensive background in conventional law enforcement, exemplified this thinking:

OSCAR: Again, it's the whole, you know, it's a whole system thing. Say you want to take a criminal case forward for prosecution. There are threshold levels. And I understand the necessity for thresholds. But it is such a high bar. Say it's two thousand dollars of fraud. If you're finding somebody cheating on two hundred dollars a month, are you really gonna let them build up to that level? And even if you do catch somebody after the fact, you're not gonna get jail time. I mean, you might get probation. And the additional work required to get a conviction: is it worth it, or is it better to stop the bleeding of public money, take administrative sanctions, and just cut 'em off the program? And if you know they're committing fraud at two hundred dollars a month, why would you allow it to go on to get to that level? It doesn't make a lot of sense.

INTERVIEWER: And I imagine the Attorney General's office feels similarly, right? They probably don't look forward to having you send them a two-thousand-dollar fraud case.

OSCAR: We are a low priority on the overall—and I'm not complaining, it's just reality. The grand scheme of crime, and we are a very low priority. And we can go, if the Attorney General will turn it down, we can go to various [local prosecutors]. . . . Some of the rural counties will take it serious because they don't have the volume of [an urban county].

But do you want it to get to that level? And you have to have, like on any type of a narcotics case, you need to a show a pattern. And you have to wait. We only issue benefits once a month, so you really want to drag this on for three months when you can shut it off now? It's not productive to extend it to get to that level. That's why you'll see very few, from our perspective, criminal prosecutions. Trafficking, when you talk to them, that's a little different. But for [eligibility], it's not—

INTERVIEWER: Would you be in favor of lowering the [dollar value of fraud required for a criminal case]? Do you think that that would help?

OSCAR: Well, yes and no. It's just—it would help us. But there's no room in the jails. There's no—you know, do you wanna kick out an armed robber to put in a food stamps scammer? You know. Even if you kicked out all the drug guys [there would be overcrowding]. And, you know, when I was at, doing my previous job, it was so rampant that like, with the US attorney, smuggling marijuana, the threshold was so high for a prosecution, it was seven hundred and fifty pounds. Do you have any idea how much weed that is?

INTERVIEWER: [*Laughs*] That's a lot.

OSCAR: You catch a guy with seven hundred and forty, you send the guy back to Mexico and you keep his weed. You see what I mean? [If] we got the threshold all the way down to five hundred dollars—wow! But you see what I mean? You just, you can fill up the jails so easily. "Oh, I got a hundred dollars' worth of free food stamps." Where does it fit in society?

INTERVIEWER: And from a purely economic standpoint, losses on the food stamps compared to the cost—

OSCAR: Of warehousing this guy? Is he a public threat? He gonna hurt you? You know. And I don't sanction what they're doing, but what makes sense for society? And that's probably a more complex question. I'm glad smart guys like you are looking into this. But what is a reasonable response, to the citizen?

Reflecting on the appropriateness of fraud penalties, Southeast investigator Danielle echoed some of Oscar's reservations about the utility of criminal sanctions, particularly felony charges and incarceration:

DANIELLE: I think [the current suite of administrative and criminal sanctions] is appropriate. Especially when we can do a diversion or a pretrial intervention sort of deal with the DA. That's appropriate for someone who hasn't been in trouble before and this is what they did and they're going to comply with their probation terms. I'm fine with that. I don't want nobody to go to jail. Or have a felony on their record if they're going to take care of it and they don't deserve it.

INTERVIEWER: Sending someone to jail is expensive too, right?

DANIELLE: Yeah, exactly. It's practical reasons [*laughs*]. . . . And I don't want nobody to lose their job either. With a felony conviction, [you] make someone lose their job. I don't want that to [happen] because they ain't going to be able to pay it [back]. [. . .]

I tell people that too. They get my letter which says criminal charges might be filed, and they walk in and they go, "Am I going to jail?" I'm like, "What? Where in that letter did it say jail?" They're all thinking I'm bringing them to jail. No, ma'am [*laughs*]. [. . .] I said, "Okay, but no. Look at that letter again, no jail in that letter. What does it say?" They [were] like, "Okay." I was like, "Relax."

RULES OF THUMB AND MITIGATING CIRCUMSTANCES IN CRIMINALIZATION   In Northeast and Eastcoast, criminal cases are de-emphasized but certainly not unheard of. In these settings, criminal charges are most often pursued in cases with exacerbating circumstances, often high dollar values. This contrasts with Midatlantic, Southeast, and Southwest, where fraud units generally aspire to criminal charges whenever possible. Again, however, individual investigators' orientations vary, with some more interested in criminal cases than others.

Investigators and supervisors develop rules of thumb about when criminal charges should or should not be pursued. Often these heuristics include mitigating circumstances that might reduce criminalization's feasibility or desirability. When they hinge on characteristics of clients or the alleged proscribed actions, decisions to avoid criminalization parallel "downward departures" in the sentencing phases of the criminal justice system.[46]

However, broader structural constraints on what is possible and practical for fraud units substantially limit their capacity to pursue criminal charges, regardless of their level of interest in such cases. Southeast, for instance, is a comparatively criminal case-oriented state, but over the five years preceding this data collection the percentage of completed fraud investigations that they referred for prosecution ranged between just 3 and 23 percent. There are a few reasons for that low rate. First, the dollar values involved must meet statutory thresholds for criminal charges.[47] Second, for referrals to go anywhere, cases must also meet whatever informal thresholds local prosecutorial authorities apply when they decide which cases to take. These thresholds may be significantly higher than express statutory requirements, and they are subject to alteration according to a range of factors, including caseload fluctuations and fraud's political and popular salience in a given place and time.

Financial considerations are very familiar to Southwest supervisor Carly, who has an explicit administrative role in referring cases for criminal prosecution. Here we were discussing Southwest's dollar value threshold for criminal prosecution and the fact that not all cases—or even most cases—that meet statutory minimums are referred for prosecution. In light of this fact, I asked Carly what other standards investigators and supervisors use to decide which cases to pursue criminally:

> We look at the strength of the case in general. So you know, is it "he said, she said," is it something that we can prove. If we can't, then we'll just go ahead and send it for the overpayment to be taken care of administratively. We look at how much the total value is as well, against our workload. Currently we have a significant backlog, so everything right now under five thousand is going to get processed administratively. We look at things like household composition—can we really prove what's happening there or not?—and likelihood of conviction.

Carly's comments usefully demonstrate the interaction of individual, subjective discretionary judgments and higher-level organizational pressures in determining fraud cases' disposition. She notes that decisions about criminal charges are shaped by perceptions of the strength of the evidence and estimates of the likelihood of conviction, as well as the dollar value of the alleged fraud. And she positions those discretionary factors within the context of the organizational operating environment: because her unit is dealing with a significant backlog, they have adopted a temporary rule of thumb dictating that cases under five thousand dollars in value get a free pass from criminal prosecution, effectively raising the bar for criminalizing clients. Like inter-prosecutor variations, overtime differences in states' welfare and criminal justice circumstances contribute to this sort of irregularity.

Commenting as a leadership figure in a pro-criminalization state, Southeast manager Jack told me his unit pursues criminal charges unless there are reasons not to. The fact that many completed investigations are not referred for prosecution, though, suggests that variables acting against criminalization frequently come into play:

> INTERVIEWER: Speaking about the criminal charge process: you send most cases you get? So there's a minimum [statutory dollar value] threshold for criminal prosecution—
>
> JACK: Right.... I guess the states get to set their own requirements.
>
> INTERVIEWER: ... And then everything over that threshold you send to the DA, and you let them sort through it?
>
> JACK: Not necessarily everything. Because [it needs to meet the threshold]. Then we also look at any other circumstances that may come into play. We don't want to try to prosecute an eighty-year-old lady that got benefits. We don't wanna prosecute someone who is on their, walking around with an air tank, who has medical conditions. We don't want the person that may seem a little off [mentally], with issues, we don't prosecute those individuals. And then too, that kinda comes down to what the investigator obtains from that person from the interview. If they see that they're not quite understanding, we may not prosecute. But that's something that we look at.
>
> The way we do our cases here, the investigator does their investigation, they write a report, their supervisor reviews that report, to see if that's the way they want to go with it. Then we have another person that ... [reviews] it also to see if all the evidence is there, if this is the way we want to pursue the case, and then they actually issue the directive to file charges against the person or not.
>
> INTERVIEWER: So it's more extenuating circumstances might prevent you from criminal charges more so than exacerbating circumstances would lead to criminal charges? Basically, if there's some reason not to pursue criminal charges we won't, but the default is that we will?
>
> JACK: Right, yeah, exactly. We're here to pursue criminal action.
>
> INTERVIEWER: So fullest extent of the law unless there's something else going on.
>
> JACK: Yeah, right. Again though, not all the cases that we do are criminal. Because, just like with these cases with the stores [involved in trafficking] that we're doing, we're not pursuing those criminally against anyone. That is basically a break for them, but we're trying to do as many cases as we can. You know, a DA isn't gonna take twenty-three cases from us over a store that's been disqualified and they're willing to pay the money back.

It's just gonna bog the system up even more than what it is now. So we'll handle those administratively.

Jack's investigators' activities, like those of their counterparts in other states, are fundamentally organized around the administrative charges of IPVs, but the way Jack sees his unit, they are there "to pursue criminal action." His comments reflect how, in addition to the statutory and administrative restraints on criminal charges, cases in which convictions seem unlikely or prosecution seems inappropriate will cause fraud units to stick with administrative sanctions—if they continue with the investigation at all. Cases in which fraud units decide not to criminalize someone because of a mitigating circumstance such as advanced age or medical problems suggest the persistence of the agency's broader provision function as a factor in decision-making, even within enforcement-focused departments, and demonstrate the influence of "deserving poor" rhetoric on fraud control outcomes.

As Jack suggested, investigators' observations are major sources of indicators that might preclude criminal charges; this is part of investigators' discretionary influence on case dispositions. Southeast investigator Danielle provided her perspective on the process of weighing observational indicators and choosing whether to pursue criminal charges:

> I went administrative on a couple [that could have gone criminal]. I had one woman who was real sickly and I didn't know she was real sickly until she came in, she's half blind. I explained it well enough, I guess, that they did go administrative on it. It was like eight-thousand-something dollars. I had one woman whose mother was living with her and the mother didn't tell her about her retirement income. The mother was included in the case and I got a statement from the mother who was like, "That was none of her business. She didn't need to know about that." And she would put most of the money in the bank, but she still received this retirement income. So that went away to administrative and that was like fourteen thousand. It ended up being a big amount, but I was like, "Look, I got a statement from the mother who said that wasn't none of her daughter's [business] . . . the daughter who applied did not know; I believe her" [laughs].
>
> There's a few situations where you think it's going to go criminal until you interview them. When I interviewed the woman and she was so upset, and I was like, "Can I interview your mom about that?" "Oh, yes, ma'am." I went to the house the next day and I sat down with the little ol' feisty lady and she

straight out told me and gave me a statement: "That was none of my daugh-
ter's business." I'm like, "Whooaakay" [*laughs*]. So that was a good one. I'm
like, "We can't [pursue criminal charges]." I want to be fair.

Southeast supervisor Peter added to this conversation, offering his take
on the organizational and administrative factors that can influence prosecution decisions:

> We could have a case where we have a large amount of agency error or inad-
> vertent error with some IPV. We may choose not to prosecute because the
> amount of the suspected IPV is much less or we're able to handle it adminis-
> tratively because some of it is non-fraud. And part of the problem with that
> is that our federal agency at FNS. Say you have this non-fraud loss. You need
> to start pursuing that recovery. Well, what we have been doing in the past is
> waiting until the fraud part, the IPV, from the court case was done, then we
> come back and do the other one, the non-fraud part. And so they're saying,
> "Because you're doing that, this part of the loss that was delinquent in its re-
> covery. You waited three years for a court case to be done." And so we get
> kind of constrained there. [. . .]
>
>   We can also have cases where a person has committed an Intentional Pro-
> gram Violation by concealing income but the agency knew about it and didn't
> follow up on that and account for it. So the loss could have been agency error
> and the person still committed IPV. So the rules are not totally hard and fast.

After echoing his colleagues' statements that certain client characteristics can forestall criminalization, Peter described the opposite—how
some cases' unusual or sensationalistic aspects increase the likelihood
of prosecution:

> [We may choose not to prosecute] when we are interviewing somebody and
> we find out, as a result of this interview we discover that their educational
> level is just not there. . . . On the other hand, we will do a case because a fed-
> eral agency may be interested in taking these cases. For instance, we had a
> lady who claimed her dog as a household member. [. . .] She gave him a So-
> cial [Security number] and all that. And they wanted to prosecute her, and so
> they did.

Although administrative pressures and interest in particular cases shape
how criminalization manifests, generally speaking, fraud workers have

substantial discretion and influence in deciding how to proceed. This, combined with fraud units' relatively small size, means that a handful of entrepreneurial actors within a state's fraud control and prosecution systems can have an outsize effect on criminalization trends for the entire state.

Southwest investigator Dusty described how the criminalization process unfolds in his state and his discretion's part in it:

> DUSTY: My supervisor . . . gives me full decision on everything. Whether I want to take it administratively or criminal. We have been on board with prosecutors who have said there is a certain dollar level where they'll take it, twenty thousand dollars or higher. I disagree with that. If I'm doing six [undercover] buys [of EBT benefits] with somebody and they're all felony transactions, I'm going to pursue that criminally instead of just doing it administratively. Because I'm gonna know that they're going to learn something from it by me doing it criminally and not doing it administratively, where it's just a slap on the wrist. So I would say that I have a lot of, what's the word I'm looking for?
>
> INTERVIEWER: Discretion?
>
> DUSTY: Yeah, a lot of discretion, thank you. A lot of discretion on making that decision.
>
> INTERVIEWER: Mm-hmm. And you think, when it's a pattern, even if it's not a particularly high dollar value, the pattern you think is very significant.
>
> DUSTY: Absolutely.

Dusty thinks relatively big cases are important but makes sure that his discretionary process leaves room for other factors, prominently mentioning perceived behavioral patterns. His interpretation of what cases merit criminalization does not always directly correspond to that of prosecutorial authorities, who in his experience fixate on high-dollar-value cases (and in the instance he describes of the twenty-thousand-dollar floor, cases that are strikingly high dollar value for client IPVs). As he processes cases, he continually navigates and negotiates between his preferred outcomes and the practical limitations imposed by the agency, the criminal justice system, and their relationship to each other.

CRIMINAL CASE OUTCOMES   When criminal cases are pursued in conjunction with IPVs, their consequences usually involve imposing financial penalties, fees, and fines on top of restitution requirements. Criminal cases also permit intensified strategies to collect court-ordered repayments. Like other criminal charges, criminal welfare fraud charges are usually settled through plea deals. In this context, these deals typically involve probation and various fines and fees. Southeast manager Jack walked me through it:

> INTERVIEWER: How willing is the DA to take cases? Do they take a good share of 'em?
>
> JACK: Yup. They'll take just about any of 'em we take to 'em.
>
> INTERVIEWER: And do they get a pretty good conviction rate or do they do a lot of deals of some kind or another, some sort of plea?
>
> JACK: Yeah, there's hardly any case that ever goes to trial. Most of the time there's some type of deal that's worked out. They usually end up paying a fine, court costs, probation fees, some type of assessment fee that some of them charge 'em, and full restitution to the agency. And then of course they have to be disqualified from the program for whatever time period.

This accumulation of payments to the state mirrors the tactics that some police departments have used in the "criminalization of everyday life."[48] St. Louis County's policing of low-level offenses and fining of minor infractions gained national attention in the wake of Michael Brown's shooting in Ferguson.[49] One recent analysis uses the term *sharecropper finance* to describe these types of measures, in which public revenues are produced through fines and fees levied against poor people, especially people of color.[50] Monetary penalties of various sorts have emerged as a key component of the criminal justice system, with major implications for the reproduction of socioeconomic stratification structures.[51]

The financial penalties imposed via criminal charges are frequently accompanied by probation (which itself entails supervision fees). Incarceration is more likely in particularly large, high-profile cases or those in which welfare fraud convictions are stacked with other criminal charges. Some fraud unit representatives and police favor such charge-stacking as a way to more seriously sanction clients who violate rules, especially when they see an individual's welfare rule violations as part of a broader pattern of lawbreaking. Adding criminal charges as part of a package of alleged offenses can also make cases more attractive to prosecutorial authorities, who may be uninterested in pressing low-dollar welfare fraud charges on their own.

Depending on allegations' nature, state criminal law, and the zeal and creativity of fraud investigators, police, and prosecutors, welfare fraud cases can sometimes be stretched to include other types of fraud or per-jury charges. Southeast investigator Danielle's anecdote above, regard-ing the state police officer who wanted to throw in a computer fraud charge, is one instance. More straightforwardly, welfare fraud charges can be tacked on in cases where someone is arrested for a conventional street crime. As examples of this process, fraud unit representatives cite cases involving the overlap of drug crimes and benefit trafficking. Their paradigmatic description is a person arrested for suspected drug sales and found to possess other people's EBT cards, implying that he was ex-changing drugs for benefit funds. Or, people with outstanding warrants for unrelated crimes may find welfare fraud charges added as part of a suite of offenses charged collectively following arrest. Such combined cases increase clients' odds of incarceration, compared to stand-alone criminal welfare fraud charges. Southeast manager Jack described how the process plays out in his jurisdiction:

> Occasionally we . . . may have someone go to jail, but it's usually because they've tied our charges in with something else. The person may be a con-victed drug dealer, or they may already have a warrant for them for some-thing else. And so they kinda just lump it all together and they may go to jail for some time. We still try to get our money back, the restitution amount, though.

The greater viability and efficiency of pairing welfare fraud charges with separate criminal proceedings is an important dimension of criminal-ization via welfare fraud investigation. Criminal cases and incarceration can and do result for a wide range of people accused of simply violating welfare program rules. However, people already caught up in the crimi-nal justice system in some way are more exposed to criminal charges and face greater likelihoods of experiencing incarceration after a conviction.

Conclusion

In principle, punishment and welfare address separate sets of problems: crime and poverty.[52] In practice, these government enterprises have long been closely related—historically as conjoined "penal-welfare" for-mations[53] and more recently as two sides of a welfare retrenchment /

mass incarceration coin.[54] Specialized units within welfare bureaucracies tasked with investigating and punishing clients are a uniquely concrete manifestation of the manifold and long-standing linkages between these worlds. Fraud units clearly demonstrate the expansion of the set of problems addressed in the United States via law enforcement interventions.[55] Fraud workers' actions result in punishments for welfare rule violations—suspensions, disqualifications, fines, and incarceration—that tend to increase experiences of economic deprivation. Thus fraud units' operations and their ties to police and prosecutors demonstrate a willingness to sacrifice abatement of poverty problems via welfare policies in favor of abatement of rule-breaking problems via punishment policies.

It is not always easy for fraud workers to recommend punishments for struggling individuals and families. Especially when they find clients particularly sympathetic, many investigators express reservations about applying sanctions, and sometimes they find reasons not to pursue charges. Such determinations partially depend on fraud workers' personal understandings of their jobs, which the next chapter addresses in detail. Criminalization, however, inheres in punitive adversarialism via dedicated welfare fraud control units. Individual feelings of sympathy or regret do not cancel out these units' systematic contribution to the net of surveillance and penalization surrounding the poor.

CHAPTER FIVE

Occupational Frames and Identities in Fraud Control Work

Some of the owner men were kind because they hated what they had to do, and some of them were angry because they hated to be cruel, and some of them were cold because they had long ago found that one could not be an owner unless one were cold. And all of them were caught in something larger than themselves. Some of them hated the mathematics that drove them, and some were afraid, and some worshiped the mathematics because it provided a refuge from thought and from feeling. — John Steinbeck, *The Grapes of Wrath*

This chapter examines fraud control as a job and a role within government, contributing to the study of "poverty governance as a labor process."[1] The fraud enforcement role is a disciplinary and punitive intervention in the public assistance system. Monitoring clients' rule compliance and applying sanctions is part of welfare caseworkers' jobs as "catch-all bureaucrats,"[2] but for fraud workers, pursuing client punishments is not part of the job—it *is* the job.

Fraud workers' descriptions of their work reveal how they conceptualize their enforcement role within ostensibly provision-oriented systems and situate themselves within that role. Fraud workers develop occupational frames, understandings of their jobs that aid navigation of their day-to-day occupational world. These understandings demonstrate nuances within the bureaucratic role's corresponding punitive orientation.

Fraud workers' accounts of their work and the occupational frames they use to make sense of their jobs are more than post hoc justifications. These understandings of work also inform the (re)construction of fraud workers' senses of who they are. Occupational frames connote the symbolism of the fraud control role to those who play it. They provide schemas that fraud workers draw upon in forming their occupational identities, particularly in locating themselves relative to police officers and conventional welfare staff. The sets of understandings that constitute occupational frames drive the ongoing process through which fraud workers become the welfare police, adopting occupational identities that reflect their investigatory and punitive mandate.[3] Ambiguity in top-down definitions of fraud workers' role creates a vacuum of meaning regarding what fraud control fundamentally is and who its agents are. Individual fraud workers fill that vacuum from the bottom up. Given their structural position's imperatives, suspiciousness and punitiveness are their default reference points.

Celeste Watkins-Hayes argues that much of what street-level bureaucracy scholars conventionally describe as worker discretion "is actually the operationalization of differing professional identities that workers create to implement public policy."[4] In accordance with this contention, fraud workers' occupational frames and identities shape their priorities and decision-making on the job, with important implications for their units' substantive and symbolic outputs.

Framing Fraud Control

Paths into Fraud Control

Welfare agency staff commonly move from working in eligibility determination or benefit administration into fraud control positions. Such intrabureaucratic transplants need to adjust to a new focus: rule enforcement through investigating clients and enabling their punishment. In other cases, people with experience in conventional law enforcement move into this different enforcement context and need to modify their approaches in response to its divergent norms and rules. Others still come into fraud control from other types of government agencies, the private sector, or directly out of school. Background is part of the calibration as fledgling fraud investigators develop understandings of the job and how to do it.

Fraud workers who come from neither benefit administration nor law enforcement share their colleagues' sensitivity to their work environments' particularities but have relatively clean slates with regard to previous work experience. They tend to describe moving into fraud control as a simple matter of career opportunity. Eastcoast manager Stephen, who was previously an analyst with the state's housing agency, explained why he made the move:

STEPHEN: "This was a better job, honestly."

INTERVIEWER: Just kind of a click up? Or just work you liked more?

STEPHEN: No, it was a click up, definitely, yes.

His colleague, Eastcoast manager Caroline, used to be in workers' compensation. A circumspect White woman in her midforties, she related similar motivation:

INTERVIEWER: The move over, from [workers' compensation] over here: you saw like a promotion opportunity available, or did you want to leave for any particular reason, or were you interested in the type of work that goes on here?

CAROLINE: Well, it was more towards my career path. There wasn't any supervisory opportunities there, and there was here, so I applied for the position here.

INTERVIEWER: More advancement opportunities.

CAROLINE: Exactly.

Carly, a Southwest supervisor, had worked in compliance for the military and the Department of Veterans Affairs, then moved into a compliance and contract position within the public assistance arena, and finally switched to investigation supervision. She described a sort of culture shock upon transitioning into a work environment with a helping occupation's norms:

It was really hard for me to come in when I first got to [public assistance] and I had to change the mindset of the social workers . . . about the punishment. They were so social work-heavy, and the contract enforcement unit, it's like, "You have to enforce your contract. We found the violation of the contract; it's your job to enforce it." And then they would have their social appeal: "Well, but if we enforce it then this is gonna happen, and then this is gonna happen, and then this hurts this." I was like, "Oh, okay, whatever," you know. "You need to enforce the contract."

Carly imported her enforcement-centered orientation from her old job and then worked to maintain—and spread—that orientation in her new context and among her new co-workers.

Those who enter fraud control from criminal justice backgrounds describe similar experiences. Southwest manager Oscar spent most of his career in conventional law enforcement. He noted how his background influences his work:

> There's a natural conflict. My biggest eye-opener was coming from a world where [it was] 100 percent law enforcement to [one that was] 99 percent social work, 1 percent or less law enforcement, and the mindsets are totally different. I got a master's in counseling, so I'm a little more "this way" than the average street cop. That being said, we're sometimes perceived as bad because [benefits people] want to give out money to everybody. That's their job. They get bonuses and whatever for giving money out to those in need, and we catch the flaws of the system. [. . .]
>
> And you don't want a police nation. This is a program to help those truly in need. But you need to check and balance. We're a necessary evil in the world that, in the mind of the social worker, [they] wish we didn't exist. Because they feel everybody's good and needy, and that's good, and cops think everybody's evil and rotten. That's too simple, but you see the worst, they see the best, and there's a natural disconnect. [. . .]
>
> Examples: "Oscar, they said they're sorry, isn't that enough?" "Uh, no, they've committed a felony by statute." "Oscar, you don't understand, they steal for need, not greed." "Okay." But an employee making forty EBT cards, sending them to themselves . . . stuff like that, that person needs to go away. . . . Those are just examples. But overall, I'd say it's probably as well managed as any place. Is there problems? Absolutely. Are there easy fixes? No. The easy fixes happened before I ever got here. Is it a constant challenge to keep trying to raise the bar? Sure. We pay little from our line of work. I make less than half what I did working for my previous job [in federal law enforcement]. I make less than a lot of when I worked for the state police.
>
> I think it's a job you do because you want to do it. And if you're a young twenty-one-year-old plotting out your law enforcement career, [will you say], "I wanna be the food stamp police"? No. When the governor asks you, "Will you take on this job for me?" and you go, "Yeah, I can do that." But is it a part of a plan? No. So you get people of various [backgrounds] on the law enforcement side coming over. One of the nice things is I doubt I'll have to kill anybody again. I really doubt I'll ever shoot my weapon in anger again. I work day shift. I have weekends off. I have holidays off. My family know who I am again. But the pay is low. Responsibility and pay is low. But the risk is low.

Oscar's description of the difference between his response and the default "social work" response to fraud cases places the clash between

identification with police and identification with welfare into sharp relief. He distills the difference in worldview when he says that social
workers "feel everybody's good and needy," while "cops think everybody's evil and rotten." In light of this conflict and other characteristics
of the job, he does not see fraud control as necessarily attractive to an as-
piring law enforcement officer.

In Eastcoast, Diego worked as an investigator for a prosecutor's office before moving into fraud control. He stressed finding balance in his
new role:

> Uniquely with this agency I am somewhere in between [social services and
> law enforcement]. I mean, when you think about it, we're tasked with a really
> difficult proposition from the fraud integrity standpoint. The primary func-
> tion of this agency is . . . to provide benefits to those who are dealing with
> whatever socioeconomic issues that don't allow them to be self-sufficient.
> And now you're tasking us, this unit, with a premise to go after those who
> may commit fraud. And the thing is, sometimes the work, the lines do get
> blurry. So I see myself in the middle. And I clearly understand why this is
> administrative and not criminal, because it would be a different sort of ball
> game. But I see myself in the middle.

The modal path into fraud control nonetheless runs through public assistance agencies' provision side.[5] Like their colleagues from other backgrounds, some assistance workers take fraud control jobs simply because
they are new career opportunities. Others, dissatisfied with benefit provision work or frustrated with clients, specifically want to police fraud.
Southeast investigator Leslie presented this perspective:

> LESLIE: I got to the [agency] and started doing the eligibility, and [when] I
> first started, everybody needed my help and everybody was just telling the
> truth. And it wasn't until I really started doing it and talking to these peo-
> ple that I'm going, you know, like, "Seriously? Do you really think I'm
> that stupid?" [. . .]
> INTERVIEWER: So you're pretty jaded, you would say.
> LESLIE: Yeah, I am. But to me, the [local] office did that to me. Y'know, so
> when it came time for a promotion of being a supervisor there or fraud in-
> vestigator, I went, "Hmm, let me try." So I tried for both, and whenever I
> came for the fraud investigator job they had a, I don't know, they had this
> letter out that says, y'know, "This is what's expected of you, this is what

your job would kinda entail." And the more I read it the more I was like, "I'm gonna call them and cancel the supervisor [application], this is what I want, this is amazing!" So from, handing them out, handing all the benefits out to getting them back, I much prefer this side of it than the other. But I think that's because I did that one for four years. Y'know, you get jaded, and everybody lies. [Fraud investigation has] helped me as a parent, especially teenage boys: they don't get too much over on me.

Peter, a supervisor in the same state as Leslie, started his career many years ago as a public assistance eligibility worker. However, he has spent most of his adult life in fraud control, having switched out of benefit administration early on. He connected conflict between fraud units and public assistance more broadly to differences between designated fraud workers' goals and motivations and those of the larger assistance agency:

Our agency's mission is helping people. We're on the side of the agency that is not giving out the money. We're taking it back. And so it seems like it's a contradiction. And our efforts, . . . administration would applaud it, but they're more interested in millions and millions served than millions in fraud.

Like others, Peter sees his work as embattled, which can beget defensiveness and the cultivation of self-protective identities.[6]

Taken together, these reflections illustrate how occupational trajectories shape the narratives and understandings that fraud workers bring with them into the job. Starting from their original circumstances as new fraud workers, they build and refine accounts of what they do and why. These accounts cluster into synchronized sets: occupational frames.

Occupational Frames

The concept of *occupational frames* builds on Erving Goffman's germinal argument that people classify their experiences and ultimately make sense of their social worlds by drawing on frames, systems of meaning that provide order to the experience of social life.[7] Occupational frames are sets of understandings of the character and purpose of work that individuals draw upon to organize and make sense of their ongoing occupational experiences. They are particularly valuable to people like welfare fraud investigators, who cross conventional bureaucratic boundaries and are subject to both external and internal assessments according to disparate metrics. Occupational frames are the backbone of interpreting fraud work and gauging its significance. Especially as conveyed in interview responses, these motive accounts serve impression management purposes, as tools of rationalization or justification.[8] However, they also contribute to self-interpretation, as narratives regarding the reasons for one's work that can be deployed in the ongoing (re)construction of the type of worker—and person—one is.[9]

Fraud workers' accounts of their jobs cluster into three main occupational frames: *catching cheats, resource preservation,* and *disinterested enforcement*. These frames have various features and implications, as discussed in more detail below. They are sets of meanings and values that fraud workers call upon in the process of forming occupational identities. While most interviewees' occupational identities correspond primarily to one of the three frames, the frames are neither mutually exclusive categorizations of individual fraud workers nor comprehensive profiles of individuals' perspectives on their jobs. Not every person who draws primarily from one of the three frames expresses all of its characteristics, and fraud workers can—and do—draw on multiple frames in their understandings of their work. All three reflect the specific pressures of fraud workers' dedicated enforcement role and provide ways to make sense of serving as the welfare police.

As such, occupational frames arise partly from individual-level factors, including political ideology and personal value preferences. Past and present workplace socialization also play a significant role; work environments influence workers' adoption of occupational frames, which in turn bear on their formation of occupational identities.

CATCHING CHEATS   Individual fraud workers, like individual police officers, hold different perspectives on their work's purposes and significance. The *catching cheats* frame is fundamentally individualistic and directly moralistic. Investigators who understand fraud control's most important outcome as identifying and successfully pursuing individual rule violators include Southwest investigator Ashley:

> My favorite part of my job is catching them [*giggles, then pauses before proceeding in a more serious tone*]. Honestly, it's getting them off of the benefits. Knowing that I stopped them from—'cause it just upsets you, it makes you so mad. You work so hard, and for them to take advantage of the benefits.

Ashley's personal anger toward individuals who knowingly defraud the system is common to those adopting the catching cheats frame. Ashley started her career working in eligibility determination. Like many of her colleagues who draw on the catching cheats frame, her reaction to rule violations in benefit provision motivated her move into fraud control.

Southeast manager Jack shares this point of view. Like Ashley, he began his career in eligibility determination but moved into fraud control when he had the opportunity. Upon learning of the fraud unit's existence, he "realized right away I wanted to be the person who takes away the benefits, not the one who gives 'em out."

For Jack and others, the catching cheats frame is not explicitly founded in a desire to punish welfare clients as a collective. To be sure, there are systematic implications of staffers' embrace of the catching cheats frame, but the frame itself does not foreground them. Instead, it emphasizes levying appropriate punishments on individual rule violators. It essentially conceptualizes fraud enforcement as a series of disconnected cases of specific wrongdoers pursued and penalized for their specific violations and focuses on obtaining the desired outcome of a substantiated IPV (and perhaps a criminal charge) in each of those separate cases. Midatlantic manager Hank originally sought a military career before "falling back" into fraud investigation management. His perspective on the fraud control occupational role in relation to the larger agency function epitomizes the character of the catching cheats frame: "Here's the breadbasket, but if we find out you're doing something, we're gonna nail you."

The catching cheats frame closely aligns the fraud control occupational role with the "junkyard dogs" that President Reagan specified he wanted as agents of government oversight and rule enforcement.[10] It also has significant overlap with law-and-order political rhetoric.[11] Like the "tough on crime" perspective, the catching cheats frame is characterized by a sense of moral or ethical outrage about individual rule violators' actions (implicitly or explicitly contrasted against law-abiding people's actions). Recall Ashley's anger toward clients perpetrating fraud; it emphasizes the *wrongfulness* of clients' behaviors. Southeast supervisor Helen depicted the frame's prominent moral disapprobation, too:

> If you do wrong, then you need to pay for it. It isn't like, "Let me slap you on the hand," or whatever. You need to pay for it. Because it's like I told you

before, a bought lesson is the best lesson. So once you pay that one time, you aren't going to want to pay that money no more.

As Helen's comments suggest, the catching cheats frame constructs the fraud investigator role as helping to advance just deserts, making sure no blameworthy misdeed goes unpunished.

Southwest investigator Ramona is a taciturn White woman in her early fifties. The idea of a one-to-one ratio of actions and consequences figures centrally in her view of her work. She laid out her support for criminalization using the catching cheats frame's characteristic black-and-white moral code and consequence-driven response model: "I think [rule violators] should be punished because they are committing theft. So I think they should be punished. [. . .] I think theft is theft."

Within the catching cheats frame, the fact that violations occur within a public assistance program rather than any other context is largely or entirely ancillary. Southeast investigator Geraldine concurred with this interpretation, taking a principled, even pugilistic stance toward fraud and its perpetrators:

> GERALDINE: I believe in locking them up [. . .] if they do wrong. Especially like thirty-one thousand dollars and you did it for five whole years. So you had time to redeem yourself, so I don't feel sorry for you at all.
>
> INTERVIEWER: So you'd like to see more jail time?
>
> GERALDINE: For the ones who do it for a long time. Five years is too long to be lying, the same lie. . . . Yeah, this one lady . . . you know she's making over six figures. I don't care about her. Then she gonna call me "You people." You people? God, the detective that arrested her called me, [saying], "I have her in the back of my car right now. She ain't too happy; she's crying. She calling you all kinds of names. What do you want me to do?" I said, "Take her ass to lockup and book her. And take a long time to set her bond. Take your time." "So you want in the morning? Or the next day?" I said, "Whatever you feel, detective." She was cussing me like it was my fault that she was locked up. [*Sarcastic*] Yeah, it's not her fault. It's my fault. I did it [*snaps fingers*].

Geraldine, a slim Black woman in her late forties, downplays distinctions between welfare fraud investigators' and law enforcement officers' functions and largely equates welfare fraud with conventional property crimes.

In her mind, higher-dollar-value fraud charges should receive more severe punishment, even incarceration. When I asked Geraldine to expound on her preference for pursuing criminal rather than administrative cases, she said, "Mostly I don't write up administrative. I go administrative if they're elderly or if a young person has a disability . . . that will look bad in a meeting of our department if we're putting a blind person in jail." Within the catching cheats frame, the only good reason to use program-specific administrative charges and sanctions instead of pursuing criminal cases is if extenuating circumstances make criminal cases untenable.

Here, the overarching objective of fraud control work is seeing justice done: ensuring that people who cheat the system are held responsible and minimizing the share that get away with it. After she expressed both concern over fraud-associated expenditures and commitment to seeing program violators penalized, I asked Southwest supervisor Carly to weigh her priorities, cost avoidance versus just deserts:

> Personally, in a perfect world, I would love to say that they're equal to me, right? But if I'm answering honestly, then I am more about the punishment. It is wrong, they need to be punished. . . . I would have to say that number one is the punishment, of going after the criminal.

Carly's invocation of the "criminal" label suggests the frame's core conceptualization of program rule violators. At the same time, her concern over illegitimate expenditure suggests she also adheres, in part, to the resource preservation frame.

RESOURCE PRESERVATION   The resource preservation frame positions the fraud control role as more system-oriented and primarily about monetary savings. This frame downplays individual cases' outcomes relative to the broader organizational and systemic implications of both fraud behavior and anti-fraud interventions.

The resource preservation frame replaces the catching cheats frame's deontological ethics with a utilitarian perspective. Conceptualizing herself in relation to a violation, an investigator drawing on the catching cheats frame will foreground that a rule has been broken, necessitating a consequence. The resource preservation frame is more consequentialist and pragmatic, focusing not on welfare fraud's inherent wrongness but its other costs, particularly its financial expense. The fraud worker, accordingly, is less an agent defending the state's idea of justice than an agent working to defend the state's coffers. Nearly all fraud control workers place at least some importance on the cost avoidances and fiscal savings they associate with their work. What sets apart those who draw primarily on the resource preservation frame is their commitment to limiting state expenditures as the most important outcome of their jobs.

Consider Carly, who is dedicated to the catching cheats frame and explicitly identifies punishment as the most important result of her work. She is nonetheless quite sensitive to the idea of cost avoidance:

> CARLY: But also . . . we need to save the money. We're in this huge financial crisis; we need the money to go other places. Or maybe even up the cap, so that the single mom might be able to get food stamp benefits in transition without popping out five more kids to be eligible, you know. It's one of those things—let's save the money and use it back in our schools. Let's save the money and use it to fix the railways. Let's save the money and use it to put towards foster care. [. . .]
>
> [*Speaking slowly, thoughtfully.*] I think that the punishment, if used to its fullest potential, will give us cost avoidance. So I think that the cost avoidance is important up front in the eligibility. I'm big on that. Let's pay attention at the beginning of the process so there's not so much catching up to do. But also, once we catch up with you, if you are prosecuted, and a convicted felon, then you're excluded, and therefore we have our cost savings there as well.
>
> INTERVIEWER: Two birds with one stone with punishment.
>
> CARLY: Yes. Yes.

Carly sees value in cost avoidance but prefers pursuing resource preservation goals *via catching cheats methods*. That is, she is happy to save money but doubles down on her commitment to punishment. Her alignment with the catching cheats frame also comes through in her suggestion of reinvesting cost savings not in SNAP or TANF but in railways, schools, or foster care. Typically, the resource preservation frame emphasizes not only the fraud worker's role as a steward of state resources but also the health and vitality of public assistance programs themselves.

Long-Term Program Viability   Usually, fraud workers drawing on the resource preservation frame highlight the importance of preserving funds for both its intrinsic value (as an exercise in frugality) and its ability to facilitate the continued pursuit of agency goals. In this sense, the resource preservation frame positions enforcement of welfare programs' boundaries as fiscally and politically necessary to protect programs' existence. Emphasizing resource preservation as an avenue to long-term program viability evinces this perspective. Fraud control, this logic goes, is crucial to ensuring that public assistance programs remain operational and available to those adjudged truly needy. Southeast supervisor Rosemary encapsulated this dimension of the resource preservation frame:

> I just think it definitely, it needs to be balanced. Because we want to help people who do need it, and if we don't stop fraud the money is going to run out. I mean, it's not an endless pot, and it needs to be there for people that need it. I mean, I truly believe that, or I couldn't have worked in social services all these years, but you have to be good stewards of the money.

Like Rosemary, resource-minded investigators tend to have backgrounds in benefit administration, and many explicitly depict fraud control as crucial to long-term program viability. This is rooted in stronger fundamental support for welfare's goals and belief in these programs' social value. Rosemary, asked about her favorite part of her job, explained,

> I believe in the programs and believe in helping, but I also am an extremely law-abiding person, and I believe it should be there for the people who deserve it and need it and meet the requirements. And I have a real problem with people that knowingly, willingly are fraudulent and get benefits, which I feel takes away from the money being there for people who deserve it. So, being able to pursue fraudulent claims is definitely my favorite part. Not that I'm, it's in a mean-spirited way. It's just like what I said: I believe that's the only way you can continue the integrity of the program.

Here, Rosemary very clearly distinguishes the resource preservation frame from the catching cheats frame. Her favorite part of the job may be identifying and pursuing fraud cases, but her justification is different from her catching cheats–oriented colleagues: she emphasizes the larger systemic value of pursuing fraud. Whereas the catching cheats frame emphasizes imposing punishment as inherently desirable and appropriate, here individual punishments are a means to the larger end of program viability.

At the end of her interview, when I asked Rosemary if there was anything else that she wanted to say or that she thought was important for
me to know, she reiterated her commitment to the resource preservation
frame. Her voice thick with emotion, she gave a heartfelt reply:

> I hope you're not in here trying to prove that us fraud workers just hate peo-
> ple that are on benefits, and we just hate people, that they're terrible people,
> and we're just coming after them. 'Cause we're really not. Like I said, almost
> to a T, just about everyone had prior eligibility experience, so we all believe
> in the programs. But we also, like I said, we see [fraud]. And it hurts; it hurts
> to know that, you know, that's going on. And people lie to your face and, you
> know, when I am trying to help you but you're still going to lie to my face.

Drawing on the resource preservation frame, Rosemary connects experience on the agency's provision side to belief in the programs' value,
with resource preservation ideas motivating career moves into fraud
control. This contrasts with the cynicism that is more prominent in the
catching cheats frame. For individuals adopting that frame, experiences
in benefit administration may have had a distinctly different effect, pushing them toward an enforcement role that they conceptualize as primarily about punishing rule violators.

The resource preservation frame, however, positions the fraud control
role as not primarily an applier of sanctions but—borrowing Rosemary's
biblical formulation—as a good steward of welfare programs. This stewardship concerns not only material resources but also public assistance
agencies' and programs' reputations and credibility. Southwest supervisor Todd, a stocky White man nearing fifty, laid out this perspective:

> INTERVIEWER: How important do you think your work is to public opinion?
>   Do you think it has—
> TODD: Absolutely, hugely important. With . . . my friends and things like that,
>   and when I meet new people, "What do you do?" And I try to shy away a
>   little bit, just because I don't know their lifestyle, and if they're on benefits
>   I don't want them to feel uncomfortable, because just because they're on
>   benefits doesn't mean they're not legit. When I get to know people and I tell
>   them, and they're like, "Wow, really? Those people are out there? Thank
>   you." I describe what we do and this and that, and he's like, "Oh, I'm glad
>   there's people out there like you, because you're actually saving money."

Taxpayer Money   Todd's remarks demonstrate the fraud worker role's symbolic dimension. Fraud workers are not only responsible for shepherding resources and limiting illegitimate spending; they also help communicate the agency's commitment to resource preservation to the public, thereby helping maintain system legitimacy and resist stereotypes of welfare programs and agencies as wasteful or overindulgent. Put differently, saving money is not the only function embraced by the resource preservationist. They aim toward a symbolic goal as well: to signal to the public that welfare programs make serious efforts to counteract fraud and limit spending to helping the truly needy.

The material and symbolic aspects of resource preservation share a foregrounding of public assistance resources as "taxpayer money." Emphasizing that public dollars originate from taxes is of course nothing new in public policy and welfare reform discourses. However, the entanglement of ideas about earning, deservingness, and work in the public assistance arena make the move from taxpayer money to public funds seem particularly direct in this context.

In some cases, fraud workers drawing on this frame will invoke their own taxpayer status, either using themselves as stand-ins for the broader taxpayer community or simply noting personal concerns with their own tax dollars being misallocated. Southeast investigator Geraldine's occupational identity is built primarily upon the catching cheats frame, but she is not immune to drawing on the resource preservation frame as well, particularly when she feels her pocketbook is implicated:

INTERVIEWER: So you took the taxpayer money thing pretty seriously. You took that as a goal of yours personally: you want to recover that money, right?

GERALDINE: That way we won't have to pay so many taxes, maybe.

Geraldine's response is somewhat tongue-in-cheek, but it reflects a genuine sentiment among many fraud workers. For Southeast supervisor Helen, too, the self-as-taxpayer dimension of the resource preservation frame is important:

You think about it when you get your check. You see them take out federal taxes. They take all these federal taxes out and you're like, "Okay," you know, what programs your money is going to or what have you. And when you see people not doing what they are supposed to that really makes you mad for the simple fact that I'm contributing to this. And if it's up to me I wouldn't be contributing to it, but I can't do that because I got to pay the federal government. And that's the way you feel, and it just goes back to like right now it's income tax season. I don't know how it is in Illinois, but here people get real excited about income tax because they are getting all this money back. The thing that kind of makes me tickled by working in here is when the taxes are seized because they didn't pay their food stamp debts. And the first thing they do is be like, "Well, I had something to do with that money." How can you do something with money that you never got in your hand?

. . . Personally, to me, I feel like if you are getting food stamps and you are not supposed to you are stealing from me. That's the way I feel. [. . .]

You are stealing from me as far as I'm concerned. I go to work. And no matter where I work at, I got to pay federal taxes. And I understand you all have your little job or whatever and you are paying taxes, but you are not nearly paying as much taxes as I'm paying for you to be stealing from me.

Eastcoast investigator Diego also exemplifies those who blend the taxpayer notion with the symbolic value of fraud control work:

INTERVIEWER: How important are fraud units to public assistance programs? Are they absolutely essential, somewhat important, not that important?

DIEGO: It's absolutely essential. It's important because it's the only way to, again, maintain the integrity of the fraud unit, which therefore promises taxpayers—myself included, I live here, work here—that, you know, the program is being administered in a fair manner. And I think anyone who's honest about what America is, and if they love the country, then I think one of the things is our country's willing to help folks. Now of course everyone's definition of how far, how much, how long we're willing to help I think varies, but overall most people would agree with that ideal. And I think that having a fraud unit maintains integrity of the taxpayer, so that they therefore know, "Okay, my taxes aren't going to a 100 percent broke, corrupt system."

Zero-Sum   The idea of scarcity is woven throughout the resource preservation frame. The understanding is, generally speaking, that any public resources going to illegitimate purposes are therefore unavailable for legitimate public assistance claimants or other government projects. Ultimately, this reduces to the idea of a zero-sum benefit system, in which there is a singular pot of money available, and every dollar that goes to a fraudulent client could have gone to a legitimately eligible client who will now go without. This construction is particularly unfavorable toward rule violators, positioning them as taking benefits away from truly needy or deserving others.[12]

Eastcoast supervisor Mary Anne is a carefully made-up White woman in her early fifties. She adheres to the zero-sum idea while acknowledging that program funding realities may differ from an idealized one-to-one recirculation of benefits obtained fraudulently to legitimately eligible clients:

> MARY ANNE: If there was less people receiving the benefits that didn't need the benefit there would be more people they could help, and maybe put the limits up a little bit so that more people could be helped. The little one that's struggling because they lost their job and they need a little bit extra to get them over the hump until they can get another job.
>
> INTERVIEWER: Do you think that would happen if there, let's say that, hypothetical, lightning strikes and there's no more fraud in Eastcoast tomorrow, do you think there would be any response towards "Okay, so let's put some of the money that would have gone wasted toward fraud back into the system and increase benefit levels or make more people eligible"?
>
> MARY ANNE: I would hope so. [. . .] Yes, absolutely, that would be nice. That's the way it should work, isn't it? [. . .]
>
> INTERVIEWER: Lightning's not going to strike and eliminate all the fraud tomorrow.
>
> MARY ANNE: Well, that's good, because I still want my job [*laughs*].

This resource preservationist positions the fraud role as potentially facilitating the *expansion* of public assistance, invoking a version of zero-sum logic to suggest that eligibility requirements could be loosened to accommodate more people should fraud control realize cost savings. The resource preservation frame casts the fraud investigator as being on the side of the deserving poor, over and against the undeserving. For Mary Anne, her role is to protect the program specifically for the people categorized as deserving.

Diego shares Mary Anne's sensitivity to the complexities, and sometimes ironies, of the fraud control world. He combined the zero-sum, taxpayer money, and stewardship aspects of the frame in explaining how he gauges his own performance as a fraud control agent:

INTERVIEWER: So you said you're a metrics guy: What kind of metrics do you use to measure your own success? Is it just dollars, is it something else?

DIEGO: I think, you know, dollars—now, here's the funny thing. Because this is tax based, I think dollars for me is strong. But I also measure my success in also how we treat people. Because at the end of the day, you're still dealing with human beings and you want to give full, full service, even to those who are committing fraud. Because at the end of the day, you want to make sure everybody gets their fair shake. But I think dollars, money, makes a lot of sense sometimes to look at. Simply because those dollars equate to what was put into the system, which is tax, taxpayer money. And ultimately you know I'm, I find myself in a fortunate position to be working and doing okay in life. I may need to utilize the system myself in the future. Who knows? So you'd like to, and that's what I think most people don't understand. Hey, if you were born into a wealthy family, that's fine. If you created a Facebook, or you're an oil baron, hey, that's fine. You'll never need this program. But I don't think that's for the majority of the population out there. And I think that even blue-collar workers these days are struggling. I think the last economic crisis proved that, the struggle of making a living. So, you know, the program can be good if it's, it's handled properly, administered properly, and money is recouped in a proper manner. It's money that's brought back to the system that potentially can be utilized to be put back, to feed benefits, right?

Diego emphasizes fairness, both in the administration of benefits and in the adjudication of suspected fraud cases. Most fraud workers espouse the principle of fair treatment for alleged rule breakers, but Diego stands out from the majority of his colleagues in his expressed commitment to "full service," even for clients who violate rules. The stress he places on balancing his enforcement work with continued advancement of the provision mission, even in cases of suspected *or confirmed* fraud, makes the place of broader agency goals in his occupational role formulation a distinct outlier, even among resource preservation types.

DISINTERESTED ENFORCEMENT   The final major occupational frame that the welfare fraud workers I interviewed employ is disinterested enforcement. While the catching cheats frame emphasizes just deserts and the resource preservation frame emphasizes systemic ramifications, the disinterested enforcement frame fixes its gaze more narrowly. Ideal-typical devotees of this approach see themselves as almost akin to automatons: machines that receive input, act on that input according to preordained rules, and produce output. The first two frames encourage unbiased rule enforcement—at least, there is nothing in them suggesting that enforcement energies should be biased in any way—but neutrality is the *sine qua non* of disinterested enforcement. This frame positions fraud control workers as technicians, disavowing interest in or allegiance to anything other than the dispassionate execution of policy.

The disinterested enforcement frame is prominent in Eastcoast, which has embraced information technology in its recent anti-fraud push. More than other states, Eastcoast looks to hire staff from the private sector or directly out of college; these types of actors enter their new work environments without many of their colleagues' experiences in benefit administration or law enforcement, and it is understandable why they might conceptualize their work here as fundamentally similar to their work anywhere else. Within the disinterested enforcement frame, a spreadsheet is just a spreadsheet. Enforcement is just the application of a set of received rules to a designated supervised population. Higher-order concerns like defending a particular ethical code or organizational and systemic ramifications are, for the disinterested enforcer, beyond the fraud worker's purview.

All the frames include a self-presentation dimension. Of the three, disinterested enforcement is most closely associated with Weberian bureaucratic rationalism; in that sense, it is particularly logical that bureaucrats might align with it. Edward provides a good example. He is a high-ranking Eastcoast administrator whose responsibilities span agency functions, beyond just fraud and program integrity. It is thus predictable that he might espouse the disinterested enforcement frame, as he did:

> Culture in this agency has evolved a little bit, or is evolving. I think it is true that at one point it was give them the benefits, give them the benefits, give them the benefits. The intent now is definitely not kick them off benefits, but there are some that feel that's what we're doing. We're always treading that line. Some of our workers feel that way because frankly, sometimes people in this office it sounds like said, "Give them the benefits." When we start doing things like program integrity, which includes a lot of things, as you know. It's not just anti-fraud. It's making sure the program is being run right, which includes not giving benefits to folks that don't deserve it. We start talking in that vein, and folks are saying, "You guys are different. This is different than

it used to be." We've got a set of rules, and we always have. We're just playing it straight. There are eligibility criteria, and we're going to stick to them.

Edward describes himself and his colleagues as "just playing it straight."
Even while juxtaposing the current era in rule enforcement with a previous era perceived to be more permissive, he argues that his agency's recent push toward program integrity and fraud control is not inherently
punitive. Tighter controls, he suggests, are nothing more than the unbiased result of following rules more carefully and consistently than in the
past.

Importantly, Edward equates fraud with any other organizational
problem, to be handled rationally and efficiently: "It's making sure
the program is being run right." This is in some ways the inverse of the
"catching cheats" frame, in which welfare fraud is understood as fundamentally similar to conventional property crime and the role of the
fraud control worker fundamentally akin to that of a police officer investigating violations and enabling punishment. Within the disinterested
enforcement frame, on the other hand, fraud within the agency is just a
public administration issue that is not fundamentally different from any
other, to be addressed according to standard bureaucratic policies and
procedures.

Eastcoast manager Caroline, who works in collecting overpayments,
adheres to the basic orientation of the disinterested enforcement perspective. While she is aware of and sensitive to the difficult circumstances of many clients' lives, she tries to detach such considerations
from her occupational actions:

> Although we do have compassion and empathy for the population, . . . in my
> unit we have to follow the mandate and what the state regulations are, as well
> as what the federal regulations are. So we do have a lot of explaining that we
> have to do with the population when it comes to what we do, meaning collec-
> tions. So we do have that empathy and the compassion for them, but we also
> have to follow what our regulations are.

Fellow Eastcoast fraud worker Andrew is a slender, bearded White data
analyst in his early thirties. Most of his job involves searching and cross-
referencing databases, seeking documentation of circumstances that
differ from clients' attestations. His comments are in keeping with the
quantitative, at-a-distance nature of his work:

I'm not on a crusade to catch, to not trust anybody caught in fraud. I'm not going to automatically assume that people are lying. I try to be neutral and just give people the benefit of doubt and go by what the evidence shows me. I don't go into it with the mindset of "Okay, everybody lies," "I think everybody's going to commit fraud," and "I'm going to catch everybody." And I'm not, that's just not me.

As he described it, Andrew understands his role as that of a neutral interpreter of the evidence and endeavors to enact that model. His East-coast colleague, data manager Stephen, said much the same:

INTERVIEWER: Where are you between a police officer and a social worker in your own approach to your work, your own interpretation of the job?

STEPHEN: Good question. For me I am clearly aligned with the mission of program integrity, so I don't have a huge conflict in respect to that. Of course I am working with people here in the central office who are not in program integrity who have started as a social worker, who work away from that perspective. And so they appreciate all the efforts of program integrity, but also they need to be operational in terms of running from the local offices as well. For me, I don't have a huge amount of conflict in respect to, if someone is doing something they shouldn't be doing, they shouldn't be doing it. We're here to detect fraud, waste, and abuse, as well to assess the instability and inefficiency in our programming, because the federal government gives us a lot of money that we are in charge of administering. Working in program integrity, that's—my eyes are pretty clearly on the prize. So I don't get caught up in a lot of these notions. A lot of people make judgments about, "Well, we shouldn't do this because they are a veteran, we shouldn't do this because they are a single mother who did blah, blah, blah." Well, we have our referral; we need to follow it to the end. That's it. This is my piece. Then if someone else makes a judgment call later on, at a hearing, or wherever else, so be it. Up front, even talking about some of the pharmacy stuff and the [illegitimate purchase of] baby formula [with SNAP funds, for resale]: there are a lot of judgment calls on that. We just have to do what we have to do. Someone else is gonna do what they do after that. But we just have to work that.

Stephen entered state employment from a private sector database management career and carried over a commitment to the disinterested enforcement frame. He tries to keep his focus on the immediate tasks at hand, thinking about fraud primarily as an organizational problem and avoiding dwelling on real-world complexities and complications. Even his language is sterile, devoid of the explicit statements about morality and values seen in other frames' perspectives. Enforcement targets are not criminals requiring punishment or undeserving people who need to be weeded out to preserve resources for the deserving poor. In this frame, they are depersonalized bureaucratic objects.

Stephen's efforts to separate his occupational role from the "judgment calls" that may be necessary in the overall fraud enforcement process are also noteworthy. Depending on the structures of their units and specific positions, individuals drawing on the disinterested enforcement frame may to some extent be able to displace discretion in the fraud enforcement process, moving it "upstream" to street-level investigative staff or "downstream" to hearing officers and judges. In these moves, discretion and judgment calls are not truly removed from the process but obscured in the conceptualization, design, and implementation of investigation and charge substantiation systems.[13]

OCCUPATIONAL FRAMES AND JUSTIFYING FRAUD ENFORCEMENT   Components of each occupational frame help fraud workers maintain perceptions of their work—and themselves—as morally upright and serving desirable social functions.[14] The catching cheats frame promotes a simplified morality tale, with fraud workers stepping in to apprehend rapacious clients. In the resource preservation frame, it's all about the big picture: stopping public funds from flowing to people who are ineligible or misuse them and conserving capital for those who deserve it. Finally, disinterested enforcement positions fraud workers as ideal-typical Weberian bureaucrats, doing their jobs efficiently and effectively on behalf of rational, methodical, and unbiased governance.

Similar processes manifest in some fraud workers' contention that their activities help ameliorate broader social problems. Before assuming his current position, Eastcoast administrator George spent many years as an investigator. He described what he sees as welfare fraud's nonfiscal costs, invoking pathologies of poverty and means-tested public assistance's intent to aid the deserving poor. In suggesting fraud behavior's consequences for children, George offered a counterpoint to those who contend that fraud charges can damage family relationships:

> I think [fraud] definitely hurts children. Because you're gonna see a lot of people that won't give to their kids what they should be giving to their kids, because it's either going up their nose or something else. I mean, these aren't real stable families. I think a lot of the kids are the ones that pay the price. I mean, I've seen some crazy shit in my years.

The idea that George raises—of protecting and helping children through counteracting fraud—is one way that workers like him position themselves and their role as virtuous. These explanations of fraud enforcement's social benefits are not just post hoc rationalizations for performing a policing function with reference to welfare provision. They are also significant factors in fraud workers' motivations to do their work and ongoing interpretations of their occupational experiences.[15] With considerable ambiguity in top-down definitions of fraud workers' role, occupational frames help them form occupational identities as they flesh out the job from the bottom up.

Establishing Occupational Identities

Fraud workers' occupational identities[16] revolve around their position as designated policing agents within public assistance systems. Their daily tasks and immediate imperatives connect them spiritually to conventional law enforcement, as does their focus on detecting and substantiating violations of legal rules. These consequences of their structural position make enforcement-first identities their default reference point. Accordingly, some look at the nature of their work and responsibilities and judge themselves as self-evidently close to police. Southeast supervisor Peter provided an example:

> We're obviously close to the police side. We can go in—we don't have guns and all stuff like that, but we can appear in court, we serve, we complete warrants. The investigators represent the agency at hearings and court dates. So they're not exactly quasi-law enforcement, but they play 'em well on TV.

Peter's comments closely link the fraud worker's identity to his or her daily activities. Unlike their counterparts elsewhere in the agency, fraud workers do not work in benefit provision; indeed, their tasks exclude clients and (sometimes) recoup resources. The enforcement function's concentration and separation within bureaucratic structure creates a clear rationale for investigators to identify with police. George shared a story communicating this sense of the fraud worker's occupational identity:

> One thing is we had a lot of people who lost their EBT cards. You know, I've had a debit card for years and I never lose it, but some people can lose ten in a year. So being the geniuses we are, we figure, "Jesus, I wonder if they're selling the damn things." Yeah, well. Now what we do is, after four cards, you have to go in and meet with the director of the office. The director of the office has our investigator there. We'll run your card and we'll see what transactions were made. In and of itself, it's a deterrent. Like I used to say when I used to get someone in front of me—I'm a good-sized guy—I get someone in front of me, the first thing I do is I usually start sliding my badge across the desk and I say, "I'm not your social worker," and then I read them their rights. And that is a whole different viewpoint. Like, "Oh, my goodness. What's going on here?" So that's what I tell my investigators. Tell them, "Look, I'm not here to give you the benefits. I'm here to be sure that card's being used properly, and if it isn't, we're gonna conduct an investigation." And it's a deterrent. Our rolls of high-volume replacements has gone down 82 percent. That was over eight cards per year.

George describes himself as a "good-sized" guy, and he is: over six feet tall, with a former football player's heavyset build. He is also notable for his sarcasm, limited patience for equivocation, and proclivity for profanity. Indeed, he hits all the beats of a "cop type" out of central casting. It is easy to imagine him as intimidating in interrogations, using *Miranda*-style warnings and displaying his badge to suggest his law enforcement association and distance himself from social work.

Occupational identities emphasizing proximity to police are especially accessible to investigators in states like Southwest, Midatlantic, and Southeast, where shoe-leather tactics involving physically leaving the office constitute a major part of the evidence-gathering toolkit. Peter's comments above flag such work as a key criterion explaining fraud workers' resemblance to police. Southwest investigator Ashley similarly invoked investigatory techniques in explaining her occupational identity:

> I wanna say I'm law enforcement? But I feel that if you're administrative, you're, it's just all office. Like, we're actually out in the field. We're going to

these homes. We're knocking on doors. . . . We're meeting them, confronting them, you know. So I would almost say that it's maybe more toward officer? But at least half and half. You know, I feel like if we were administrative, I would be doing all my investigations in an office. You know, I'm not, I'm surveillancing, I'm driving my car, I'm going out to where they're living, their home. So yeah, I would say maybe it's more toward law [enforcement] than administrative, just 'cause we're out in the field, and we're actually working out there.

Acting like a police officer seems to lead Ashley to think of herself like a police officer, even while working for a public assistance agency. She walks like a cop, talks like a cop, and uses her badge like a cop. Her unit's inclination toward criminal sanctions and cooperation with criminal justice authorities similarly precipitates strong identification with criminal justice actors. Fraud workers' perceptions of their jobs in more intensely criminalizing states bear out the fact that they gather evidence not only to substantiate administrative, program-specific charges but to become part of criminal cases, on which they work collaboratively with prosecutors.

Southeast supervisor Peter relishes moving cases into criminal proceedings: "My favorite part of the job is reading the prosecution reports and referring people, referring cases for prosecution." His colleague, supervisor Helen, also sees herself as police-adjacent:

I'm closer to the police. The reason I'm closer to the police is because, guess what, if you act a fool I got to deal with you. Here, people come up in here and act a fool, you pacify. . . . Sometimes no matter how much help you put out there for people, they still are not going to be satisfied. No matter how much help you put out there for people, people are still going to act crazy with you. It's just so many things. Yeah, I prefer the police to be there [when I interview clients]. Okay, we having an interview and you want to cuss and holler, with the police in there you are going to sit down. Most of them are not going to sit up in there and be like, "Well, I want to leave; I'm finished." They are going to sit there and talk to you because they know they could go to jail. Which is bad to say. But if you know this up front your attitude changes. With us it's like, "Okay, we are going to file charges, we going to do this." And they be like, "Well, all right, you do what you got to do." Then the sheriff will go out there and it's like, "Oh, they are not here." You're ducking and dodging the sheriff. But if you get a traffic stop you are going to jail.

To me, with what we do, it's like okay, well, we need a police function. You need to show them that you do have the authority to do whatever. Some people view it as "Well, okay, you aren't nothing but a paper pusher." So if you are a paper pusher, then you can say whatever you want and nothing is going to happen. And they don't believe that anything is going to happen. And then when the police come to arrest them for food stamp fraud they are like, "Are you serious?" They don't take it seriously. If you put it up front, "This is a crime," they will do it much more different.

Helen draws on several components of the fraud control position to evoke its proximity to conventional policing. Off the bat, she notes the reactive, punitive character of fraud control work, drawing a parallel between her work and police work as both dealing with people who "act a fool." She also explicitly invokes the criminal justice system's role in what she does. First, she describes how presenting the fraud unit and police as a united front helps garner compliance and cooperation from clients. And second, she argues that criminal sanctions are crucial to efficacious fraud control, demonstrating to clients that fraud workers are more than just "paper pushers."

In Southwest, supervisor Carly's unit heavily utilizes fieldwork and actively pursues criminal charges. Carly is not a field investigator, but she plays a pivotal role in the preparation of cases for criminal prosecution. In that capacity, she has close ongoing working relationships that lead her to identify with criminal justice authorities:

INTERVIEWER: If we think about social worker on one pole and police on the other, where do you see yourself, your personal approach to your job, on the social worker to police officer spectrum?

CARLY: I see myself leaning more toward the police officer spectrum than the social work side . . .

INTERVIEWER: Yeah, that's one of the things that's interesting to me about these units, is that you're right there in the middle.

CARLY: Right, yeah. I predominantly fall towards that police, you know, consequence, action, consequence, action, consequence, more than the social work side. [. . .]

INTERVIEWER: So you're the law-and-order type, more than the social work type?

CARLY: Right. Yes. However, I can very much sympathize and see the point of

> the social worker. But I, predominantly, my roots are, no. You have to do
> something about it. There's an action and a consequence.

The connection between Carly's use of the catching cheats frame and
her occupational identity is apparent. The punitive orientation of her
work setting encourages such perspectives.

The situation in Midatlantic further evinces the impact of work setting on occupational frames and identities. Midatlantic is the only one of
the five case study states in which the fraud control unit operates parallel to the assistance agency rather than within it. Without broader public assistance goals and motivations as a bureaucratic superstructure for
the fraud unit, this arrangement is especially conducive to identification
with law enforcement.

Although this state was willing to grant interviews with only a handful of high-ranking figures in its fraud control enterprise (and not street-
level investigators), those representatives clearly indicated that their bureaucratic separation from the state's assistance agency begets a law
enforcement habitus. Hank, the would-be military man turned Midatlantic manager, unequivocally described himself as "definitely on the
law enforcement side." Beyond the occupational identity effects of being
removed from the assistance agency's bureaucratic culture and broader
objectives, Hank also associates this separation with greater regulatory latitude. Recounting a conversation with someone from the benefit
agency, Hank said,

> The person told me that FNS regulations say you can only call [clients] in to
> do this or that. Well, I don't care what FNS says about how many times we
> can bring someone in about eligibility. I am under a separate mandate, and I
> can investigate anything I want, even a tip.

Hank's colleague, Midatlantic administrator Penelope, shares his view
of their unit's alignment with criminal justice. A cautious White woman
in her late forties, Penelope ascribes some advantages and some drawbacks to the unit's bureaucratic separation and criminal justice identification. Penelope said that the independent fraud unit is "perceived to
be external muscle" and that their independence may lend credibility
by sidestepping "fox watching the henhouse" critiques of blended provision and enforcement setups. Overall, she said, "we're probably bet-

ter off [separate] for investigative purposes." Still, the separation comes
with some loss of easy access and other bureaucratic hurdles that she
thinks might be less pronounced were they under the assistance agency's umbrella.

Enforcement Identities in Welfare Contexts

As even fraud workers who strongly identify with the police note, their
jobs are not identical to conventional law enforcement. Southwest investigator Dusty began his career as a police officer and is employed as
a sworn peace officer in his current position with the Southwest public
assistance agency. These circumstances prime him to strongly identify
with police. Yet he has had to adjust his occupational identity in light of
his new surroundings:

> It seems like sometimes they don't want to put people in jail, because we're
> here to help people. We're here to give benefits to people that need them,
> needy families, needy people that actually need them. That hard part is when
> you find people abusing them, when you need to take action, and you actually
> need to take somebody to jail or take their benefits away. It's a little more dif-
> ficult. Instead of me being a cop in [my old job], where, "Oh, somebody com-
> mitted a crime, I'm taking them to jail, you know, mark a little stat for me, I
> took someone to jail, blah blah." But it's different on this aspect of the social
> work because we don't want to ruin our reputation, and a lot of people don't
> know that [the agency] has sworn officers.

Dusty pointed to considerations of the assistance agency's broader helping mission as precluding an unqualified embrace of a law enforcement
identity. Legally speaking, jurisdictional limitations also impose fundamental differences: fraud investigators' legal authority is limited to program applicants and participants. They may function as law enforcement
agents but have far less expansive discretion and jurisdiction. Southeast
investigator Danielle used the descriptor "law enforcement lite" and recounted this appellation's origin in an exchange with a police officer: "I
think a [state] trooper told me that, because we can't do our arrests. So
he said, 'Oh, law enforcement lite. Well, you got a badge.' I'm like, 'That
don't mean nothing! [*Laughs*] It's just shiny!'"

Their assigned tasks and objectives are enforcement-specific, but fraud control workers are part of the welfare system—and that context bears on their occupational identities. Justifications of fraud control as necessary to preserve scarce benefit resources and defend public assistance programs' long-term viability evince their employing agencies' influence. And they commonly move into fraud control from benefit provision backgrounds. Although they may be disenchanted with welfare, many nevertheless enter fraud control identifying with public assistance work. Adapting to investigative and enforcement tasks makes suspicious and punitive thinking—with particular restrictions of jurisdiction and authority—their new default.

Yet limitations on their legal power constitute important caveats to identification with conventional police. Southwest supervisor Todd, for instance, downplayed the significance of their enforcement and punishment goals and motivations and highlighted how his unit's boundaries separate it from criminal justice agencies:

> I would say my staff are closer to the social work [side] because, like I said, we're just fact finders. My unit doesn't do prosecutions like that, we're fact finders. It has to go through the other entities to get to that point. We're like just the first step and there's two or three other steps in the middle before it would actually get to an attorney general's office, so we're actually closer to that [side].

Todd is a pragmatist who primarily frames welfare fraud control as a matter of limiting (illegitimate) government spending. However, discussing efforts to streamline allegation adjudication processes (for both administrative and criminal charges), he described how the unit is bringing in more investigators with policing backgrounds. With this more strongly police-identified new blood, Todd expected to see an uptick in their efficiency processing the sorts of consequence-focused cases he associates with the criminal legal system:

> In-house here we are trying to develop a way to streamline that process to get us more things going to an administrative hearing or prosecution-type thing. So the outside people [with law enforcement backgrounds] will not change that, per se, us inside people will, but the outside people coming in will have a better idea of how that works and they'll be able to help us get there. We know we need to do it without them, but when they do show up, they'll be a help [in] getting it going.

Todd's use of insider/outsider language again points to how occupational backgrounds influence occupational frames and identities. His comments also suggest distinctions between different types of fraud workers, with implications for fraud control outcomes. Over time, bringing in and socializing outsiders changes the makeup of insiders. Recruitment from particular groups—here, people with law enforcement backgrounds—has consequences for direct fraud control outputs like IPVs and criminal convictions. And it also has symbolic consequences, shaping meaning-making and shared understandings of who fraud workers are.

Other respondents placed more emphasis on assistance-focused goals and motivations in locating their occupational identities. However, even those strongly committed to the helping orientation expressed commitment to stopping fraud. Robert, a White man in his midsixties, is a longtime veteran of the Eastcoast public assistance agency, where he has held wide-ranging responsibilities:

> INTERVIEWER: Could you talk a little bit about where you might see yourself on that spectrum between a law enforcement–type ideology or orientation and a social work–type orientation?
>
> ROBERT: I'm probably about as liberal as you can find. I'm sort of of two minds, and I think my inclination is, by and large, people are honest. By and large, they try to do the right thing. However, as they would say in *The Big Lebowski*, to paraphrase, "Just because I'm a liberal, doesn't make me a sap."
>
> INTERVIEWER: [*Laughs*] I think there might be another two-syllable word somewhere in there, but yeah.
>
> ROBERT: [*Laughs*] I don't want to be taken advantage of.

Robert is not a fraud unit representative, but his observation that he is "sort of of two minds" with regard to the fraud issue reflects the "multiple and contradictory logics"[17] that apply to designated enforcement agents within an ostensibly helping-oriented system. Southeast investigator Danielle described herself as "right in the middle" of police and welfare. She pursues suspected violations doggedly. At the same time, aspects of her approach nod to the broader agency's assistance mission. She said she tries to help people avoid violations when she can, even suggesting to clients how they might better access resources:

I've even called a woman and said, "Look, I know he's in your house. Is your husband in your house? You can add him and get more food stamps." They think they just can't report the husband in the house and it's like, "No, you're eligible. Is he working? Is he self-employed or anything?" "No, he's just not working." "Okay, add him." I mean, because I want to help people. If you're eligible for it, the program is there; take advantage of it, but don't lie to get it. [. . .]

We're right in the middle. I'm going to help somebody. Like calling them when it's to stop them from committing fraud, I think that's social services, and I still want people who are eligible for the benefits to get the benefits. I don't think it's wrong to need assistance, because that's why it was developed. Just don't lie to get it. I think I'm doing a social service when I sit and talk to somebody in an interview and make sure they understand. I'm not one to be like, "You did this wrong." I'm not going to do that. We're going to talk about the weather and everything and be cool about it, and I'm going to be like, "You know why I called you in here today?" Sixty percent of the time: "Yeah." They know why they're in there. Twenty percent, they play dumb, and then the other ones will say, "I don't know why I'm in here." "Well, let me tell you." And it all goes fine.

Although some fraud workers, like Danielle, stake substantial claims in social service territory, the imperatives and responsibilities of their day-to-day work make an enforcement-first orientation the group default. Most say they are closer to police than social workers. Southeast manager Jack embraced this perspective, personally and on his staff's behalf:

INTERVIEWER: So, most of you come from [an eligibility] background, [Jack: Yeah.] from that world, that's where you started [Jack: Right.]. But where you are now: How you do see yourself? If we think about police, public safety, traditional law enforcement organizations over here, and think about social workers, welfare caseworkers type of thing over here, where do you see yourself on that spectrum? Are you closer to the police side, or closer to the social workers' side of things?

JACK: [Interrupting] Oh, we're closer to the police.

INTERVIEWER: Methods closer to police?

JACK: Yes.

INTERVIEWER: Goals, motivations, ideology maybe closer to police?

JACK: Yeah, I think so.

INTERVIEWER: You think [that's the case] for most people in your office, or is there kind of a range?

JACK: I think for most people they would say more close to the police. Especially those that have been around for a number of years. And most of my staff are at least two years and more.

INTERVIEWER: So you think maybe the longer you work here, the more you're coordinating with those agencies, and day-to-day work maybe shifts the way you think about yourself and your job, closer to that end?

JACK: Right. And I mentioned too, I've changed over the years. You know, I wanted, I was the gung ho [one], trying to catch everybody. But you learn that you can't catch everybody after a while. You do what you can do, you come and give a hundred-plus percent every day, but it doesn't always work out to what you expect, on what you want to be doing.

Describing his personal occupational evolution (and transition into middle age), Jack indicated that his policing strategies have shifted, tilting somewhat more heavily toward practicality. But he also described a general move toward identifying with conventional police as staff become more accustomed to fraud control work's accompanying tasks and associations. His comments encapsulate how the bureaucratic separation and concentration of rule enforcement functions produces a labor force that sees itself like police. In Jack's experience, the job's duties and exigencies push people toward such identities.

Conclusion

Welfare fraud control is a compelling context for examining how people process their working worlds and position themselves within them. Occupational frames help fraud workers make sense of their role and offer resources for ongoing self-interpretation. In turn, ideas about fraud control work's core character and most important results inform how individual fraud workers identify their relative proximity to police and traditional welfare work. The enforcement-specific nature of their work and their incentives to maximize successful investigations make carceral logics their default. Still, their location within the public assistance system prevents wholesale identification with law enforcement, even though they work in separate and specialized fraud control units that foster the catching cheats frame. These consequences of bureaucratic structure illustrate how organizational forms and divisions of labor systematically shape on-the-ground policy implementation.

Occupational frames and identities' significance transcend fraud workers' individual meaning-making. Understandings of fraud work involve basic conceptions of clients and fraud workers' relationship to them. And they influence how fraud workers pursue cases and punishments. Whether a given investigator sees the job as primarily involving the apprehension and punishment of wrongdoers or protecting the flow of government resources affects which aspects of which cases are deemed significant. As the next chapter describes further, fraud workers definitely want to present their activities as worthwhile and desirable. Their accounts of what their jobs are and who they are in their occupational capacities are more than just self-presentation strategies, however. These distillations inform their ongoing interpretations of their occupational experiences and constitute guides to action that shape discretionary decision-making.

CHAPTER SIX

Fraud Control as Performance

Welfare fraud workers recognize that their work has symbolic aspects. They know that, in addition to their substantive consequences, their activities send impactful signals to multiple audiences, including their political and administrative superiors, other government agencies, client populations, and the general public. The signals they send to these different parties have different implications for their efforts to stake out and defend bureaucratic territory. To their governmental higher-ups, they endeavor to signal efficiency and effectiveness to secure budget appropriations. In their relationships with other agencies, signaling professionalism and reliability helps build strong reputations, facilitating ongoing evidentiary access and investigative cooperation. And as they orchestrate their activities to signal swift and certain fraud detection, punishment of rule breaking, and a sense that welfare provision is regulated by sweeping surveillance and strict sanctioning, they work to bolster their programs' legitimacy and encourage rule compliance.

Fraud units' particular location within government lends their signaling efforts some distinctive features. Compared to conventional criminal justice agents, their identity is somewhat ambiguous, and they often feel they need to do more to justify their resource allocations and defend their unique jurisdiction. At the same time, they sometimes feel conflicted and subject to critiques from both the welfare and police sides. To help negotiate this terrain, they highlight their expertise and specialized knowledge as they make the case for their importance and due respect. Through pointing to the skills and capacities that fraud workers have but mainstream welfare workers and police do not, they delineate and claim their bureaucratic territory.

These efforts necessitate generating narratives and numerations that signal disinterested, rational action, (cost-)effectiveness, and the efficient production of substantiated fraud cases. Such reputations help fraud workers access resources and build fruitful relationships with relevant actors outside their units. Viewed systemically, they also influence the substance and consequences of fraud investigators' ongoing work: reputations for agent and unit effectiveness help garner funding and inter-agency cooperation, further entrenching punitive adversarialism.

Accessing Funding

Welfare fraud units' relationship with money is multifaceted. Working for agencies assigned to help people who do not have enough money, they are part of a system that officially recognizes and classifies that condition, then issues circumscribed and caveat-laden versions of money intended to help meet basic needs.[1] When violations of the rules governing agency-issued funds are suspected, fraud units come into play. Following investigations of household finances and client behaviors, fraud workers present evidence justifying agencies' suspension or discontinuation of quasi-money benefits, as well as efforts to recoup funds and possible criminal proceedings.

At the same time, fraud units run up against typical bureaucratic funding limitations. Many fraud workers feel that state governments shortchange public assistance administration in general and connect this observation to problems they see in welfare agencies. They say that low wages cause employee disengagement, as well as high turnover, leading to inefficiency and underperformance. They also argue it perpetuates fraud-specific problems if eligibility interviewers and caseworkers lack motivation to actively contribute to program integrity efforts.

Amid the practical necessity of securing funding, fraud units' budgetary appropriations differ between jurisdictions and over time. Policymakers' inclinations toward budget requests shift alongside variations in fraud's salience. Broader economic and fiscal conditions also play a role; the Great Recession, for instance, brought cuts to fraud units, despite their attestations that their work stretches government dollars through suspensions, disqualifications, and restitution orders.

Although conventional law enforcement agencies have their own budgetary concerns, fraud workers envy police departments' standing within government and default funding support. Southwest supervisor

Carly juxtaposed her unit directly with police departments, which she sees as advantaged amid a general trend toward public sector austerity:

> I think that local law enforcement now is finding that they have to justify their numbers more and more these days. And historically we've always had to justify our numbers. And it all stems down to funding. All of us. I think that before, local police departments were just given money, because this is your function, this is what you do. And if you need more money, people were always pretty willing to give that to them. So the need to justify hadn't been as great. People aren't necessarily willing to give us money. We have to fight for every dollar that they give us to spend toward this problem. So I think that's the different views on it.

Carly connects fraud units' comparatively lower profile and the lack of consensus about their social function to greater difficulty securing funding, suggesting that fraud units must explain and justify themselves in ways police departments may not.[2]

Conversely, heightened fraud salience can also generate waves of support and budgetary windfalls for oversight offices. Such effects are apparent in the national fraud control boom headlined by Reagan-era "welfare queen" rhetoric and "junkyard dog"–style aggression and tenacity in government oversight.

Eastcoast's recent history evidences a smaller-scale fraud control boom. In a high-salience environment, state political leaders provided an influx of resources, facilitating a fraud control overhaul. Eastcoast administrator George was brought in specifically to lead the new efforts and given leeway and financial support to reconfigure the fraud control system according to his vision. Here, he reflected on this unusual budgetary windfall:

> We have tons of support. Because what happened was, I come in here and we had an absolute shit show going on. It was in the front pages of the paper, I had the [local paper] sitting in here taking my picture, interviewing me for an hour. I was like, "What are we doing?" It was like a bad *60 Minutes* interview. So right away they get into "We've gotta do something about this." So then they went head over heels, and we sort of got whatever we wanted.

Responding to elevated fraud salience, the state granted George and his team nearly free rein. George brought in Eastcoast manager Vincent to serve as his right-hand man. Vincent is a physically imposing White man in his late forties with a shaved head. Like George, he has a lot to say about fraud control and expresses his thoughts in a thick regional accent. He spent much of his career in Las Vegas casino security and thus has experience working with capital and freedom uncommon in state government bureaucracies. Yet he shares George's sense that the agency has provided plentiful resources:

> INTERVIEWER: Do you think that the agency appropriately values fraud control? That you get the resources you need?
>
> VINCENT: Oh yeah. Without a doubt. . . . Probably more now than ever before. Because I think they understand the importance behind it. I'm not saying that's always been the case, but I think we had [an agency head] here before who came in right after all this, with the [scandals], and it was a big push. That's when all the [fraud control] stuff came into play. And I think that, that's about the time I came in here, on the second wave of introducing matching: more matches, more frequently. Those that we could do in real time. And that was when I first realized that folks on the outside were talking with no insight as to what was going on. Because it was nice to see, and probably never done before, to ramp up the [fraud control] as much as they did, as quickly as they did, and put enough resources behind it. That's one of the other instances that I tell is, that they've invested in us, now we have to keep this going. Because you can't just say, "Okay, we got these in place, everything is there, let's just lay back and now everything will come out in these matches." It's just not the case. You have to keep going. You have to keep them going. You have to keep them fresh. You have to keep constantly checking these programs, because you never know. Because there's some system that shuts down and you're not getting the information as quickly as you were or as readily, or correct, and that's usually when something bad happens. So we're always working to keep these things stimulated and keep them moving, keep them fresh, and keep them out there so people know that we're continuing to do what we're doing.

As Vincent pointed out, fraud units cannot take funding for granted. Managers and administrators make signaling a consistently high priority: not only do they want to *be* efficient and effective, they need to be *recognized* as such. Demonstrating productivity cultivates ongoing support for fraud units, perhaps insulating their budgets from resource contractions.

It is a different story in Southeast. Southeast investigators are paid less and lack Eastcoast's technological tools. They also reported more tension with the agency's benefit administration side and less support from agency administration. Investigator Geraldine described their situation:

> INTERVIEWER: Do you think [the agency] appropriately values the fraud unit? . . . They can only put so much money into one area, but do you think they put enough money, enough emphasis here? Do you think they fairly assess what you guys do?
>
> GERALDINE: No. [. . .] They don't think fraud is all that. They don't think there's a lot of fraud, but there is. No, we can't get anything. Sometimes we can get supplies.
>
> INTERVIEWER: [*Chuckles*] Like tape and pencils?
>
> GERALDINE: Pencils. Yeah. But we have a tape recorder and we just got some new laptops. So it's not that bad. It's getting better. [. . .] They need to pay us more. [. . .] We just got an increase, but we were getting paid the same thing as a [case]worker almost, and we do way more. We go to court, we prosecute, we testify, we go in the field, we are pounding the pavement, them reports we write, oh my God, they are like something that a law student would write. [. . .] And I've had DAs tell me how awesome of a job [I did on] a report, "You say you want to come work for me? Just let me know because your report writing [is good]." We all on the same templates, we all pretty much on the same page when writing reports. They are fabulous. One attorney said he told his client, "You might have to plead because I went through her whole report and there is no scapegoat in that report; she got you sealed up." He said, "That report was awesome!" [*laughs*].

Geraldine pointed to fraud workers' duties and skills to support her claim that they are undervalued. Specifically, she asserted that her fellow investigators have greater responsibilities than benefit administration staff and that their jobs require additional capacities. Invoking her experience working with prosecutors, for instance, Geraldine suggested that her work approaches the work lawyers do. Differentiating fraud workers from mainstream agency staff grounds her contention that the agency should more fully recognize and support her unit's work.

Northeast investigator Tabitha's unit has experienced more pronounced funding restrictions, especially with state cutbacks after the Great Recession: "It's the [separated] investigative model that is problematic. It delays things and leads to rippling efficiency effects. They felt the trade-off wasn't proving worth it, and it was causing issues in the other end of the shop [in benefit administration]." Thus the state government assessed—and altered—fraud control practice based on cost-benefit analysis. Across the country, fraud unit representatives, too, call on cost-benefit arguments, but in the opposite direction—to make claims for greater fraud control resources.

Overworked, Understaffed

Fraud units find opportunities for government to recover funds (through restitution orders) and avoid expenditures (through client suspensions and disqualifications) and for state governments to obtain federal dollars (through incentive programs allowing states to keep some recovered benefit funds). Accordingly, fraud units invoke return on investment in arguing for maintaining or increasing their staffing numbers. These claims hinge on the idea that fraud workers "pay for themselves"; as evidence, fraud units tally overpayments identified, funds recovered, and estimates of "cost avoidance" connected to illegitimate benefits that presumably would have continued without client suspension or disqualification. This logic presents robust fraud control enterprises as a source of long-term cost savings and fraud control cuts as penny wise and pound foolish. Southwest supervisor Todd elaborated:

> When our clientele went down [in the early and mid-2000s], the legislature reduced the number of staff. They did it everywhere. They did it at the local office. Reduced everything. Then when the economy took the crap, we actually reduced even more, but clientele and fraud went up. They even say the crash was in '07, but I think for us, we were affected in '08 and '09—[that's] when we started getting hit hard with it. [. . .]
>
> I think outside the box really weird. Each one of my investigators over a five-year period will save the state approximately one million dollars in what we call cost avoidance. We get cases shut down or get benefits reduced to their correct rate from what they were being paid out. One investigator is not making a million dollars in five years. I also think that if the legislature gave me more people and paid them, then those people [who] are being paid are going to pay taxes, [and] legislators will get more money back. They're going to go out and spend their money, which will then be taxed. Actually, you should be giving us money because you're going to get it all back [laughs].

Cost avoidance and fund recovery also figure centrally in occupational identities, particularly among those who draw heavily on the resource preservation occupational frame (see chapter 5). The notion that one "pays for oneself" through recovering funds and preventing illegitimate payouts is a common resource for defending one's position and, by extension, the broader unit one represents. Some fraud workers extend this logic by musing about tying recovery percentages to personal compensation. Investigators entertain the hypothetical of what their paychecks would look like if they included some of the benefit funds reclaimed via their investigations. Geraldine, referring to her current work and her prior job as a child support enforcement agent (chasing "deadbeat dads"), discussed this prospect:

> INTERVIEWER: You do get some percentage back, though, from recovery of overpayment though, right? For Intentional Program Violations, like 35 percent or something like that?
>
> GERALDINE: Mm-hmm.
>
> INTERVIEWER: I know you personally don't [laughs].
>
> GERALDINE: No, our agency does. We've been getting millions of dollars back for the government.
>
> INTERVIEWER: No, I know, I've seen the reports. But no incentives for you personally?
>
> GERALDINE: I wish they would give me an incentive. I'd be out there busting them like—just 1 percent.
>
> INTERVIEWER: That would be a lot.
>
> GERALDINE: That's what I used to say about child support, though. . . . I'd collect a million dollars. Just give me 1 percent of that one million and I'd be happy. . . . Because without me working the cases, they wouldn't have gotten anything. That's how I feel.

George, recalling his time as an investigator during the Reagan administration, recounted an experience with a federal bureaucrat who inquired about the possibility of awarding investigators percentages of their investigations' recoveries. George liked the idea's implications for his own pocketbook, but he worried too:

> INTERVIEWER: Welfare fraud has always been a popular target. I mean, go back to Reagan's first campaign. He liked the idea of the "welfare queen." That came about then, that's still in popular discourse. You remember—?

GEORGE. Yep. His saying was, "I want all my welfare fraud investigators to be as hungry as junkyard dogs."

INTERVIEWER: Junkyard dogs, that's right, that's right.

GEORGE: I had a guy from the feds at that time come out and interview me to see if they paid us a percentage of what we brought back. And I said, "Buddy, you know, you're singing to the choir." I said, "I'll be a millionaire." I was an inner-city officer at the time. I was like, "Yeah, pay me a percentage." And I'm thinking, "Jesus, then you'll see the *investigators* going off in cuffs, from charging people inaccurately."

Although George sees the incentive's appeal, he has reservations about how it might influence investigators. His lighthearted outward embrace is tempered by a more serious and skeptical internal monologue. The hypothesis that such an arrangement would lead to "investigators going off in cuffs" also connects to a personal experience with an investigator pursuing criminal enrichment through his job:

You can also attract the wrong type of person, too. I hate to say [it], but an investigator that did work for me, but worked in another region when I was [first working in welfare fraud], that, he had a special recruitment process. He'd have some people come in that might, you know, they'd say, "If you can pay this back in cash, I'd like to keep it out of court." And he always carried his briefcase with him because his briefcase usually had cash in it.

For George, then, not only could "commissions" affect investigators' actions; they could also attract problematic people to the position in the first place. Like his counterparts elsewhere, George sees recruiting and developing high-quality staff as essential to successful fraud control. Anything that could compromise the unit's labor supply is met warily.

UNDERSTAFFING AS A PROBLEM   Fraud unit leaders want the right people—and more of them. In all five case sites, workers cited understaffing as a problem. Even George, who said he "can't bitch too much" given his resources, would like to hire more staff. As an Eastcoast investigator predating the recent boom, Patricia is well positioned to reflect on the impact of adding agents:

PATRICIA: Our unit has greatly expanded recently. . . . All those law students [who had been hired as investigators], for one reason or another, they left, and then [our staffing] was totally untenable [*laughs*]. And then we [had low numbers] for a number of years, and that's when I had [responsibility for] all of [my region] and then hired more people. So we need to have the numbers out there, we need to have the people to do the job. Since hiring a whole bunch, where we are now, we actually had [a few who] left for different reasons shortly after they started. So, you need the staff to do this job. Even though my jurisdiction greatly reduced, I am still overwhelmed with work. And like I say, trafficking alone needs some dedicated staff people to handle that. So I guess that's the only thing I can think of off the top of my head is we need the people. And it's definitely improved! There is no doubt about it.

INTERVIEWER: But you could still use more?

PATRICIA: Yeah. Because every time—we all get 'em, run into these confusing and complicated cases. All of us are like, "I don't have time." And know there's like so few cases that are quick and like everything's online, or it's only one issue, or the case file can be found right away, or you request the calculation of the overpayment and you get it back, you know, within two weeks, which is wonderful. Like months go by before you get it back and you've gotta reacquaint yourself to the case. There's so many issues. So, yeah, we need more people, and then we could always be as thorough as necessary. When we [hired more people], I'm like, "Oh my gosh, am I gonna get bored with my job?" Noooo! Not at all. Not by any stretch of the imagination. I don't know how I did it all when I was doing it before.

Although their fraud control system remains robust, Southwest fraud workers reported a recent decline in their ranks. Southwest investigator Sue is a lean, dark-haired White woman in her midforties. She said the number of investigators working in her assigned county is half of what it was a few years ago:

SUE: That's it, for [my] county. That's a big difference. That's half. And we're increased in referrals.

INTERVIEWER: And you're supposed to complete thirty-six investigations a month, right? And even that's obviously a ton, and that's difficult, and even that's not enough to keep up with the load.

SUE: No, because we get more than thirty-six a month. [. . .] So it's like, it's just increasing. I know I get more than thirty-six referrals a month, so I mean there's no way, there's no way you're going to. No way at all. So they're just going to sit there.

SUE: Yeah, well, they get kind of upset. "Well, that was like six months ago
or eight months ago," and I'm like, "I'm sorry, we're just now getting to
the investigation. We still have to question you on that part of the time
frame." Some of them get upset.

Timing creates complications for both investigators and clients. Charges
may relate to financial and household circumstances and statuses with
the agency that no longer apply or involve alleged misrepresentations
that have already been corrected. Allegations of months-old violations
disconnected from their current situations are understandably frustrating for clients and complicate their efforts to assemble exonerating evidence. They can also take up investigator time on fruitless chases, further draining agency resources without the measurable returns agents
need to justify their work.

Return on Investment

Arguments about the financial value they provide are a crucial part of
fraud units' efforts to send their preferred signals and thus defend this
governmental response to welfare administration questions. While
they perceive public outrage about the social phenomenon that they are
tasked with counteracting, they also feel they lack police departments'
default levels of support from public coffers. Thus they continually at-
tend to self-presentation and specifically attempt to demonstrate their
activities' value in dollars and cents. This revenue-centric framing foregrounds fraud units' fiscal impact, evoking some conventional police departments' function as revenue generators for municipal governments.[4]

Southwest coordinator Keith exemplifies this approach and the influence of New Public Management (NPM) ideas more broadly. An en-
ergetic and upwardly mobile White man in his late twenties, Keith was
trained in business and explicitly prioritizes efficiency. He aims to reconfigure his state's fraud unit—and ultimately its entire public assistance program—to run more like a business. Speaking about how his
fraud unit measures its outcomes, Keith said, "We can look at numbers
of prosecutions and that kind of thing. Different parties might prefer different outcome measures, and how you choose among the various possi-
bilities is an important question. But ultimately, what we do needs to satisfy the value calculus."

The fraud control occupational identity is linked to both police officers and welfare workers, but it also contains a "superaccountant" element that corresponds to other government oversight roles. Fiscal considerations figure centrally in their activities' substantive consequences: they identify areas where state funds can be recovered and facilitate that recovery, and try to prevent expenditures through front-end detection efforts, client suspensions and disqualifications, and presumed deterrent effects. Driven by neoliberal thinking and the more immediate pressures of austerity-minded government, fraud units as collective entities defend their positions by arguing that their resource recovery and cost avoidance provide fiscal benefits that meet or exceed states' budgetary investments. Individual representatives often demonstrate a corresponding personal dedication to self-justification (and by extension collective justification), emphasizing their individual efforts' return on investment.

Southwest supervisor Carly fundamentally interprets her work through the catching cheats frame, but she also highlights fraud control's fiscal implications. Furthermore, because she is married to a local police officer, she is uniquely situated to reflect on the relationship between conventional law enforcement and welfare fraud control. As she commented on the different stakes that she and her husband associate with their work, she illustrated the comparative need for self-justification, specifically in economic terms, that fraud control workers feel. Referring to her husband, she said,

> Yeah, he's so funny, 'cause he's an officer, and he doesn't care. . . . He's been in the police department for twenty-one years, something like that. . . . He doesn't understand why I care so much about the conviction. Or why I care so much about the restitution. Or why it was a really big deal, that $58,000 in collections that just went out at the beginning of the month. And I was like, "Well, that just shows that we're extremely efficient. We've already brought money in." We care about how much—for every dollar I spend on fraud, in fraud prevention and investigations, what's our return on that? Like a business thinks. And local law enforcement, they don't think about that.

The $58,000 that Carly mentioned refers to a recent assignment in which she and a colleague went through old case files to calculate overpayments and initiate restitution actions. When we met, her cubicle was still crowded with Bankers Boxes; we had to relocate a stack just to make a place for me to sit during our interview. Clearly, the task had been arduous and tedious, but its results made Carly proud. Wading through box after box of case files of varying quality and completeness to calculate overpayment figures is nobody's idea of a good time and is certainly duller than the fieldwork investigations that substantiated many of the violations involved. Carly's satisfaction with the work despite its apparent dreariness is tied to the calculable $58,000 figure, which demonstrates the importance she assigns to advancing the fraud unit's case for cost-effectiveness. By contrast, she feels that her husband and his police colleagues are able to focus more directly on their primary duties, without the same concerns about demonstrating their value.

CALCULATING RETURN ON INVESTMENT   Calculating fraud investigations' net fiscal impact is complicated, even impossible. Fraud units emphasize their "cost avoidance," or the benefit funds that, without the suspensions and disqualifications permitted by IPV charges, presumably would have been issued to clients. A common approach for estimating a given program exclusion's associated cost avoidance is to multiply the average monthly benefit amount received during the period of fraud by the suspension's length.[5] However, especially given the instability of poor people's lives and the ubiquity of intermittent program participation,[6] not everyone who is kicked off programs would have otherwise continued consistent enrollment.

The most solid data on fraud enforcement's return on investment come from numbers on what the investigations actually bring in. The USDA reports that, in fiscal year 2016, state agencies nationwide completed 963,965 total SNAP client investigations and collected $89,632,055 in associated overpayments.[7] These figures show a basic return per investigation of $92.98.

More than half of these investigations, however, were pre-certification "front-end detection" efforts; there are no overpayments to potentially recover from investigations completed before benefits were issued. There were 374,064 post-certification investigations in fiscal year 2016;[8] including only post-certification cases increases the per-investigation return to $239.62.

The monetary savings associated with preventing ineligible people from receiving benefits are doubtless significant and should not be disregarded. However, like calculations of client suspensions' fiscal impact, they are inherently uncertain. Focusing on the directly numerable average of $239.62 recovered per post-certification investigation gives reason to doubt that fraud workers concretely "pay for themselves." Given the complexity of worker-hours and other implicated resources, it is difficult to calculate what the typical post-certification investigation costs, but something more than $240 seems likely.[9] Further, there are additional costs associated with investigations that are launched but not completed, as well as efforts to collect restitution, pursue criminal prosecution, and supervise or incarcerate people.[10]

Echoing police departments' use of crime statistics,[11] fraud units want to use dollars and cents to signal effectiveness and efficiency. The most concrete numbers on their activities suggest that, in the immediate sense, the idea of fraud investigations producing net fiscal gain seems dubious. This has led critics to characterize such interventions using phrases like "the fraud control game"[12] and "the false promise of administrative reform."[13]

Again, though, fraud workers themselves stress that their actions also have symbolic value that produces substantive consequences. Fraud investigations do not just result in restitution orders and benefit recoveries; they also communicate that public assistance systems are engaged in active surveillance and punishment for rule breaking. This signaling of state oversight and coercive power may encourage clients to obey rules and can result in "administrative exclusion"[14] if the climate of punitive adversarialism discourages eligible and otherwise interested people from participating.

Reputation and Credibility

Internal Fraud

Seeking to manage both their own reputations and those of their broader public assistance programs, fraud workers also report prioritizing cases involving agency staff. Though the vast majority of their efforts are outward-looking, focused on the general client population, they are highly concerned with the optics of cases implicating their own.

Above, Eastcoast administrator George described a particularly brazen instance: the investigator who collected and pocketed off-the-books cash payments from clients. More commonly, fraud workers describe employee malfeasance involving fabricating clients and then personally collecting the benefits allocated to these fictitious parties. Such offenses, based on exploiting positions of responsibility and trust, are pernicious and often difficult to detect.[15] Eastcoast administrator Robert explained, "One of the most effective ways of committing fraud is to have a worker set up a case that doesn't exist and keep pumping benefits into it." Midatlantic administrator Penelope was even more succinct: "Caseworkers that will dummy up cases. . . . We see a lot of that."

Fraud units take employee fraud cases very seriously. Southeast, for instance, gives cases involving employees their highest prioritization, the same status given to cases referred from the office of the governor or a state legislator. Jack, the Southeast manager, added that, alongside client fabrication, these cases can emerge following a natural disaster. He described how the USDA FNS relaxes normal SNAP eligibility rules and validation processes under disaster conditions and said that Southeast encountered agency employees committing the type of straightforward eligibility fraud that they typically look for in the nonemployee client population:

> We had a thousand-something employees with the agency apply for benefits. [*Looking over the top of his glasses, chuckling.*] Many of them were not eligible for the benefits that they applied for. And so [the next time there was a natural disaster], there was a lot less employees that applied for benefits. 'Cause they saw what the circumstances that came out of the first one [were]. And [after that] we just had a very few number of employees that applied for benefits. 'Cause what happens is management took a very strong stance against people who intentionally got benefits that they knew they were [ineligible for]. They terminated 'em. So, which is fine. That's the way it should've been. It took care of 'em. People learn.

Antoine, a supervisor under Jack, described being redirected to focus on cases of employee fraud that reflect poorly on the agency: "If it's a personnel investigation then that takes priority, so everything you're doing gets kinda shoved aside until you get, take care of that." Antoine's personal feelings correspond to the agency's official position:

> Probably doing personnel investigations has been the one irritating factor of my job, when you have to interview your own people. And you realize that, well, you've been entrusted with the faith of the state. And you've been entrusted with this job because you're supposed to know better. And you don't.

Antoine disdains such actions, which he feels demonstrate failures of character and harm the agency's reputation. With some levity, he retold a specific case of employee fraud that his unit prosecuted and the convolutions that can result from pressing charges against agency employees:

> One of our employees, one of the eligibility workers that we processed in court, the judge, the DA, wanted to [plea bargain] her as a misdemeanor, 'cause it wasn't a great dollar loss. . . . [But] she wanted her day in court. She represented herself. So we go into a civil service hearing, she's representing herself, she's her own lawyer, and she's asking herself questions in the fourth person [*laughs*]: "Did you sign that?" "No, I didn't sign that."

Antoine's recollection brings up some of the unusual elements of substantiating these types of charges. The caseworker in question is in an atypical position. Normally, the fraud unit might call on her to help support their version of events in an Administrative Disqualification Hearing or in court; here, she takes the opposite role, seeking to contradict the fraud unit's account and exonerate rather than incriminate.

Not all employee misconduct occurs among street-level workers whose quotidian working lives are so closely connected to fraud units' standard detection and investigation processes. Public assistance agencies are vulnerable to the same types of embezzlement and other white-collar crimes that occur in other organizations. Higher hierarchical positions entail more trust and responsibility and thus open up more opportunities to commit larger crimes.[16] Southeast supervisor Helen recalled,

> HELEN: We had one of our [administrators] who got arrested. . . . He defrauded the agency.
> INTERVIEWER: Oh, so he was just embezzling?
> HELEN: Yeah, large sums of money. He got jail time and all that for it. He got federal jail time, because you know that's federal dollars. So to me, you should take it a little more seriously. Sometimes you have got people stealing from right under your nose and you don't know. . . . They said he had been doing it a year after he started working here. And he did it up until a month before they caught him.

This individual enjoyed significantly better legal representation than the *pro se* eligibility worker Antoine discussed, in line with research on white-collar criminal processes more generally.[17] But his case also incurred a strong reaction and ultimately incarceration. In Southwest, manager Oscar shared the perception that large cases merit such punitive responses, saying "an employee making forty Electronic Benefit Transfer (EBT) cards, sending them to themselves, you know, stuff like that, that person needs to go away." In an arena where workers regularly talk about deserving and undeserving clients, where morals and ethics are foregrounded, fraud workers suggest that it is a particular insult to find someone charged with upholding the rules undermining them instead.

Managing Multiple Audiences

Fraud units are concerned about signaling legitimacy and credibility, building their reputations with multiple audiences, including state politicians, other government agencies, and the general public. Eastcoast administrator Edward, who holds agency-wide authority, summed up, as though with practice: "My responsibility [in my position] is to work with different constituencies, internal and external, including, of course, the [gubernatorial] administration, but [also] advocates, FNS from USDA, legislators, and the general public." As he depicts it, Edward's job largely involves managing and maximizing relationships with various groups while minimizing any risks.

Southwest coordinator Keith employs similar risk/benefit thinking, especially risk aversion. Keith's unit's risk management and prioritization endeavors are multifaceted. At the most basic level, he said, "individuals receiving noneligible benefits is a risk, with many controls." Forward-looking fraud control efforts strive to manage the risk of clients violating program rules. Yet, Keith continued, "people committing fraud is a risk, but our daily operations entail many other risks as well." He noted, for instance, how their work processes involve information risk management, with the unit responsible for adhering to federal and state law and policy regarding client confidentiality and data protection. Particularly important is the fraud unit's engagement with what Keith called "reputational risk," evoking organizational studies scholarship on the topic.[18] This logic further evokes the NPM effort to refashion public sector organizations after private sector models. As bureaucratic departments specifically organized to increase oversight, enforce individual accountability, and ultimately roll back the scale of the welfare state, fraud units help advance this agenda. People like Keith actively seek to make their units "run like a business," spurring changes in organizational culture and practice.

For Keith, managing reputational risk means presenting an image of the fraud unit as "prudent and professional." He echoed Eastcoast administrator Edward in pointing to multiple audiences with whom that image needs to be cultivated: other departments within his agency, other social service–oriented agencies, local law enforcement, the governor's office, the legislature, federal authorities, and the public. Like many of his colleagues in Southwest and counterparts elsewhere, Keith foregrounds the public as taxpayers. And he takes quite seriously both the obligation to serve them well *and* the responsibility to communicate to them the idea that they are being well served.

PUBLIC PERCEPTIONS

In the creation and spreading of appraisals, affect and emotion become part of the meaning of signs. Physicians exposed to the phrase "compulsory health insurance" react not to the dictionary definitions of three words but to a powerful set of economic and moral anxieties. Language becomes a sequence of Pavlovian cues rather than an instrument for reasoning and analysis if situation and appropriate cue occur together. — Murray Edelman, *The Symbolic Uses of Politics*, p. 116

Perhaps more than any other term in US domestic policy, "welfare" is loaded with "a powerful set of economic and moral anxieties." The basic lexical denotation of "welfare"—meaning health and prospering—has given way almost entirely to negative connotations as it has become shorthand for public assistance programs. This goes beyond a simple Pavlovian relationship in which an ostensibly neutral stimulus becomes associated with a response, in that it has imbued an ostensibly positive term with a new, negative meaning.

Along with concepts like dependency,[19] the idea of rampant fraud, driven by media portrayals and political rhetoric, has played a central role in the transformation of public assistance and the idea of welfare in the United States. Today, simply participating in public assistance may be equated with committing fraud[20] or broader criminality.[21] This study's respondents provide evidence, reporting, for instance, that when their work comes up outside the office, they hear sentiments about clients like "they're all crooks."

Fraud workers are state agents tasked with policing public assistance

programs that many believe are "out of control" and rife with rule violators and rule violations. They take these assigned responsibilities quite
seriously but do not believe that their efforts are well understood. Even
though many agree with outsiders that fraud is common in their programs, few think the public actually understands much about public benefits, fraud, or fraud control. Fraud workers wish their work had more
of a public information impact, but their experiences leave them skeptical that any is forthcoming. Eastcoast supervisor Mary Anne referred to
fraud workers' frustration with ignorance and misunderstanding of their
function:

> It's just the frustration of it, you know, that it gives. You hear people, you go
> anywhere and people start talking, if we are in the newspaper, and they'll
> be saying different things. And it's just frustrating because that's not the full
> story. We are working hard to stop fraud and I feel that people don't, the gen-
> eral public don't realize how hard we are working to stop it. [...]
>
> I think they feel that everybody is frauding, and it's not the case, because
> of welfare reform. And you know, [clients] are allowed to work and make a
> certain amount of money depending on their household, and, like, they are
> allowed to have a car. There's different things that, I mean, it's not neces-
> sarily [the public's] job to understand the rules and regulations because they
> don't work here, but it's just frustrating to have their opinion that, you know,
> we're not doing our job and trying to stop it, because we've come so far.

Eastcoast administrator George shares Mary Anne's perception, connecting it to their state's shift away from fieldwork-based investigations
and criminal cases. In his estimation, a return to previous generations'
more invasive and punitive methods would augment popular understanding of and support for fraud control:

> I think on the [criminal] side they've grown too laid back. I think you have
> to have those big cases go to court, make a splash with—granted, it's gonna
> draw attention that there's welfare fraud out there, but you've gotta hit on the
> bigger cases so that they don't come up and bite you in the ass when the [lo-
> cal papers] or [local TV news] goes up and does a study and survey, and says,
> "What about this?"

George wants the public to know more about big cases, but also the cost
avoidance and restitution numbers his unit produces:

Yeah, the numbers look great, but also it lets the taxpayer know, you know, you're doing something up front, and you're also legitimizing the family that just needs a leg up. "I need some help. I'm hopefully gonna be off this damn program in six months, but I just need that leg up to get me through this." You know, make it available.

Like many of his colleagues across the country, George believes that fraud unit activities have the potential—provided appropriate communication channels—to shape public opinion about assistance programs and fraud controls within them. What's more, he suggests that active fraud units and robust front-end detection systems can help counteract common misconceptions equating receiving welfare with committing fraud. As this logic goes, the more people understand the strength of program integrity systems, the harder it will be for them to assume there are many people accessing benefits on the basis of fraudulent eligibility claims. Evoking resource preservation thinking, he connects these presumptive public opinion effects with better prospects for long-term program viability. To his mind, increased fraud control efforts that are publicly known will promote willingness to "you know, make it available" for those who officially qualify.

But that caveat—*provided appropriate communication channels*—is a real barrier to fraud workers significantly influencing public opinion. When, for instance, members of the public report fraud suspicions, these units have limited ability to follow up or provide feedback to tipsters. Mary Anne, the Eastcoast supervisor, took a pause to consider before answering when I asked about her least favorite part of her job:

The frustration of, like, with the hotline, and not being able to get the knowledge out there to them that we are looking into this. We don't want fraud any more than the general public wants fraud, you know. We are working on it. But you know, we can't tell them. If they call and they say, "Sarah Smith is working at Dunkin' Donuts," and we look into that and we see that Sarah Smith can work, we can't call that person and say. But they are going to call and say nothing was done. And that makes us look bad, but we really did look into it. So that part is frustrating with the job.

She feels her unit has little ability to build awareness of its activities or change perceptions about their dedication and effectiveness. I mentioned to her colleague Diego my sense that fraud units were fairly low-profile, even among social scientists interested in poverty and punishment. Unsurprised, Diego said few people in his state have any real idea what his unit does:

> Yeah, they don't, and that's one of the things. I constantly hear, "Oh, they don't do nothin' to people on it." We actually do. People would be shocked. I think people would be shocked to hear that when people, when we bring solid cases forward that the evidence shows, 100 percent, beyond a shadow of a doubt, that they are committing fraud. And I mean a case where you have all the applications that they signed, they took on a job, they made $10,000, and they filled out an interim report. That last interim report was during the period of fraud, and on the section where it says, "Has there been any changes in income? Has anyone in the household worked?" they sign "No," they check that box, and it's a signature below. That's pretty much the intent is there to, not necessarily defraud the system, but the intent is there to hide the truth as to what your earning capability is, to then utilize the system for benefits. When you get those solid cases, I think the general public would be shocked what people get. They lose their benefits for a year.

Diego was unabashed in adding that he, too, was unaware of what the state's fraud control enterprise comprised before he transitioned into the agency from a position in the conventional criminal justice system:

> I think people . . . may have sort of misconceptions or myths built up. Again, myself included, until I started working here. There were a lot of things that shocked me. There were a lot of things that I thought, "Oh, I never knew that." I thought differently. So I think unless you learn what the program's about, match it with reality as far as what the program allows, does not allow, what it gives, what it does not give, you're gonna be surprised at the things that you thought. "Wow, I didn't know that" or "Why are they doing that? That doesn't make sense." So I think the general public probably has a worse slant on it because they don't understand some of the rules. Plus the other thing, they don't understand fundamentally how the program works. You know, I think you have to be sort of a higher-level person who follows politics, news, government to know: it's a federally funded program, but states get to administer it. And that we do have a fraud component, that people *are* disqualified and people *do* have to pay back to the system . . .

Cash benefits: you're not allowed to buy liquor, you're not allowed to buy prohibited items, and we take those cases very serious. . . . I think the general public would be impressed to know that if they were to buy prohibited items on an EBT card, that [*snaps fingers*] it does, it gets caught like that. It comes up on our side, we see it, we flag it, we seek to sort of sanction the location, then they have to deal with certain penalties. We bring the person in for a hearing, sanction them. So I think the public would be shocked to hear that as well.

The sense that the public is under- and misinformed about public assistance programs and state efforts to prevent fraud within them was nearly universal among my respondents. They want to get better information out there to improve their positions moving forward, but also as a way to deter fraud.[22] To them, it's a frustrating public relations problem without clear solutions.

Public assistance agencies make some efforts to promote fraud control awareness within their own spaces. These are generally focused on the proximate goals of deterring fraud and encouraging fraud reporting, and their reach is primarily limited to program clients or applicants. Materials posted in local offices remind visitors of fraud surveillance, detection, and investigation mechanisms. Agency websites also feature anti-fraud initiatives, particularly in advertisements of phone hotlines and online forms for reporting fraud suspicions.[23]

Funding for broader advertisement, however, is limited. Some states pay for advertising, announcing fraud control initiatives or soliciting public reports on billboards or at bus stops, in spaces that might otherwise contain ad copy for soft drinks or summer blockbusters. But for the most part, as Midatlantic manager Hank put it, "We're not out in the public's face. It's not a big marketing presence. You can tell when you meet someone and you introduce yourself and say what you do [chuckling]. No one knows who we are."

Apart from an aspiration for an expanded media presence, Southeast investigator Danielle decried even her agency's *internal* sharing of enforcement information:

INTERVIEWER: How often do you hear about public assistance fraud in the media? I know they were all over that [scandal].

DANIELLE: Not often enough.

INTERVIEWER: Should be more?

DANIELLE: Yeah, because every time I have somebody prosecuted, I write a press release and I send it to [my manager]. It's supposed to go on our intranet. It doesn't. What? Put it on the intranet. At least put it on our little intranet. I'll send a letter to the [eligibility] analysts after somebody's prosecuted, thanking them for the referral, letting them know what's happened to the person. They really appreciate that. I tack it on the bulletin board in the local office. I don't think they've had any of our press releases on the intranet, at least two years. We know we're writing them and sending them, and [the manager's] sending them to the information person, which throws them in the garbage. That's sad, because the analysts want to know we are catching the fraud. As an analyst, I enjoyed knowing. "Oh good," I knew. But I never heard anything from the previous investigator. I try to be proactive with that and let the [local office] know we're doing our job.

INTERVIEWER: If it made to the media, it would help with the morale of analysts and it would help—

DANIELLE: And it would help the public see. We're trying to be proactive. It would also get the word out to the people who were thinking about committing fraud or currently committing fraud that there are people out there checking you out.

At the same time, many fraud workers lament that the messages that do reach the public are frequently overly inflammatory. They want to publicize their commitment to pursuing cases and securing penalties and remunerations to protect program integrity and ensure that public money is wisely allocated. Instead, the public rarely receives information from agencies themselves; messages from politicians and the news media are much more prominent. These external entities have different agendas than welfare agencies, and they fixate on scandalous fraud incidents (both real and fictional) that often reinscribe stereotypes.

Fraud workers broadly embrace communications invoking resource preservation ideas. However, even facially dispassionate communications hold implications for reinforcing the equation of benefit receipt with deceit and criminality.[24] Communications intended as strictly informative or factual are no match for tabloid tendencies and prejudices. Fraud workers would also like to see attention brought to the catching cheats frame, emphasizing punishment in ways that could bolster deterrent effects. At the same time, they see how more lurid and sensationalist approaches are especially conducive to the reproduction of stereotypes and stigma. These contradictions further complicate their stance toward publicity.

Although historically deep rooted, stigma against recipients of means-tested public aid, tied to racial and gender stereotypes, has grown steadily in recent decades and has taken on particular virulence since the rise of Reagan-era "welfare queen" rhetoric. Even clients themselves can favor harsh policies and share negative perceptions of other program participants, regarding themselves as exceptions to a generally blame-worthy recipient population.[25] The predominant ways that the public receives fraud-related messages exacerbate these trends. In Midatlantic administrator Penelope's words, "Because people only see the bad pieces, they're inclined to be skeptical." Dominant representations of benefit recipients and fraud contribute to the ongoing construction of popular opinions and attitudes.

RELATIONS AND COLLABORATIONS WITH OTHER ORGANIZATIONAL ENTI-TIES Fraud units cultivate presentations as capable, effective, and efficient to political and administrative leadership to defend their funding. This manner of self-presentation is also an important consideration as they look to build and protect cooperative working relationships and information-sharing agreements with other departments, agencies, and organizations, including multiple non-welfare organizations. This latter group includes the various private and public sector organizations that provide them evidence, as well as other administrative and criminal enforcement authorities. In all of these relationships, reputations for competence and professionalism serve fraud units' interests.

Proximity is an important consideration: fraud units particularly need strong relationships with public assistance agency administration, as well as the local office caseworkers that generate most of their referrals and provide other information. Individual investigators aid in this effort as they cultivate rapport with local office staff to encourage case referrals and investigative cooperation. Midatlantic manager Brian—a stocky White man with close-cropped hair in his late thirties—said: "The cooperativity of the [local] offices makes a big impact on our referrals. It's up to our local person in the office to establish that relationship; a good relationship means that they'll give us more work." Suggesting NPM-style thinking, Brian indicates that their fraud unit sees the assistance agency like a business sees its customers. They need to provide good service and manage their brand to establish, maintain, and extend favorable relationships. In return, they get business—in this case, high-quality investigation referrals.

Fraud investigators also need to coordinate with their enforcement counterparts in other states who can provide residency and income information and help on duplicate benefit cases involving allegations of receiving SNAP benefits in multiple states simultaneously. Southeast supervisor Helen explained: "The ones that I like are the duplicate participation. With the duplicate participation I get to disqualify you for ten years. I like those." These long-term suspensions make duplication cases particularly valuable, reinforcing the importance of unit-level reputations and interpersonal ties with out-of-state colleagues.

State bureaucracies' accountability mechanisms do not apply to other states' employees; therefore, fraud workers need to be particularly thoughtful in building and maintaining cooperative interstate relationships. Southeast supervisor Antoine has a process:

> ANTOINE: We also have to keep relationships with other states. I get contacts from other fraud units in other states 'cause they have someone from Southeast that's now living there, and they may have somebody that's down here that they're trying to find. Some states are much more receptive. I think [one nearby state], I think I've personally talked to every investigator in [that state]. They all got my phone number. And sometimes I get a call from a strange state and the first thing I say is "What dirty dog gave you my number?" and he starts laughing: "We got your name from somewhere else; if we call you, you will return our phone call back." I got word from Alaska last week. . . . Something that they wanted to verify. So keeping those relationships open is important. Because to be able to pick up the telephone to call somebody, to avoid—I try to avoid as much red tape as possible, because if I need something, I need something.
>
> INTERVIEWER: And that personal tie can help you bypass a lot of bureaucratic channels.
>
> ANTOINE: Yes, yes, oh yes. Without having to go through fifteen people to get something done. Old school.

Other investigators share Antoine's perception that some fraud units are more receptive and cooperative than others. Interestingly, across the country, one specific state repeatedly comes up as both the site of a disproportionate amount of fraud activity and home to notably unresponsive and difficult fraud unit staff. For this study's purposes, exposing this semi-notorious state is less important than documenting the implications of its staffers' behavior. While fraud workers try to avoid being spiteful or vindictive, more than one suggested no particular sense of urgency upon receiving a request from a unit that has been less than helpful to them in the past, or even one that simply has a reputation for being closed off or poorly run.

As discussed in chapter 4, similar cooperative relations between welfare fraud investigators and criminal justice agents can help investigators avoid red tape and locate evidence more quickly and easily. Federal, state, and local law enforcement agencies constitute an important subset of the organizations with which fraud units try to cultivate good reputations and close ties. Accordingly, keeping those working relationships open and productive is a major component of fraud workers' thinking about their reputations and investigatory effectiveness. Southeast investigator Danielle emphasized her relationships with police officers. She is proactive and considers building close ties with both law enforcement and benefit administration a major component of that approach:

> My first goal when I became an investigator was to go out there and meet everybody in the sheriff's office. I've got my state police contacts. I went out there and met people and I was surprised how many agencies—state police, local—are like, "What do you do? Didn't even know they had a fraud unit in the [welfare agency]." And I'm like, "That's me!" They're all happy to help me out because they want to be proactive too, nipping fraud in the bud. That's about it, but I just couldn't believe people didn't know that my position existed [laughs].

Prompted to identify her single most useful investigative tool, Danielle spoke about cooperation and personal relationships with external agencies and agents:

> It depends on the case. DMV's pretty darn useful. And [child] support enforcement; we look on [the child] support enforcement database. That's good. I use probation and parole. We can't get into their database, but I have a few parole officers that I call to. They've been useful. Especially if somebody's on monthly monitoring. That's usually "Oh yeah, that's where we go. He's there every month when we go check on him." So it's like "All right, bingo!" [laughs].

Danielle maintains a sort of mental Rolodex, allowing her to bypass administrative divisions and information silos to access some external resources directly (like the child support enforcement database) and others through skillful bureaucratic work-arounds. Southwest supervisor Todd echoed Danielle's valuation of such informational conduits as he bemoaned losing a connection at Child Protective Services: "I used to have a couple friends here and there over the years. I would pick up the phone and they'd look it up: 'Absolutely. We took [the kids] away this date, this time.' They've moved on so I've lost my contact."

Not all investigators are equally skillful at building such relationships, but they universally recognize their value and point to networking, communication, and collaboration as essential components of successful investigation. Leadership figures may try to deliberately engineer cooperative relationships, though they often emerge organically. Investigators trade tips and accrue experience regarding to whom they can reach out for what and to what effect. And in all cases, successful relationships hinge on the mutual respect and trust that good reputations foster. Southwest investigator Dusty, like Danielle, called cooperative and coordinated actions across agencies his most effective investigative tool:

INTERVIEWER: You think you've got the tools you need; what do you think is your single most effective tool . . . ?

DUSTY: I think it's, I think our best tool is, whether it's the hotline, or USDA, where we all work—it's kind of like a triangle, where we all work together.

INTERVIEWER: It's coordination.

DUSTY: Yeah, it's coordination. Reaching out, kind of networking with each other. Finding out what's going on at this store [where SNAP benefit trafficking is suspected], finding out what's going on with this recipient. And you would be surprised, the phone rings all the time [like it did earlier in the interview].

INTERVIEWER: [*Chuckles*] Just once.

DUSTY: But it's always ringing, and it's people from [this city, that city], you name it. "Hey, I got this food stamp trafficking case, blah blah blah." It's just unbelievable.

INTERVIEWER: It's usually just civilians? Cops?

DUSTY: Civilians. There's law enforcement officers that will reach out to us. We work hand in hand with the FBI as well. We've helped run a couple task forces where we will go in with them. If they can't get the federal charges, we'll come in and assist them and do the state charges for the food stamp fraud, whether it's fraud schemes and artifices, or money laundering, or something to that nature.

INTERVIEWER: So the next question up was what government agencies you work with. I know we touched on that, and you network pretty broadly, and that's one of your best tools.

DUSTY: Yeah, we do, we do. So the agencies we work with: we work with the FBI. We work with the local police departments . . . with all the sheriff's offices as well. USDA. . . . We also work with [our state's health care agency]. . . . If they need health insurance or any medical that runs hand in hand with us because if we're running a case with food stamps and they're also getting [medical assistance], we get a dollar value from them and then throw it all together and slam dunk with it. We work hand in hand with them.

And Jack, the Southeast manager, brought it back to unit reputation:

JACK: Over time we've worked with a lot of different agencies. Everyone from local sheriff's departments to USDA OIG, the Office of Inspector General, Secret Service. . . . And they know what kinda work we do, they know we do quality work. And so they will reach out to us for help, and then we know that if we need help I can just pick up the phone and make a call. What, fifteen years ago I would've never thought I could pick up the phone and call Secret Service and say, "Hey, I need a little help with something." 'Cause you think, Secret Service, they're there protecting the president and that type of thing. But I could do it now [*gestures toward phone.*]. I turn around here, pick up the phone, and call Secret Service. Because of the quality of work that they know we do they're willing to help. It's, we work hand in hand on cases. I think we work more, I think we do more during investigations than the feds do [*chuckles*], but they do their thing, we do our thing, our part of it too.

INTERVIEWER: So that reputation is one of your long-term goals [as a manager]? Maintaining that position, connection with other agencies that's built on a foundation of good work?

JACK: It is. We've always worked well with OIG—USDA OIG—and that goes back before my time. The people before me, as I came aboard, they would say, "Well, we gotta get you in contact with these agents, these OIG agents." And when I first came on board I got to run around with those agents sometimes. They would, they would take their undercover out to a store and if they were coming through [town] they [would say], "Hey, you wanna ride with me?" And I'd ride along with 'em and let 'em run their undercover in, see if they could make a deal. And it just grew from there.

Asked if working to maintain the unit's reputation to protect their co-operative relationships with other agencies was something he took seriously as part of his job, Southeast supervisor Peter replied,

Oh yes. Because I want to work with them as well, and then they depend on us, if we are able to assist them. And we are happy to assist law enforcement. There is that feeling of being an instrument of justice in that as well. [. . .] Most of our times we've been helpful. I've been able to help them find the guy they're looking for. For whatever it is they're [doing]—they don't always tell us what they are doing.

In his leadership capacity, Southwest manager Oscar positions cross-agency collaboration first and foremost and considers his department's cultivated reputation and credibility the backbone of its effectiveness. He formalized this emphasis in a tripartite formula, with three ingredients each connected to reputation management:

I think what we have over the rest of the country is the, ah—I don't think that anybody has what I'd call a very good system. I think what we have unique in Southwest is we've blended the three elements that are important for us: partnership, commitment, and trust. And those sound nice, but they're very hard to execute. When I say partnership: we've partnered internal [to the public assistance system] with our shareholders, whether it be [benefit administration], sworn and civilian investigators, as well as the different things, the unemployment, all that. Keeping that all under one roof is good. . . . We can get videos from stores real quick, bank records real quick. That gives the bank cover from lawsuits, and it gives us speed to go get what we need to either clear or find violations. [. . .]

Partnerships are hard to form. People need to know you're committed. And I think we've demonstrated that. But more important we've all earned each other's trust. It's real easy to break it, it's real hard to build it.

RESPONDING TO ADMINISTRATIVE SUPERIORS   Fraud units also have responsibilities and objectives pertaining to hierarchical bureaucratic relationships, made plain by activities like their ongoing efforts to demonstrate return on investment. These come with a slew of informal demands and pressures from administrative and political superiors. Jack offered an example of how these informal influences shape fraud control implementation:

> JACK: Another factor [in case prioritization decisions] is who made the com-
> plaint. [. . .] Sometimes we get these calls that come in through our
> [agency head] or from a political person or whatever, or through law en-
> forcement. We try to give those more priority because those are the ones
> that we're going to be asked later, "What are y'all doing on that? What
> came of this case?" and whatnot. So we give those a higher priority. If
> we have complaints on an [agency] employee that may have been doing
> something wrong, those get the highest priority. And then we work 'em
> from there. But you know, if our [agency head] says that so-and-so from
> the governor's office called about this complaint, well [snaps fingers],
> we're on it.
> INTERVIEWER: What kind of cases does the governor's office care about?
> JACK: Well, they actually, evidently people call in to them with complaints
> also, about neighbors, people that they know. And they get funneled down
> to me also.

Sometimes demonstrating effectiveness entails responding to specific demands from superiors. These can come from state government as well as federal agencies and officials. All state public assistance agencies are subject to federal oversight. This oversight is particularly close with SNAP, in which all benefits are federally subsidized. Eastcoast administrator Robert, a longtime public assistance veteran, summarized: "There's more stringent rules about how you go about things in the SNAP world than necessarily, that I'm aware of, in the TANF world. . . . Because it's a hundred percent federal money, so they're a little more protective of it." His administrative colleague George described how accountability to federal authorities influences his unit:

> I mean, I know people don't realize this, but a lot of this is playing partners.
> And every year I'll have FNS come in, and they'll say, "How many cases do
> you have? How quickly have you acted on them, how much time?" So you
> have the long-timer saying you have to get stuff done. So I think you have to
> play to that audience. It's kind of like these kids taking, you know, some of

the [standardized] testing in school. You know, you teach to the test. Well, sometimes I have to work to the audits.

Demonstrating Effectiveness and Avoiding Blame

Defending the fraud unit's position comes down to assessments of effectiveness—indeed, sometimes George feels he has to "work to the audits." In any organizational entity, simple hard work may not be enough to evince effectiveness, or even show a fundamentally sound approach. Documentation—especially quantification—is essential, and so it makes sense to invest organizational energy in constructing narratives and numbers demonstrating successes.[26]

Tales of reputation management demonstrate such narratives' prominence in the minds of fraud unit representatives, particularly those in leadership roles. They also demonstrate the perceived benefits of positive, outcome-focused accounts of the unit's work. Above, George described how official federal requirements shape how he conducts and depicts his business. Southeast manager Jack explained how accounts of effectiveness pay off in less formal ways:

> The one thing I say here with the agency: we have a lot of support from the people here in the agency. Again, it's reputation. They know what work we do here within the unit, within the department, and they're quick to stand up for us when it comes to anything that comes into media.

The flip side of seeking credit is avoiding blame.[27] Bureaucrats try to not only accumulate credit by doing things well but also avoid blame resulting from perceived errors; some argue that blame avoidance is in fact the primary concern of the modern public officeholder.[28] Fraud workers understand self-protective impulses, and their self-presentations demonstrate both credit seeking and blame avoidance. Southeast supervisor Antoine illustrated this point:

> ANTOINE: So I think as a supervisor I don't supervise everybody the same way, because everybody is a little bit different. And some people I may have to nudge a little bit. Some people I may have to nudge a lot. Some people I may have to pull back [chuckles]. But as a supervisor, though, I have to control that. And it's not that I want everybody to be an aggres-

sive bulldog. I want you to look at your cases, and we want to make sure that the work we do is correct the first time out the box. I'm not the kind of person that believes in yellin', screamin' in somebody's face. Nah. I will tell you, "You're not meeting my expectations. Now what can we do to fix this?" Or tell them, "Don't waste time looking for something that's not there. Don't assume there's a loss if the evidence you find does not substantiate the complaint; this is an active case, and we move on to the next one."

INTERVIEWER: You gotta know when to fold 'em.

ANTOINE: [*Nods*] Know when to fold 'em. Yes.

When he was an investigator, Antoine picked up a piece of wisdom that he applies in his supervisory capacity: the fraud unit needs to act deliberately and carefully, because overzealous or imprudent enforcement activity can damage their desired narrative. Speaking about pursuing criminal charges as their default course of action in substantiated fraud cases, he said,

Unless there's mitigating factors, complicating factors. There's some issues where there's documents that we can't find, there are things that we can't verify, as far as our loss is concerned; we can't find an application that this person supposedly did, or we find out that the person submitted the application and the information was on the application, but we just didn't, the [agency employee] didn't process it. That's not a case that you're gonna pursue criminally. 'Cause you do not want that coming back on you in court. So sometimes we do have to eat cases. But you do that because of, the information you're looking at just is not, just doesn't meet it.

. . . My philosophy is that I don't try to make an apple an orange. If it's an apple, it's an apple; if it's an orange, it's an orange. I'm not trying to make stats because I wanna push something through. I'm only gonna push something through that is legitimate and there is no problems with it. Most of my cases that's in certain areas we never get subpoenaed to come to court, 'cause those cases are usually pled out in court, especially if the person has no prior offense. They're pled out; they get a suspended sentence with active probation.

In addition to trying to protect their units from blame, unit leaders are sometimes asked to defend themselves before administrative or political superiors. Jack was called upon to represent his unit in a session of the state legislature:

> I think [politicians] are quick to jump on "Well, why are we not doing certain things?" But again, they don't know the rules and regulations either. A couple years ago, I was asked to go over to the session when it was in. And the person that asked me to go with him over there, some bill or whatever was up for committee, and he said, "Well, you may have to testify, or talk about this or that." And I was like, "Ahhh, I am not this type of person." I am not a public speaker. I can sit down and talk to you all day, sit down and talk to a group of friends. But I am not one to get up in front of a group and talk. I try to connect with people, and I cannot connect with a group. But he did tell me this: "Just, when you get there to talk, just know this: you know more about fraud than anybody else in that room. So don't let them persuade you on something that is not, that's not right or is not true. Speak what is the appropriate action," and such. Luckily, I didn't have to say anything. But I was sweatin' it out. I didn't know what was gonna come of it. But it happens. They're just as quick to say, "So-and-so is committing fraud," and, you know, "Why aren't y'all doing something about it?" Well, when we get those referrals [from political figures], I tell ya, we make 'em a priority. . . . As their leader, their government leader, if they don't make that out, they may not get that vote the next time.

Jack relays how his expertise and specialized knowledge about fraud provided him a resource for deflecting blame and defending his unit's position in this high-stakes environment (albeit one he did not end up having to use). Such expertise and specialized knowledge are valued tools for sending the right signals.

Expertise and Specialized Knowledge

Fraud workers' intersectional positions engender unusual collections of knowledge and skills. They point out that this makes them scarce and valuable human resources (more valuable, perhaps, than their compensation and budgets reflect). And in their personal narratives, fraud workers distinguish themselves from other agency employees through reference to their investigative knowledge and skills, their grasp of policies and statutes, and their ability to write reports meeting the standards of adversarial legal proceedings. Such arguments allow them to separate and elevate themselves from stereotypes and stigma attached to case-workers and eligibility technicians within welfare provision.[29]

Fraud investigators also distinguish themselves from the law enforcement side, emphasizing their skill at effectively utilizing a different range of evidentiary resources than what police typically use. More significantly, they stake their claim to providing a service that the conventional criminal justice system cannot on their deep knowledge of public assistance program policies and regulations. Southwest supervisor Carly argued that good welfare fraud control requires specialized knowledge and a specific type of thinking that police do not have:

> [Police officers] also aren't program people. They understand the law, and they understand the laws in their communities very well. On a broad thing: "You can't do that." We have to understand a program *and* the laws in the communities and figure out how to take the statutes and federal codes across the board and apply them to the situation that we're in at the moment. So it's different, a totally different level of thinking. A lot of times what will happen is we, in the past, a lot of retired police officers would try to come and do this job. And just absolutely be horrible at it. Because it's not what they ever did. They didn't ever investigate anything. It's always great when you have to interview a retired cop, 'cause I'm like [*exasperated sigh*], come on. Really? What did he do? What was his job while he was retired? That's what I want to know before I even talk to him.

Eastcoast investigator Patricia further suggested that fraud workers with benefit administration backgrounds have in-depth rule and policy knowledge that gives them an advantage over fraud workers with other backgrounds:

> PATRICIA: When I came over [from benefit administration], I was actually an example or trial for them. I just, I was just like in the right place at the right time [when] I came over into this position. In the past, up to that point they hired, like, law students to do this job. And it was just because of my previous job that at the time—it was the same unit as this unit, it was a combined thing so I was already in the unit, and they just needed some help in dealing with these cases. And in doing that it was just like, "Whoa, I like this. I would much rather be doing this than that." And I had the

casework background, and so what turned out to be is I understood way more than what the other investigators understood, because I had been doing it and they were from off the street.

INTERVIEWER: You knew the terrain.

PATRICIA: Yeah. And so they hired caseworkers after that.

Southeast supervisor Antoine provided a higher-level perspective, describing how fraud workers' specialized, intersectional knowledge positions them as inimitable and indispensable government functionaries:

ANTOINE: . . . You pretty much stay in the middle, because [police] don't understand this side.

INTERVIEWER: And they don't understand each other a lot?

ANTOINE: They don't, they don't. And their perception of this side is skewed. A lot of times we get a lot of contact with law enforcement agencies because they're trying to use us as the investigative side to find something they're looking for. They may have a drug case, but all of a sudden they think that this person's committing food stamp fraud, and we end up doing all their work for them, in essence. So we're always in that middle. [. . .]

[And] sometimes you have to be very temperamental as to how you deal with the agency side. Because I've really had to pull back sometimes, talking to a supervisor that's completely ignorant of the fact that if this person's rent is $500 a month and they have no income but say their rent is paid up. How they getting the money to pay it? And I guess a lot of that goes back to my own training. When I was an eligibility worker we did management reviews at every interview. "This is your expenses, this is the income side." And if one didn't match the other, we actually asked, "Mr. [Interviewer], how you gettin' your bills paid? Is someone helpin' you, or are you getting some assistance from somewhere?" And we had to document that in the case record. Because I've seen your rent receipt, I've seen your lease, I've seen your doctor bills, I have a pretty good picture of what's going on with you.

But the way it is now . . . we don't have to verify this information. I'm looking at this person, saying, "Wait a minute. Tell 'em to stop. Why is this person's mailing address thirty miles away from their residential address?" People want their mail. This is on the other side of the river, so she's—and to me, I instantly see that, I guess because I've been all through the state, things like that instantly pop into my head: "Well that don't—no, no. There's no such address there." I've had cases in [one town] where people will call, and [I'll] say, "No, that's [an agricultural] field. No-body lives there."

Conclusion

Force relations are also symbolic relations.[30] States pursue monopolies over the legitimate use of not only physical violence[31] but symbolic violence as well,[32] and the exercise of coercive power entails the exercise of symbolic force. The power of states and state actors derives from societal recognition of their authority, not merely their monopolization of legitimated physical force. Indeed, establishing and strengthening state agencies of formal social control, which call upon the threat of physical force, relies on "the concentration of a symbolic capital of recognition (or legitimacy)."[33] Fiscal matters are an immanent component of this symbolic capital of recognition. Tax collection is a key power of the state, and disbursement of tax funds for accepted purposes is a key attribute of legitimated state authority.[34]

As state actors, fraud workers seek credit and avoid blame to defend their positions within government and their control over their allocated bureaucratic territory. Good reputations with the general public and other components of the state entrench their positions. Their accounts of effectiveness and (cost-)efficiency justify their claims on fiscal resources and ground their requests for additional staff and other forms of support. And they invoke unique specialized knowledge to bolster claims of bureaucratic terrain for which other state actors are ill equipped.

Compared to police, fraud workers' intersectional bureaucratic domain and official duties are less well known and understood, a status that they feel generates different requirements of explanation, justification, professionalism, and reliability. Their legitimacy cultivation strengthens their ability to enact punitive adversarialism by helping secure resources (especially more staff) and access information through formal and informal means. Interpersonal relationships with bureaucratic agents in both public assistance and law enforcement further help fraud investigators achieve their immediate objectives, including producing the IPVs, criminal prosecutions, and restitution orders so valuable to narratives and numerations of unit outcomes in business-inflected metrics like return on investment.

   Alliances across bureaucratic fields are both cause and consequence of fraud units' intersectional nature. Responding punitively to poverty management issues, investigators build cooperative relationships with people on both sides of the ostensible division between policing and provision. As oversight responses to critiques of government expenditures, fraud workers also work to build positive public perceptions and argue for more effective communication about their mediation of provision and punishment through rule enforcement. Above all, they emphasize that such communications should highlight their dutiful stewardship of government resources, advancing legitimacy through signaling circumspection and regimentation in public administration. Looking at the directly measurable fiscal returns of their efforts on a per-investigation basis, however, suggests that this bureaucratic intervention is not just about fiscal substance. Client surveillance and punishments offer value that goes well beyond the numbers.

CHAPTER SEVEN

The Blame Game

Punitive adversarialism in welfare has multiple meaningful consequences. In symbolic terms, how fraud workers conceptualize, pursue, and depict rule-breaking clients constructs "welfare rule violators" as a functional category. Fraud workers mostly concur about who rule violators are and how they stand out from the general client population. Espousing bureaucratic norms of formal neutrality, they largely disavow racial/ethnic differences in fraud proclivities; instead, they link fraud to morally blameworthy patterns of individual and familial behavior. Even as investigators say popular welfare stereotypes are inaccurate, they invoke ideas familiar from welfare reform arguments. They contrast fraud perpetrators—characterized as lazy, uninterested in labor force participation, and over-fertile—with more commendable groups, including more deserving program clients, nonparticipating wage earners, and agency staff (like fraud workers themselves). Among program clients, fraud workers associate shorter-term participation with deserving poor status and longer-term participation with undeservingness. That is, to fraud investigators, chronic poverty constitutes grounds for a measure of moral suspicion.

Constructions of rule violators as fundamentally blameworthy and deserving of censure are evident in law and policy and administrative priority setting. They are also built through on-the-ground practice. As investigators engage in their day-to-day work and fraud investigations proceed, they refine the subset of clients they see as likely rule violators. That shapes how they do their jobs, which involve substantial discretion. Unofficial classification into a more suspicious or less suspicious group guides decisions about which cases to pursue and recommend for prosecution, for instance. In this way, investigators' experiences and hunches affect the substantive outcomes of the fraud control effort writ large; iteratively, through ostensibly neutral metrics, those intuitions are reinscribed in refinements of fraud control approaches.

Perspectives on Clients

Social differences of class, race, and gender suffuse welfare fraud enforcement. While large percentages of people arrested, prosecuted, and convicted in conventional criminal justice processes are also poor, fraud investigators' jurisdiction is specifically socioeconomically disadvantaged people. The programs that fraud workers oversee are also highly gendered and racialized, especially as they are reflected in popular mythology and political rhetoric.[1]

Northeast administrator Roger, a White man in his early sixties, said "class and racism play into" the demonization of welfare clients in his state. As he put it, others in his agency share his sense that their clients are commonly (if implicitly) regarded as second-class citizens: "Our former director has a quote: 'When there's a line out the door at the DMV, there's an outrage, but if there's a line out the door at the welfare office, that's not an outrage.'" Midatlantic manager Hank sees similar asymmetries in public reactions to paper crimes committed by the poor relative to those committed by people elsewhere in the socioeconomic hierarchy; he notes that welfare fraud upsets people, but "No one cares about tax fraud!"[2] Southeast investigator Danielle, who is White, sees race and racism as major factors in perceptions of public assistance:

> INTERVIEWER: What do you think the public perception of public assistance is like here in Southeast? What do most people think about it?
>
> DANIELLE: They think they're all Black. They think they're all trashy. I tell people, "No." I think most of the people who are getting assistance aren't unwed mothers with eight hundred kids who've always been on it their whole life. That's a small percentage. I try to tell people that. That's not how it is. [In one area I work], I want to say that's mostly White. And it's mostly people who might be on them for maybe a year or two years and then they get off of them. The public perception isn't that. They all think of the welfare queen, and that's not the majority of people who need the assistance.

White Northeast administrator Ken evoked the sociological conflict perspective and referred specifically to Michael Lewis' ("Not *that* Michael Lewis [of *Moneyball* and *The Big Short* fame]," he cautioned) book *The Culture of Inequality* in discussing this phenomenon. "There always has to be a 'them,'" Ken said. "If they look different, that's all the better."

Southeast manager Antoine, who is Black, agreed and even described an inverse phenomenon, in which a person cued with his fraud enforcement affiliation was surprised by his race:

> [People] tend to lump everything together. The person may be in SSI [Supplemental Security Income]: "Where's she gettin' all this welfare money?" Well, it's not [TANF]. That's Social Security; she's not getting welfare money. Yeah, there's stereotypes. I mean, I've had to deal with it personally. I remember talking to a guy on the phone one day, and we'd talked several times. I had a new investigator down in [another city], and I told her, "I'm gonna come down there and we're gonna go by this guy's office and talk to him." And we walked in and the secretary looked at me and she said, "Who are you?" I said, "I'm Antoine." She said, "Ohhh." And my staffer looked at me, she said, "Why are you laughin'?" I said, "I guess I used my White accent on the phone. I shouldn't have done that" [*laughs*]. And it's just funny to me, but you, there's always been this misconception of what is welfare. And everything is lumped under that same umbrella.

Cultivated Neutrality

Fraud unit representatives foreground their opposition to what they consider to be largely inaccurate popular understandings of public assistance programs, fraud, and fraud controls. For many, this includes committed expression of modern bureaucracies' officially status-neutral, race-blind policies. Yet presentations of neutrality and color blindness sometimes crack.

One White fraud worker in Southeast, asked about impressions of between-group differences in fraud perpetration, responded with formally race-neutral language about generational dependence, stating that "you can't really define it by race." A couple of minutes later, however, the same interviewee said, "And again, by race, I would probably say African American more so than White," suggesting that ideas of racial difference were implicated but unspoken in the previous response. In Southwest, a White fraud worker appeared to blur the line between popular stereotypes and personal stereotypes while discussing public opinion: "It's such a stigma to be on [benefits]. Because, you know, Shanequah has five babies so that she can get public benefits. And you have a stereotype of the baby factory, and then just the lazy person. Or, you know, the criminal." A different White fraud worker in Southwest assumed a stereotypically Black style of speech, adopting an inflection when imitating a client: "She goes, 'Jesus been payin' my bills.' And I was like, 'Jesus—?' And she was like, 'Don't you go to church and pray for Jesus?'" Several interviewees also mentioned perceived patterns among immigrants. Eastcoast administrator George provided this perspective:

Different areas have different populations. [One area] has a large section of Russians who were pretty darn good at what they used to do. Nigerians were very good. . . . If you go around [certain] offices, there's a large Hispanic population, so it depends on where you are. And it's, you know, everyone's got an angle. [. . .] You can go down the street probably ten minutes from here and buy a Social Security card, you know. . . . [We are dealing with] illegals that we didn't know about their driver's licenses. Guess what? I hate to say it. They're probably gonna be on freaking aid too, so I gotta go out and find them before I get a call about them. [. . .]

Years ago we did have a Puerto Rican connection where they were falsifying Puerto Rican birth records. And that was organized. They were running up people through the [local] offices. . . . And there was a slew of those that we had.[3]

In our interviews, most fraud workers were disciplined in presenting status blindness and formal neutrality in responses to questions about between-group differences. They acknowledge that they mostly investigate women; this fact corresponds to women's representation among SNAP and TANF clients.[4] Most, though, deliberately disavow race and ethnicity as variables relevant to fraud control work. This position reflects the role of statutory and common law antidiscrimination provisions, as well as the related environment of "legalized accountability" in public offices,[5] and echoes criminal justice professionals who say they just see cases, not races.[6] In broader terms, this orientation represents the ideal of bureaucratic duties executed dispassionately, "objectively," "without regard for persons."[7]

I used the language of "social groups" when asking about perceived between-group differences in fraud behavior. I wanted to encourage interviewees to discuss their impressions of category-based social inequality in the welfare fraud context, avoid cuing specific axes of difference, and minimize defensiveness and reticence. Responses demonstrated race's salience as a master status generally and in this context specifically; most interviewees' reactions to questions about social groups suggested that they interpreted these as questions about race or ethnicity. Eastcoast analyst Andrew's response is exemplary:

> INTERVIEWER: In terms of patterns and what you see in fraud: if we think about the entire population of people who receive benefits and then the population of people who you catch committing fraud, do you see systematic differences between those two groups? So maybe it's, like some examples might be, it's more people who have lived here for a long time, or people who just moved here, or people who have been on benefits for a long time, or just got on benefits. Or any particular social groups, anything like that where you see patterns?
>
> ANDREW: No, no. I [*pause*], I really haven't. You know, a lot of people make the assumption that this group of people or this ethnicity is the one who commits fraud, when really, it's, I haven't seen any such pattern where I could say, "Okay, it's by group." I really haven't seen that.

From there, fraud workers commonly invoked ideas of randomness in fraud behavior's distribution. Eastcoast investigator Tiffany, who like Andrew is White, paused and expressed uncertainty, suggesting some discomfort with the topic:

> TIFFANY: Ummm—I'm not [sure]—I don't know if I would really, especially with social groups. I think the matter, depending on what office you cover, what the general demographic [is], that doesn't seem to matter. I think it's, um—ah—I don't know. To be honest with you, it seems to be so widespread, I'm not sure if I could pinpoint—I know, ahhh—I know typically they say, you know, younger, younger clients, but I mean you really do see a wide range of all different types of, um, types of people, and different, whether they've been on it a long time, short time, or—so, to be honest with you, I don't know if I could pinpoint any trends.
>
> INTERVIEWER: Pretty, kinda randomly distributed?
>
> TIFFANY: Yeaaaah. I wouldn't say it's one class over another, or that it's younger—I mean, you don't see a lot of elderly clients doing this [*chuck-*

les], sixties and seventies. But I would say below that you do get a wide range.

A number of interviewees mentioned only relatively innocuous notions of group-based differences, like the idea that they do not see many older people committing fraud. Others linked perceived patterns in fraud behavior to regional demographics, suggesting that patterns in referrals and investigations tend to mirror local populations. Several, for instance, described investigations of Black clients as comparatively common in urban areas with larger Black populations and investigations of White clients as comparatively common in Whiter rural areas. Southeast investigator Leslie is assigned to a region with mostly White clients:

> You have to realize that the majority, especially in [the area] that I deal with, the majority of the clients are young, between twenty and thirty-five years of age, White women, who just feel entitled to it. That is their perception— that is, their husbands or their baby daddies, or however you want to consider them, y'know, are out making the money, but they've never worked a day in their life and they've got three kids, all school age, and she's never worked a day in her life and the husband pays all the bills. Those are the ones that are just red flags, y'know, big sirens going off in your head: "Hey, that's the one you need to look at."

But overall, the modal response is that fraud is fairly equally or randomly distributed across different demographic categories. Tiffany herself suggests this, combining her semi-agnostic position with a conclusion that her experiences ultimately do not allow her to "pinpoint any trends." Where Tiffany struggled to find her words, Southeast manager Jack had a straight-ahead certitude to his vision of fraud as widely dispersed:

> I think it's just random. Because I've seen the person that has never gotten the benefit before, they commit fraud right off, and then I've seen the people that have been on the system for years, and then they commit fraud. I can tell you this: one of the things that I do note that, just working with different law enforcement, many times the people that they may be looking at, we already were looking at also. If they're committing fraud in one program, they're probably committing fraud—not probably, there's a chance that they're committing fraud in another program. I don't see that's being any certain group or any certain area of the state. There's fraud all over the state.

Latino investigator Diego works primarily out of an urban Eastcoast office that serves an especially destitute client population, many of whom experience homelessness and addiction. Yet he too expressed the belief that welfare fraud offenses are distributed widely across the socioeconomic spectrum and other axes of social differentiation. He consciously framed his reply in terms of debunking popular misconceptions, even his own prior beliefs:

> You know, quite honestly, I deal with it *all*. That's, I mean, before I started with the [assistance] office, I pretty much knew it as the welfare office. Even my previous time, which was ten years at the [prosecutor's] office: you know, welfare office. And there's a lot of misconceptions and stereotypes that revolve around welfare, and it wasn't until I worked here that a lot of those were sort of dispelled. One is, it's across the socioeconomic range. Blue collar, to middle class, to even folks who are trying to clearly gouge the system, making good money. Gender, race, age, ethnicity, just *around*-the-clock. You know, I would say that's what's probably the common thing, is that it's equal.

Speaking from his position as a manager in Midatlantic, Hank emphasized his unit's commitment to demographic-blind standards of operation and the virtues he sees in that approach:

> When a report comes in, we don't even look at the name [to make judgments about the client's demographic categorizations]. We don't keep metrics on demographics because it's not important. We avoid any bias by just looking at the referral and going off that. A lot of our people wouldn't even know the ethnicity codes because it's just not something we look at . . .
>
> In the early '90s, there was a study of fraud-prone situations, but it was shut down for targeting because they were worried there would be profiling—you can't pull over the Benz in the bad neighborhood, you know. Thankfully no one pushes the demographic stuff. I say thankfully because we could be forced into an engineered fraud control situation, with quotas and that kind of thing.

This study can provide only limited insights into fraud workers' racial opinions and attitudes. However, across interviews, workers used the language of neutrality while also evoking stereotypes that conflict with the "color blind" mantra. Discussions of Mexican immigrants coming to the United States "just to get on benefits" are one example, especially prominent in Southwest, where fraud unit representatives presented it as more geographic than racial/ethnic. And fraud workers across the country invoked racialized ideas about "generational dependency," the "culture of poverty," or the characteristics of "ghetto" areas and people who live in them. But even when their statements suggested racialized and racist tropes, interviewees mostly avoided explicit racial language. Some of the express commitment to formal neutrality doubtless reflects social desirability bias and fraud workers' efforts to defend their units' and agencies' legitimacy, and fraud workers may personally embrace tropes about color blindness or a "post-racial" society.[8] Of course, claims of racial/ethnic neutrality do not mean that fraud enforcement is actually non-biased; indeed, even in the absence of animus or conscious discrimination, racial schemata can influence street-level bureaucrats' discretionary action and shape people's experiences in social service and criminal justice settings.[9]

Work, Earning, and Deservingness

Anti-welfare rhetoric consistently invokes the decline of the Weberian Protestant work ethic.[10] Many fraud workers demonstrate similar tendencies. They are more prone to explicitly discuss work, earning, and deservingness than race and ethnicity, and they frequently connect welfare fraud to ideas about willingness to work and earn one's keep. Asked about differences between the overall client population and those who perpetrate fraud, Southwest manager Oscar said,

> Oh, I don't know if I would be comfortable with specifics. You see people that are on, abuse things like alcohol, drugs. They're very difficult to employ sometimes. And those that aren't marketable in the workforce are more likely to take advantage of the benefits. Those who lack, uhhh, education. Those who lack social skills. If nobody will hire them, if they get comfortable with just, this, this lifestyle, and that can lead into generational continuation. "My mom did this, my dad did this" or whatever. "This is just how we live. Whatever money I make, I'm not gonna tell anybody, I eat for free. . . ." It's a mindset to a lot of people. Not all. Those who really use it as a hand up in a time of need, I think those cases are really significant. But where we work we see only the fraud piece. We don't see the good side.

In addition to invoking ideas of dependence and a culture of poverty, Oscar links unwillingness to work and illegitimate claims to benefits. These comments support the identification of modern welfare—or "workfare"[11]—as valuing people only according to their contributions to the market economy, not their social or familial contributions.[12] And that raises an important gender perspective: that welfare organizations "try to transform welfare-reliant women into a particular kind of masculine worker-citizen."[13]

Gender is an omnipresent issue in welfare programs past and present, particularly in the context of work, earnings, and claims to social valuation.[14] In the abstract, motherhood is a respected and cherished status; however, race- and class-charged backlash over "cheaters" begets harshness toward welfare-participating mothers.[15] Through forcing parents, especially mothers, into the paid workforce, the US welfare system recognizes and respects the breadwinning aspect of parenthood traditionally marked masculine, but not the domestic caregiving traditionally marked feminine.[16] Post-PRWORA, choices between caregiving and wage-earning are denied to poor women but remain available to better-off women, furthering class-differentiated concepts of womanhood, motherhood, and femininity.[17]

Fraud control policies enact welfare reform ideology, and fraud unit representatives largely embrace the embedded idea that all people, including single mothers, should undertake wage-earning work. George shared an anecdote:

> I remember talking to a social worker once. She was so proud. She loved her job. She was very good at her job. She was always reporting [suspected fraud] to us and everything else. And she said, "You know why I love my job so much?" She said, "I was a sixteen-year-old teen parent." She said, "And welfare helped me get through school. Let me intern for them and they hired me." She's now a housing coordinator for a different agency.

Recalling a previous question asking how he would spend an unexpected windfall grant to his agency, this Eastcoast administrator continued:

> I think if I want to see an improvement, rather than give my division a hundred thousand dollars, I think I'd rather see someone come in and give the work participation division thirty million dollars to develop a jobs program for these people that really is a fucking jobs program. You know, not some-

thing when you come in and say, "Okay, this guy Dale was working all his shifts. Find a folder in there and try to figure out how to get him just busy time." I mean, teach these people. Give them something that they can go out and be employed with . . .

I think that's where, I think, if there's a possibility [clients think], "I can make some decent money in my life and make something of myself," I think some of these people would go for that. I mean, it depends. I've had interns come in here that, we'll use some of the participants of the programs. You can see why some of them never make it. Because they come in, they're half asleep the first day, they don't show until three days later. They call and say, "I can't make it. My baby's sick." You know, it isn't working.

George contrasts the "good client," who conforms to work expectations and ultimately becomes a valued employee, with "bad clients," who make excuses and fail to meet expectations. Southeast supervisor Peter strongly supports work requirements and tightly links what he sees as unwillingness to work, government dependence, and fraud inclinations. He put it bluntly:

And this [public assistance] program, while it has some benefits to some people, is a perpetuation of liberal failure. Put that in your blurb [*laughs*]. [. . .]

And there is this perpetuation of this mindset of "The government will help me." It seems [to me] that the government's job is to defend the borders, and fight wars, and, you know. The government shouldn't be responsible for feeding you. Communities are different; not the government. And there is a lot of truth to the words of the apostle Paul: "If a man does not work, let him not eat."[18]

Connecting work and self-reliance to individual dignity, some fraud workers contend that reduced stigma surrounding program participation engenders comfort with protracted participation and rule breaking. Reflecting on why some clients commit fraud and not others, George said,

I think a certain amount of that might even be your upbringing. . . . My father used to call it "being on the dole." It was a certain stigma. "Jesus, you're on the dole," you know, like "Oh, shit." I mean, yeah, I think there's a little bit of, you wanna do the right thing, you know. At the end of the day you wanna say, "Hey, you know what? I started with very little and look where I am today."

Speaking about fraud's effects, Southeast supervisor Antoine similarly highlighted his impression that reduced stigma begets familial patterns of extended participation, to the detriment of paid work:

> [Fraud] gives people a disillusion of what's the purpose of the program. But it also, in my opinion, it has a deeper effect. Because it affects the overall children. Because if you don't see mama go to work, then you grow up with a psychological condition that "This is the way life is." That "I'm supposed to get these benefits." When I was a case manager it used to always be funny when a lady would tell me that her daughter was now making eighteen, who had a child. "So she gonna get her own check." I used to look at them and say, "*This is not a job*" [*"chhh" sound, dismissive*]. . . . "Her having her own check, *it's not a job*." So I think there's some social ramifications on that, where you start to think, "This is the way we're supposed to live. Somebody's supposed to take care of us. We're supposed to get these benefits." And a lot of people that I've run across over the years have always felt that. "I'm supposed to get this." No you're not. Nah, that's not the way it is. And those individuals that have those social scruples that don't want the stigma attached to them— now, nowadays there is no such thing as a stigma, 'cause no one worries about the stigma.

Like many of his colleagues in fraud control, Antoine said that the stigma attached to welfare participation has diminished and characterized that as an undesirable development. Such comments also foreground fraud control's symbolic impact. Problems in public assistance, they propose, result at least in part from clients growing too comfortable with participation and too relaxed about strict rule adherence. Thus a core function of punitive adversarialism is adjusting these symbolic valences: reaffirming stigma and disciplining clients through publicly performing close surveillance and consequential punishments for rule violations.

Policing Fertility

Echoing the issue's centrality in broader welfare reform rhetoric,[19] fraud workers key on "over-fertility" as a typical trait of the welfare rule violator. That perception has the potential to influence their discretionary decision-making such that fraud workers concentrate enforcement on mothers and further entrench these stereotypes. Southwest manager Oscar's criticism of welfare-participating mothers spotlighted childbearing:

I have two children because I can afford two children. If you can't afford children, do not give incentive for popping out more and more and more children. First two or whatever, we will help. Beyond that you're on your [own]. You know, I know that sounds cold and heartless, but if I give you a bigger check to have another child, you're gonna have another child.

Investigators who mention the idea that people have more children to get better welfare benefits typically place responsibility for regulating fertility with women, not the men in their lives. Although fraud control focuses significantly on ascertaining men's places of residence, sanctions for misreporting fall primarily on women. Fraud control staff's informal assignments of blame follow suit, emphasizing women's failure to limit childbearing. Southeast investigator Geraldine depicted these gender dynamics:

> GERALDINE: Half of [clients] are lying. They're hiding income and resources. That's why they say they're not married. "Oh, we're separated, but he pays all the bills." Who's gonna be separated and all their money's coming into the household? How are they surviving? Unless they make mega money to support two households. You see what I'm saying? It's crazy. I have that all the time now. "He doesn't live here. He pays all the bills in lieu of paying me child support." Really? "Where you get him from? 'Cause I want to find me one." I'll tell them anything. "He don't live here. We're separated but he paying all my bills." "Girl, where'd you find a man like that? I want one!" You're a fool. He paying all your bills and he over there living somewhere else? "So where does he live?" "Oh, I don't know. He lives with his mom and his sister here and—" Yeah, right. Or "He lives in the trailer in the back."
>
> INTERVIEWER: In the back? Behind the house?
>
> GERALDINE: Yeah! I say, "Really?" Then she came up pregnant six months later. So what happened? They met in the middle?

The Truly Needy and Deserving

Lust, gluttony, greed, and sloth headline the sins fraud workers assign to welfare rule violators, encapsulating the worst traits more broadly attributed to the "undeserving poor." They describe the "truly needy," on the other hand, with positivity, empathy, even pride. Oscar spoke about the truly needy as his lodestar on the job:

The reason I like to come to work is I truly believe that sometimes people need help. I grew up, I was very poor. We did not have these wonderful benefits fifty years ago that they're out here now. And I think those people truly in need should have access to it. But I spent my life in public service, as either law enforcement or a soldier, I believe in the rules, the rights, and that resources are limited, and people who are getting them through fraudulent means should not, basically. They should be stopped, and if [it] meets the criteria, prosecuted.

Consensus on deservingness typically revolves around people thought unable to self-sustain: children, the elderly, and those with disabilities. Outside of these categories, many fraud workers' assessments of deservingness hinge on relationships to the paid labor market. They favor short-term over long-term participation and especially disfavor nondisabled, working-age clients. Asked about the appropriateness of available benefit amounts, Peter described differences in deservingness:

> PETER: I would say normally that the benefits are appropriate for the household size within the parameters, how they base the figures. However, if there is a contingency of people where the assistance system doesn't really help them as much as it could have . . . the big example would be: you have two extremes. The guy on the street corner who is chilling and that type of thing, he gets two hundred dollars per month.
>
> INTERVIEWER: In food benefits?
>
> PETER: Yeah, right. Elderly widow who is getting [Supplemental Security Income] and maybe a little Social Security survivor benefit—single woman, living in her home, seventy-five, eighty years old, unless she has incredibly high medical expenses, she is only going to get ten dollars to twenty dollars per month. [. . .] But the single guy hanging out on the street corner, cutting grass every week somewhere and makes forty dollars a week and is at his parents' house or whatever, they get two hundred and the elderly person gets sixteen.
>
> INTERVIEWER: That doesn't seem quite right to you?
>
> PETER: No. I think what we could do is have some sort of program for the elderly that gives them the maximum for that person's household. I mean, you're only talking about two hundred dollars, and that just seems more helpful. That's the kind of assistance that people could really support, that kind of idea, as opposed to the perception of the guy hanging out on

the street somewhere in Chicago that's kind of just there all the time and doesn't seem to be—you know, he's just hangin'.

Comfortable versus Struggling Clients

The translation of inmate behavior into moralistic terms suited to the institution's avowed perspective will necessarily contain some broad presuppositions as to the character of human beings. Given the inmates of whom they have charge, and processing that must be done to them, the staff tend to evolve what may be thought of as a theory of human nature. As an implicit part of institutional perspective, this theory rationalizes activity, provides a subtle means of maintaining social distance from inmates and a stereotyped view of them, and justifies the treatment accorded them. — Erving Goffman, *Asylums*, p. 87

Like Goffman's institutional staff, fraud workers construct visions of clients that help them carry out and justify their work, which is fundamentally adversarial to those clients. Along with constructions of clients (especially rule violators) as undeserving, fraud cases involving clients seen as financially comfortable are reference points for moral justification.

Notions of financially comfortable people receiving—and abusing—welfare share space in reform pushes with attributions of perfidy and indolence. Ronald Reagan's gubernatorial agenda contended that permissive policies and loopholes enabled comfortable people to access programs.[20] Reagan proposed workfare systems to serve the truly destitute and sought to close programs to those he deemed not genuinely poor. Claims that many clients are not truly impoverished recur in calls for modifying public assistance, and anti-fraud rhetoric commonly depicts welfare participants as deceptive criminals who are essentially financially comfortable.[21]

Fraud workers' discussions of their investigative caseloads echo these ideas. They accentuate fraud cases involving better-off people, whom they see as especially blameworthy. In part, the comparative emphasis on such cases suggests their disproportionate impact and memorability. That they foreground these cases also tends to imply that ignominious cases of blatant abuse are rhetorically useful for justifying their undertaking, to themselves and to outsiders.

While many fraud control workers stress such cases, estimations of their prevalence vary. Some, like Midatlantic administrator Penelope, believe this kind of fraud is rare:

Generally, [the percentage of people caught for fraud who are financially comfortable] is very small. We get a few more comfortable nurses and doctors [defrauding the medical assistance system]. The egregious piece is even smaller, but that's the splashy stuff that the press gets a hold of and gets it in the paper.

Others depict these types of offenses as common. Southwest investigator Dusty told me he regularly encounters people who are rather well off but still engage in SNAP trafficking:

DUSTY: A lot of it that I found is greed, you know. They're also selling [their EBT] because they don't need it. They're making $85,000 and they're getting benefits. That makes no sense to me. They're not going to fess up and say they don't need their benefits anymore. They're going to start selling them. They'll just have more cash in their pocket.

INTERVIEWER: It that something you come into on a regular basis? Someone making six figures and still receiving benefits?

DUSTY: Yep.

Some even said that a minority of fraud cases involve clients who are really struggling or violate rules just to make ends meet. Southeast investigator Danielle is one example:

DANIELLE: Maybe 20 percent [violate rules] out of necessity. Forty percent, just normal people seeing if they can get away with it and then the higher percent—

INTERVIEWER: That'd be 40 more.

DANIELLE: I think it's women whose husbands have these great jobs and everything, they don't have a great relationship, he gives her an allowance, and she's applying for food stamps because he's probably working out of town, working overseas, and she's still driving her fancy-ass SUV and got her big ol' diamond ring on Facebook. She's like, "I'm going by food stamps, because he's technically not really in the house, and my friend said I could get food stamps, and that's going to get me extra spending money, because I can use this for food for the kids." I don't respect that at all. . . . That's one I'm working on right now.

INTERVIEWER: You interpret those like the person [thinks], "I need a little more?"

DANIELLE: I don't find that's necessity, because she's just trying to get one over. Well, then there's people that are like, "Well, you know, maybe I just don't have to report my job that I just got." They know better than that.

INTERVIEWER: You think about those kinds of cases differently, one bothers you more than the other?

DANIELLE: Yeah. When I look at DMV and I see the eighty-thousand-dollar Infiniti, I Google Map the house and it's parked in the driveway. It's in both their names. Or it's in his name, actually that one. I'm like, "Oh, okay." It's amazing what people put on Facebook. I'm like, "Privacy settings, people, and I can't find all this!" Those kinda make me mad. Not mad: more motivated to try to get all the information processed quick. I send an email to the worker when I find enough. Husband's in the house, and I get the worker to request the verification and then usually the woman will close the case. She'll just let it go, because she's like, "Oh, caught." That'll make it easier for me, because then I have an endpoint and I can finish my part of it.

Danielle's colleague Rosemary feels similarly and was even somewhat more cynical about the percentage of fraud perpetrators who are truly impoverished:

INTERVIEWER: About what percentage of [SNAP fraud perpetrators] would you say are those people who are really hard up versus people—and this is a subjective assessment, of course, but—versus people who are more comfortable? [. . .]

ROSEMARY: That's a hard question. But of the cases that we work, I would say the percentage is really small.

INTERVIEWER: Of people who really need it?

ROSEMARY: Of people who truly need it and are really just trying to get by versus they are doing everything they can, working it, every angle to get benefits they don't deserve. I would say it's small.

INTERVIEWER: Like five, ten, twenty, twenty-five [percent]?

ROSEMARY: Definitely less than twenty.

Designating an investigation and enforcement role within public assistance systems engenders suspiciousness and punitive orientations. To a substantial degree, the role's organizational position predetermines how employees will approach it. While they are certainly not the only people who downplay clients' circumstances and highlight individual responsibility for breaking rules, their position's character and imperatives induce such thinking. This includes contending that for many clients—especially welfare rule violators—the struggle isn't real.

Comparing Clients to Oneself

Distinguishing between "struggling" and "comfortable" clients hinges on interpretations of those terms. Fraud workers observe and infer things about fraud suspects and compare those observations and inferences to their mental models of "struggling" and "comfortable" lifestyles. Investigators' own lives provide touchstones for comparatively assessing their impressions of clients' lives. Southwest investigator Ashley, for instance, described her suspicion when she sees clients at the grocery store, and how she juxtaposes her own lifestyle and spending habits with what she observes:

> I guess my perspective of it is like, you know, I go to the grocery store and I see someone pull out an EBT card, I'm automatically just suspicious. Just, "What's going on?" Just thinkin', like, you know, "Oh, must be nice to buy steak every night for dinner." . . . You don't think it's always good, you don't think it's being used for the actual need of the family. Like, if you're actually needing it, why aren't you buying just the needs of it? Why are you buying like—you just see them all misusing it.
>
> . . . In general, if I'm not even working, if I'm just at the grocery store, it's like, "Oh, she just walked into an Escalade, that must be nice!" [*laughs*]. It almost makes you want to write down the DMV, the license plate number, and do like [a lookup] [*still laughing*]. . . . I think it makes us mad because, you know, you go to these houses that have housing given to them, food stamps, and you know—I'm a mom of three and I work a full-time job, *and I don't get my nails done. I don't drive an Escalade.*

Ashley's comments reflect multiple recurring themes in fraud workers' sentiments. The notion that others are living comfortably without her commitment to paid work frustrates her. And her feeling that it "must be nice" implies that some clients are not just comfortable but more comfortable than those investigating them for fraud. Similar opinions appear in attitudes about client drug-testing proposals; several respondents thought there was evident irony in requiring drug tests for state employees but not for clients. Recalling his history of random drug testing in the military and law enforcement, Southwest manager Oscar encapsulated this perspective: "If it's good enough for me, what makes them so privileged?" Oscar also used his life history to model a responsible approach to poverty, of which he feels policy and many people fall short:

> It should be not a way of life, but a stopgap. I'll give you an example. And I'm old. We were broke before Lyndon Johnson's Great Society of the midsixties. My dad, World War II veteran, highly decorated, he had what they call now PTSD. . . . Some of the churches would help us. But if we wanted to eat, they had, in [our] area, they had church farms. You worked At the farm. If you're a ten year-old, twelve-year-old boy—and we're talking a long time ago, I know, child labor law—if you're a seventy-year-old man, they would find an appropriate job you could do. And you showed up, you did what you were capable of. At the end of the day, you got a little voucher: you went to the church storehouse with your voucher and they gave you food for your family. And if you didn't work if you were able, you didn't get a voucher. And if you needed money for rent, you mowed the yard at the church. You polished the wooden pews. You waxed the preacher's car. Whatever.
>
> It was a, I did not feel bad about taking the assistance, 'cause I worked, and my brothers and I worked very hard to get the money. And we were very grateful for the opportunity. Something like that, I don't know if it's realistic in 2015, but it gives dignity. You know, if you're missing a leg or an arm, different story. But if you're capable and just, "Oh, I don't want that job, it only pays minimum wage." So what? Why should we pay you if you don't want to go take this job? Take the minimum wage job and we will have a program to get you up. Or quit.

Asked if the consequences of substantiated fraud cases weighed upon him when he was an investigator, Jack, too, called upon his own history:

> No. I knew I had a job to do, and I was fine doing that job. And I have so many people—when I interview people for positions, I ask them basically a question, saying, that as part of this job, you have to investigate people. That results in them being arrested; they lose their job, they may go to jail—most people do not go to jail because it's small-dollar and there's a lot more bad people out there than just what we have and what we do—but I ask them, "Well, how does that affect you?" And most people tell me, "I have no problem with that: if they did the deed they have to pay for it." And that's kinda the way I felt too, as an investigator.
>
> I've been working since I was fifteen years old, and have always worked hard, and always had a job. Worked my way through college, and such, and

there was a lot of sacrifice, growing up, getting to this point and such. But as an investigator, getting to be that, to that level, I knew that I had worked hard, and here we got people that cheated, don't tell the truth, to get something they were not entitled to, so I had no problem with it at all.

Like distinguishing between the deserving poor and less-deserving rule breakers, drawing distinctions between oneself and dissolute clients constructs the welfare rule violator through reference to her contrasts. Fraud workers' conceptualizations do not just include attributes they assign to "cheats" but also invoke attributes cheats supposedly lack—compunction, personal responsibility, self-control, even self-respect.

Fraud investigators—like other welfare workers[22]—can be socially proximate to clients. That is, they may come from the same neighborhoods, share interpersonal ties, face similar financial struggles, and even be former or current clients. Southeast supervisor Helen used herself as a compelling contrast, as a former client who now investigates potential fraud:

Sometimes you feel sorry for people who don't know how to get out of a bad situation. The reason I'm saying it is because, like I tell people—I always use myself as an example—sometimes you are a young parent. I was a young parent. But you have to decide if you want to have a crutch of the system or if you want to get off the system. And that's why sometimes I have to tell them. Because people used to tell me, "Well, you've never been where I've been." And I say, "You don't know where I've been. You don't know, just because I'm sitting on the opposite side of the desk, you don't know if I sat on that side of the desk." And sometimes I have to tell them, "I have sat over there. I have been through that. Which means if I've been through that, you need to figure out what you want to do. Until you figure out what you want to do, you're going to still be sitting over there."

I take pride in being able to take care of myself. I take pride in being able to feed my family. Some people don't do that because, one thing that I learned by working, usually their grandparents have benefits, their parents have benefits, now they are getting benefits. It's just a generational curse. You can break the curse if you decide to go do what you need to do. But some people don't want to do that.

Helen says her experience helps her understand clients' circumstances. Yet she takes pride in having "switched sides of the desk" and discontinued her program participation. Like her colleagues, she ultimately comes down on the side of individual responsibility and concludes that extended welfare involvement—and especially welfare rule breaking—is indicative of bad personal choices.

Bracketing Sympathy and Empathy

The job of investigating disadvantaged and marginalized people and enabling their punishment can engender ambivalence. Fraud workers' expressions of sympathy and empathy often foreground the archetypal deserving poor: the old, the young, and people with disabilities. Geraldine chronicled how fraud punishments can tug on the heartstrings, especially when applied to members of these favored categories. Her comments are worth quoting at length:

> GERALDINE: To be honest, the government is all messed up, sir. I have been doing this for seven years. A young person like me or you, we can lose our job today, we can go in there . . . and they are going to give us a two-hundred-dollar food stamp off the bat because we don't have any income. But you and I are healthy. We can find another job. But that little sixty-, seventy-year-old lady, who only gets a check once a month, that's her only income. They are going to give her fifteen dollars. [. . .]
>
> I think it's backwards. To me, they should give the [old] lady the two hundred dollars because she has no other means of income. She's old, she's not able to go and get a job. She's old. You and I, you give us the fifteen dollars, that would motivate me. I'd say, "Oh no, I got to get off the system. I can't make it on fifteen dollars. I got to hurry up and find me another job. I've lost my job, so I'm gonna hurry up because I can't do anything with fifteen dollars." But if you give me two hundred, I'm gonna take my time trying to find a job because I know there's two hundred dollars coming.
>
> I think it's backwards. Poor young lady. Poor old woman. You know what I'm saying? It's just backwards. They done their years in their system. Whether it worked or not, they get a check, that's all they gonna get. They gotta get medication off that check, they gotta buy their groceries, they gotta do it [all], and you gonna give them fifteen dollars? Some get eight dollars. They save their eight dollars. I ask them what they do with eight dollars. They say, "I buy me a pack of meat, ma'am." I said, "Okay." That's horrible.
>
> That's the only thing. When I incriminate old people for food stamp fraud, you know, their younger children have got them and then lied for them on those applications. Half of the older [ones], they are illiterate; they can't

even hardly understand the applications. They go and get one of their kids, or granddaughter, or somebody, or friend, who can read to fill it out. [That person] lie on there for them. They don't even know. I'll say, "Ma'am, did you know this person is on your application?" "He shouldn't be on there!"

But you gotta get them, because [they] signed it and [they] said [they] submitted it. So [they're] responsible for whatever information they put on there. I hate doing that. But I go get on that other person harder than I do that old lady. I'll tell them, "You need to help her pay this money back. She's on a set income." But they don't care. How could you do that?

. . . I put two people in [jail] in seven years. But one of them ended up getting probation because she had medical issues; she just wouldn't have made it in jail. I put a pregnant lady in jail. Well, let me stop, she lied to me. I asked her how many convictions, has she ever been in trouble, be- cause if you've been in trouble the third time, you gone. But if you haven't been in trouble, I can talk to the DA on your behalf; because you cooper- ated with me, you gonna pass. You talk, you'll get PTI [pretrial interven- tion]. We'll put you into PTI, you'll get probation, blah, blah, blah, a little slap on the—you just gotta pay, then do what your probation says. She lied to me that she had never been in trouble. It didn't show up in my system when I looked in my computer, because we can look at it too. I couldn't, I didn't see it. But then the DA, the people looked her up and said, "Baby, this is your third time." I looked at her. They gave her eighteen months. She was pregnant; she had the baby in jail. I didn't feel sorry for her. I said, "You lied to me. Had you told me the truth I still could have talked to the DA because you're pregnant and he probably would have gave you a [lighter sentence]." She screamed, hollered . . . she passed out on the floor. I'm just sitting [there]. Oh well. She lied to me.

INTERVIEWER: But the old people, that's the hardest part?

GERALDINE: That's the hardest. Don't you think?

INTERVIEWER: That's brutal.

GERALDINE: But they do the crime.

INTERVIEWER: Even if they don't know? Even if somebody else wrote it for them?

GERALDINE: Ignorance is not an excuse.

Geraldine does not take sanctioning and prosecuting clients lightly. She uses a sort of strategic detachment, even fatalism, to help manage her emotions.[23] Even in the case of the despairing woman forced to deliver her baby in confinement, Geraldine points to how cooperation could have improved her situation. And although she sympathizes with older people, she falls back on rule-driven bureaucratic rationality and the imperatives of her office to justify their punishment.

Such coping strategies are valuable to fraud workers. Eastcoast manager Vincent described how he negotiates welfare fraud control's emotional stakes, compared to his previous casino security work:

> The way I think I look at it, in respect to fraud, you just have to work within the parameters that you are given a lot of times. Because it's human services, [not] casino credit or comps. There's a face to a lot of these kinds of things, children, there's a lot of things, you know. [But] when people do make that algorithm and [get charged with fraud], I'm not put out by it. I don't think it's anything more than. . . . Social workers do this. Advocates do this. . . . I do what I do, and my people do what they do. We all have a horse in the race. It's just that some of those horses are a little more sensitive versus what I do. It's a little more colder; it's a little more, you know, matter of fact. We don't necessarily look to give away a lot of benefits. We're finding that people have been overpaid and owe us back, thus they aren't going to get anything going forward. It's a little more negative, which is what we use in our interviews. I mean, I always find that people have to understand when they come to work for us that they need to go home feeling good, when you say you saved the state or the taxpayers or the agency x amount of dollars. Doesn't always translate well to the clients or to the recipients, but it's just a necessary part of the business for shortage control.

Fraud workers recognize that their work takes place in a particular context, with particular implications. Vincent's enforcement-specific assignment, however, begets conceptualizing investigated clients as suspects first and foremost and bracketing the circumstances surrounding their alleged rule violations. As he says, this is their role; establishing dedicated enforcement workforces within public assistance systems creates this role, and constructions of welfare rule violators as accountable actors who merit punishment are a corresponding result.

Conclusion

Fraud workers largely express commitment to formally neutral, disinterested bureaucratic logic when asked about group-based differences among program clients and fraud suspects. Forswearing race and ethnicity as meaningful factors in fraud enforcement, they foreground constructions of rule violators that emphasize behavioral and generational patterns. These constructions draw on key welfare reform tropes, contributing to an aggregate construction of clients in general and rule violators in particular as undeserving, lazy, and greedy.

Fraud workers explicitly identify rule-violating behavior as a characteristic of the undeserving poor. To delineate this group, they juxtapose them with more favorable comparison groups: wage earners who do not participate in public assistance programs (sometimes using themselves as examples) and the more deserving, rule-observant subset of clients. Some fraud workers are more broadly critical than others of clients as a whole, but many express positive sentiments toward clients they see as deserving, including sympathy and empathy.

These comparatively positive sentiments toward children, the elderly, people with disabilities, and short-term program participants demonstrate fraud workers' negotiation of provision and punishment. They justify punishment by emphasizing its application to people who are just greedy, who would rather draw public assistance than work wage-earning jobs, and who break rules imperiously. Provision, they argue, should be reserved for those who need and deserve it more; their jobs nobly help protect resources on behalf of the deserving poor.

As chapter 6 highlighted, fraud control is not just a substantive intervention designed to protect government resources. It is also a public performance, designed and implemented in ways that send signals to multiple audiences. Identifying the archetypical welfare rule violator as dissolute and self-serving and contrasting her with other, less blameworthy figures supports the notion that surveillance, administrative sanctions, and criminal charges are appropriate governmental responses to the misallocation or misuse of program benefits. Highlighting the welfare rule violator's undesirable characteristics follows from the history of pathologizing and punishing poverty and helps justify punitive adversarialism. At the same time, expecting to encounter such actors primes fraud investigators to find them, further reinforcing preconceived notions about who is—and who is not likely to be—a welfare cheat.

CHAPTER EIGHT

Finding Welfare Rule Violators

This chapter addresses fraud control's substantive consequences in two parts. First, it extends chapter 7's discussion of how fraud workers construct welfare rule violators through showing how such working knowledge shapes the realization of fraud control policy. This influence manifests in fraud workers' informal criminology of welfare fraud, a working understanding of fraud's causes and punishments' function that informs enforcement action. Fraud workers say moral failings underlie rule breaking; they emphasize greed and opportunism as causal forces and express particular interest in pursuing cases that they see as fitting this framework.

The focus on intentionality and culpability that their position engenders similarly surfaces in their vision of penalties' purposes. They explain enforcement as discouraging fraud behavior. In deterrence terms, they argue that awareness of fraud units' enforcement actions reduces clients' general likelihood of attempting fraud. They also see their work as having specific deterrence effects, with punishments discouraging future violations by sanctioned clients. Further, they highlight incapacitation effects via suspensions and disqualifications that foreclose re-offending opportunities. Both deterrence and incapacitation imply certain approaches to enforcement. Implementing fraud control effectively, the informal criminology suggests, hinges on quickly identifying "problem cases" and dealing with them punitively. Fraud workers' arguments for stricter penalties invoke these ideas, proposing harsher sanction structures to counteract rule breaking.

This chapter goes on to describe how fraud workers' discretion implicates social inequalities and their reproduction. Fraud workers are drawn to cases that correspond to their established visions of the phenomenon of welfare fraud and its perpetrators. They also express interest in acting on larger cases, cases with greater evidentiary availability, and cases that they believe to be part of individual, family, or geographic patterns of perpetration. These tendencies suggest how fraud enforcement can disproportionately fall on particular groups: people whose characteristics correspond to welfare fraud stereotypes; mothers; and people with more substantial histories with government agencies, especially with their explicitly disciplinary components. Differences in how fraud units see different types of clients and their cases connote differences in how they allocate their energies. Several facets of their approaches lend themselves to cumulative disadvantage processes, in which liabilities or discrediting characteristics expose people to further disadvantageous experiences. Such effects counteract welfare programs' ostensible purposes of assisting people in difficult circumstances and helping them move (back) toward financial self-sufficiency.

The Informal Criminology of Welfare Fraud

Fraud workers' understandings of fraud behavior include ideas about its causes and the functions of punishing it. These shared models are vested within the context of state agencies with substantial influence in people's lives. When legally empowered actors apply heuristics in their discretionary action at work, there are substantial real-world effects.

Welfare Fraud's Causes

NEED VERSUS GREED

As chapter 7 described, fraud workers commonly discuss "need versus greed": the question of whether rule-violating clients act more out of material desperation or acquisitiveness. This is related to the question of whether clients who commit fraud are struggling or comfortable but focuses specifically on the causes of clients' behavior rather than their material conditions.

The dominant model of client rule breaking dictates that most violations arise from greed. This perspective is notably prevalent even in comparison to the position that a significant portion of clients who commit fraud are comfortable. That is, fraud workers' descriptions of fraud perpetrators' financial situations are more varied than their descriptions of fraud's motivations. Even those who believe that most fraud perpetrators are not truly impoverished leave room for some destitute people engaging in fraud. Their commitment to greed motivations is more uniform. This suggests fraud workers' emphasis on assigning blame to clients' active behaviors. It also implies that investigators believe—consciously or subconsciously—that there are situations in which rule breakers are really struggling but nevertheless commit fraud out of greed.

Southwest investigator Sue illustrated the moralistic dimension of fraud investigators' informal criminology, emphasizing greed motivations and describing other types of blameworthy behavior she associates with fraud:

> The type of people we go out and actually do these [investigations] with always want to know everybody. Like, they want everybody to know their business. So the people that keep it private are more the people that are in need. I feel that way. It's just my opinion. [. . .]
>
> It's mostly greed. [. . .] They're few, far and in between that you do find that are need. And then you find those that they're need, but they want to get caught up on their stuff, so that's why they don't report their income or whatever the case may be. They were laid off or having a hard time, so they go a couple of months without, six months without letting us know, hey, they started working again. It's not that they are trying to supplement; I think it's just that they are trying to get caught up on all their bills. So that's helping them. But it's still fraud regardless.

In Southeast, investigator Geraldine agreed that greed can supplant earlier need motivations in driving protracted fraud behavior. Even if fraud started in a moment of acute need, these investigators intimate, it continues as a patterned behavior:

> People who are doing this fraud, let them see, some people did what they had to do at that point. They lied to get it because they needed it at that time. But I told them, "Why did they continue to do it? After you got on your feet, you should have stopped. But you continued to do it, because you got comfortable and you got used to it." That's what I tell them. Some people really needed the money. They was just in a financial bind at that time and after they paid their bills, they didn't have any money. Either they's gonna let some go back or whatever or do what they needed to do. But like I told them, "You . . . shouldn't have filled out that next application. When it was time to recert[ify],

you shouldn't recert. You should let your case close. You would have gotten
away with it." You will, because the government got it made like that. They
got it so easy now, they could get illegal benefits, and we can't do anything
because they got so many days to report a change or so many this, they can
get away with it. But no, you got greedy. You wanted to continue to get it because you got greedy, you was used to it. You had gotten on your feet. It don't
take more than six months or whatever to get out of the situation you're in unless you continue to do the same thing that got you there. I tell them. [My co-
workers] think I'm crazy, but I tell them.

OPPORTUNISM   In discussing transitions from need motivations to greed
motivations in continued fraud behavior, Geraldine fundamentally describes opportunism and associates low barriers to fraud commission
with the behavior's prevalence. These ideas are woven throughout fraud
workers' informal criminology. One motif is that most welfare fraud
does not entail conventional property crimes' typical stealth, threats, or
acts of violence. Indeed, many eligibility fraud offenses do not require
doing anything but involve only sins of omission, such as failing to report
a source of income.

Claims about opportunism invoke perceived shortcomings in social
control mechanisms. These include fraud workers' reservations about
their own ability to constrain fraud, as well as the perceived weaken-
ing of informal social controls that might otherwise reduce fraud proclivities. Southeast supervisor Antoine, who studied sociology, conjured
Robert Putnam's *Bowling Alone* as he correlated a rise in fraud with a
decline in informal social controls:

ANTOINE: There's not as much [stigma] as it used to be. 'Cause you can do it
without being known. You're not coming into an office [to apply]. When
you go to a store, you swipe a card. Unless someone really pays attention
as to what's going on, everybody uses debit cards now, so it's not like the
paper food stamps, where you're in the line at Walmart and everybody
sees you doing this. So a lot of the stigma of receiving benefits has been removed just by the way the system has evolved over the years.
INTERVIEWER: Is that good, bad, just different?
ANTOINE: I think it's different. I mean [*sighs*], you have to change. You have
to evolve with the times. But I think that because I don't have to see
you, you don't have to see me, in the back of my mind: "I can do this and

nobody's gonna ever know." 'Cause I'm not worried about my church members seeing me going to the food stamp office. Not seeing the guys from the club see me going to the food stamp office. I'm not in the civic center or the civic organization knowing I'm on food stamps.

Beyond low barriers, fraud workers see low risk as the other major contributor to fraud opportunism. They portray fraud as relatively easy to attempt and say clients believe that they are unlikely to be caught or punished severely. Antoine explained,

They think they can get away with it. Some people have their own personal scruples: "I'm not gonna do that. I'm not gonna do anything to bring attention to myself, I'm not gonna do anything that I don't think is right," and some people just don't think about it. Just, "Okay. Catch me."

Comparing welfare fraud to more conventional property crimes, Eastcoast investigator Tiffany agreed:

I think it has a lot to do with the people who think they're gonna get caught, and people don't think they're gonna get caught. I mean, I think that if you have an agency like this, and the odds of you getting caught are kinda slim, people are gonna do it. Whereas, a lot of people are not gonna go rob a car, steal a car, because they know they're probably gonna get caught, you know what I mean? So to them, this is an easy way to get extra money, and the odds of you getting caught, you have a fifty-fifty chance of getting caught. So I think that has a lot to do with it too. . . . And a lot of referrals we get are from caseworkers, and not all caseworkers do referrals. So if you get a caseworker who just doesn't do fraud referrals, then you could get away with stuff for a long time. So it's like, really your chances of getting caught with doing something like this are a lot less than doing something like stealing cars, even stealing [stuff from a] car, or whatever, the odds of getting caught are a lot less.

As Tiffany points out, variations between clients' circumstances—such as their caseworkers' predilections to refer cases for investigation—underlie irregularities in exposure to fraud investigations and charges. Nevertheless, some fraud workers say that generally low barriers to fraud attempts make opportunistic stabs at deliberate rule violations all but inevitable. Eastcoast manager George holds this perspective:

[Fraud] used to be a huge problem. I think we've clamped down on it a little bit. It's still always gonna be a problem. They're always a step ahead of the game. If I hit you with a whole dollar, they'll find seventy-nine cents. So it's always gonna be there. I mean, the federal government—I think for the SNAP program—estimates a 3 percent fraud rate. I think that's probably a little low. I think, you know, there's a fair share of fraud out there. I mean, is it really egregious fraud? Not really. I mean, you know, there's an uptick in cases around Christmastime. People go out and get a job [and don't report it]. Wanna get their kids something. I mean, you know, again, they're not wearing a ski mask.

George suggests that means-tested assistance programs will always include some amount of fraud. His account of the Christmas uptick puts a pronounced human face on the issue, spotlights the kinds of expenses that benefits do not generally cover, and implies that there is not always a straight line from committing need-based fraud to becoming a fraud recidivist. Southeast investigator Leslie related a similar understanding of clients' calculus regarding rule compliance:

I think the majority of the ones that do it, do it to see if they can get away with it. "I'm just going to try it for six months, see if they catch me. If they catch me no harm, no foul. Right? Hmm. I got away with it for a year. Hmm. Got away with it for eighteen months. Hmm. They're still not on to me, they're never going to catch me." And honestly, the percentage of them not getting caught versus the ones that actually do get caught, it's like one in a million. So it's like they're playing the lottery. "They caught you but, guess what, they didn't catch me. And just don't piss off anybody that's going to turn your butt in." Y'know, so it's kinda that, that's what I think, anyway [*laughs*]. That's to me what I get most of the time, is: "Yeah, well, you got me this time. I didn't think you would. Y'know, but it was worth a shot." I mean especially the hand slaps that they get. It just drives me insane.

Fraud workers' criminological framework suggests that many clients weigh risks and benefits and then violate rules because they believe they are both unlikely to be caught and unlikely to be severely punished. Despite skepticism about their ability to alter this arithmetic fundamentally (with their current staffing levels, at least), fraud workers' arguments for fraud punishments' functions show how they think they can shift it incrementally.

Functions of Punishment

In addition to a theory of fraud's causes, fraud workers' informal criminology includes a shared understanding of the functions of punishment. Sometimes punishment justifications draw straightforwardly from ideas of retributive justice and just deserts. However, even the most decisively catching cheats–oriented tend to make room for some additional utility of punishment. Evoking mainstream criminological ideas, they see deterrence and incapacitation as welfare fraud punishment's major functions.

DETERRENCE VIA PUBLIC PERFORMANCE   Deterrence figures centrally in justifying punishment and was an important rationale for the twentieth-century punitive shift in the US criminal legal system. In emphasizing deterrence, fraud workers evince how criminal justice principles inform punitive adversarialism in welfare. Fraud workers consider clients an audience for their actions and conceptualize the performance of their jobs as creating a climate of deterrence. Southeast supervisor Helen suggested how stronger sanctions might bolster specific deterrence effects:

> And I understand you want to help the kids, but to me, it is if the head of household does wrong, you need to shut the whole case down. And let them feel something and they are going to realize, "You know what, they are not playing with me." Like they say, I'm from Missouri: show me. You need to show them, and you show them one good time and they have to go into the store a whole year and pay for groceries and they might be hungry some of that time, they will appreciate it when they get it back. And that is just the way I feel. You should take everybody off.

Helen indicates deterrence's importance to fraud workers, but also their sense that lax sanction structures undermine its effectiveness. Expanding her comments about "hand slaps," Southeast investigator Leslie echoed Helen's concerns about current sanctions' power to deter specific clients:

> The available penalties, we use and we use often. I just think there should be harsher ones, there should be something extra. Penalty, administrative fine—I mean, something. Because unless you're hittin' 'em in the pocketbook, they just really don't learn. Cause we've had 'em—you bust 'em once,

and then three years later they're doing the same thing. And they got arrested, and they're still doing the same thing.

The effectiveness of general deterrence—aimed at discouraging fraud among the whole client population, rather than specific individuals' repeated offenses—hinges on awareness. Clients must know that they are vulnerable to surveillance and sanction. Accordingly, many fraud workers support publicizing their operations and maintaining prominent places for fraud control, including physical prominence in local offices and cognitive salience in clients' heads. They urge higher-ups to communicate fraud units' activities via statements from caseworkers, posters in local offices, and banners on agency websites. Southeast investigator Geraldine Harris is particularly invested in press coverage. She described how a personal relationship with a public relations officer in a local law enforcement agency helps her broadcast fraud control actions:

> [I have strong relationships] with the courts and the judges. They like me to go talk to the [prosecutor]. They say, "Girl, you got great [access]. How did you get in there to see him?" I can email him that we need this. The [sheriff's office public relations officer] that puts the stuff in the news, she says, "Oh yeah, Ms. Harris, what you want to get in the news?" We've been trying to get the high-profile cases that we do—we try to get them in the news so the public can see it and maybe it'll stop some; [grins] it can scare 'em a little.

Geraldine is cognizant of her work's performance aspect and believes publicity makes her more effective. Rather than seeding stories in the press, her boss Jack highlighted the performance of community-based fraud control fieldwork. To him, investigators' community presence—like community policing patrols—has general deterrence effects:

> I definitely believe that [the fraud unit] acts as a deterrent for people. . . . Whenever we hire people, I want to make sure that they're, one, that they're self-starters, and two, that they're not afraid to get out in the field. Because I like to see people out in the field. . . . Just that presence alone I think helps. . . . I really do believe that the presence is a deterrent. And like I said, I do like to see staff getting out in the field.

Public assistance clients, of course, often experience the entire system as intrusive and overbearing.[1] Limited familiarity with fraud control interventions, however, suggests some limitations on the deterrent effects that Geraldine and Jack propose.[2] Many fraud workers recount clients under investigation being befuddled—they didn't know there *was* a fraud unit. Therefore, investigators believe greater publicity about agencies' investigation and punishment mechanisms could drive down fraud by amplifying their work's deterrent effects.

CONTRADICTIONS IN DETERRENCE, STEALTH, AND CLIENT AWARENESS
Even as fraud control workers believe cultivating awareness of their activities among the client population is an important element of the broader effort to counteract fraud, they value stealth. These conflicting priorities present a paradox. Both prescriptively and descriptively, fraud workers may hold conflicting views on broadcasting or concealing fraud control activities. Prescriptively, many feel that advertising unit activities is a deterrent, but also that operating below clients' radar enhances their chances of successful investigations. They recognize the tension between the big-picture goal of deterrence and the immediate goal of establishing IPVs, and even demonstrate it in interviews in which some say both that their work dissuades rule breaking and that clients are frequently unaware of fraud units' very existence. Investigations provide something of a bridge: a fraud worker can use clients' ignorance to aid in their investigation, and the investigation itself raises awareness that clients will presumably spread by word of mouth, thus deterring fraud.

In both conventional law enforcement and welfare fraud contexts, it is often helpful to gather information in this way—before targets realize they are under suspicion. Southwest investigator Ashley prizes catching suspects unaware: "When I've gone to these houses, they [say]: 'Who are you? Where are you from?' They're just so surprised. Which I guess I think is good in a way for my position at that time, because, you know, the biggest thing is getting them when they're not aware that we're around."

Investigators' conflicting but coexistent beliefs about their work deterring fraud and their relative obscurity aiding investigations may reflect rational myths[3] that justify fraud control activities. Their coexistence also suggests the common conflict between the abstract aspirations that can motivate street-level bureaucratic careers and experiential learning gained on the job.[4] People report moving into fraud control believing that their enforcement work will have significant effects, including in the area of deterrence. Experience with day-to-day fraud control work, its observable outcomes, and the structural constraints upon it may not harmonize with those preconceived notions. The dissonance, though, can stay subconscious.

INCAPACITATION   Fraud workers suggest that some clients are immune to deterrence and need to be incapacitated via suspensions and disqualifications. Eastcoast investigator Tiffany encapsulated this perspective: "There's some clients where I feel like, 'Oh, that wasn't enough, they'll do it again.' And then there's other clients where I think, 'Oh, they really learned a lesson.' So I really think it depends on the client too." Outlining her perspective on appropriate sanctions, Southwest supervisor Carly exemplified the argument for counteracting fraud via expelling offenders, thereby eliminating their opportunities to reoffend:

> If you're an individual, criminal charges [mean] you don't get to get food stamps anymore. You're gonna have to figure out another way. And nine times out of ten they weren't using them for [food] anyway. If we caught you getting food stamps you weren't supposed to be getting, you've probably sold them to someone else, or you're probably using them for some other reason. We just didn't catch it; maybe we did. Jail time? I don't know that that necessarily helps the situation, because we're just paying to put them in jail then. But just the exclusion: "Okay, you no longer can get money this way, so you're gonna have to figure out another way to go get it." So that would be mine— [permanent] exclusion from the program.

Constructions of rule breakers as incorrigible justify program policies permitting suspensions and disqualifications as well as individual fraud workers' actions driving such outcomes. Arguments that some determined or wanton rule breakers can be stopped only by incapacitation appeal to a wider constituency than just deserts arguments; kicking people off SNAP or TANF is more palatable when presented as the only way to stop further fraud rather than as simply punishment for past misdeeds. This is a narrower version of justifications for long prison terms in conventional criminal justice, which argue that public safety demands removing certain people from the community.

The prevailing emphasis on IPVs is intimately connected to incapacitation arguments. The sanctions that accompany IPVs are an avenue to reducing welfare rolls through temporarily or permanently removing those found to have deliberately broken program rules. From the fraud

unit's perspective, imposing IPVs also counteracts rule breaking by removing perpetrators from the environments in which they committed
offenses. This preventive value, in turn, connects to what fraud workers
see as some clients' tendency toward protracted fraud activities.

Disrupting Patterns   Incapacitation figures prominently in fraud workers' desires to disrupt perceived patterns of rule violations. Mainstream
criminology includes similar concerns with habitual offenders and breaking patterns of criminality. In the welfare context, prevalent beliefs about
generational dependence and the culture of poverty underlie special emphasis on such interventions.

Midatlantic administrator Penelope recounted how a private company "hawking a data-mining program" recently analyzed their public assistance agency's data: "They did a study . . . that showed different
patterns of fraud: single mother cases, mostly clients who are eighteen
to twenty-five, low education, no driver's licenses. They also found that
those who have defrauded once are more likely to do it again. . . . We
weren't shocked by that."

Southwest investigator Dusty similarly believes that fraud tends to be
part of a behavioral trend. He specifically depicted fraud offenses as indicative of criminality that, once established, becomes essential to the
individual and endures over time: "I say once you're a criminal you're
always a criminal. Then they're always going to try to find some way to
commit fraud. Whether it's, you know, they've been doing it their whole
life or they just started doing it."[5] Accordingly, Dusty invests particular
energy in building criminal cases when he identifies an individual with a
pattern of rule-breaking behavior, even if the serial violations do not aggregate to a high dollar value. Asked if he sees that type of case as representing a "pattern of behavior that isn't going to change with an administrative sanction, with a suspension," he replied, "Yes. If I keep seeing the
same pattern, yeah, absolutely."

Southeast manager Jack similarly prioritizes patterned behavior. Discussing which factors other than cases' dollar values he takes into account in deciding where to invest his unit's energies, he highlighted perceived behavioral patterns, not just of individuals, but of groups:

> I would say there's other factors too. But dollar amount is nice to have. We do
> want to try to establish large-dollar cases. But, you know, if there is an issue
> in a certain location with a group, I don't mind hitting that local, that area.

> With interviews, with making a presence there. Because it's my belief that we
> may deter for a little while. Now, it may come back, but maybe our presence
> will stop it for a little bit or slow it down for a little bit.

Beliefs about clients' orientations and the pathologies of poverty shape
fraud enforcement practices, from federal- and state-level policies, to
agency and fraud unit leadership's priorities, to individual investigators'
discretionary action. Constructions of rule violators and their behaviors
inform decision-making at each stage of the process that culminates in
welfare fraud punishments. When these constructions include stated or
unstated ideas about group-based differences or fraud's prevalence in
certain "problem areas," they hold significant implications for reproducing social inequalities.

The Social Distribution of Welfare Fraud Punishments

Inequalities suffuse welfare fraud control. From the start, only socioeconomically disadvantaged people are eligible for means-tested public
assistance. To certify formal eligibility for assistance, programs impose
obligations of informational transparency and personal documentation
that generally do not apply to better-off people; the poor must prove
their poverty. These obligations recur consequentially when clients are
called to defend themselves against fraud charges. Social inequalities
also surface throughout fraud investigations, from the ways in which
fraud suspicions arise, to their formalization in charges, to processes of
substantiation. Together, these factors suggest variations in exposure to
surveillance, investigation, and punishment.

Social Inequalities and Informational Transparency Requirements

Clients who violate program rules may see their actions as resisting op-
pression and as a means by which to defiantly claim their rights as citizens.[6] That is, welfare fraud might be considered a "weapon of the
weak"[7] or a form of "everyday resistance."[8] But for many, simpler and
more personal reasons underlie violations. Broken rules may be the predictable—or even inevitable—results of regulations that are complex,
confusing, and poorly suited to poverty's characteristic exigencies and
uncertainties.[9] One might analogize to a builder working in the rafters

of an unfinished house who lays down makeshift board bridges between ceiling joists to expedite movement. Occupational Safety and Health Administration (OSHA) rules disallowing such informal work-arounds might be less salient to the builder than the task at hand—to the extent that the pertinent regulations are known at all.

Despite the day-to-day unpredictability and subsistence pressures many poor people face, social service agencies place extensive documentation requirements upon them. Prisoner reentry organizations provide a poignant example. These reentry agencies are spaces in which people carry backpacks "overflowing with a library of documents from public assistance, parole, and transitional housing."[10] These documents include a slew of different agency records, certificates, passes, and identification materials. Most directly paralleling the welfare fraud context, they also include various pieces of paperwork relevant to program eligibility, such as financial statements and proof of residence.

The various pieces of evidence they require of their clients are a crucial ingredient in social welfare organizations' "people processing"[11] work. Making their lives transparent and legible to program authorities is one of the ways that the poor pay for public assistance. Participating in programs like SNAP and TANF requires compliance with a bevy of rules and regulations and careful attention to the official documentation that welfare bureaucracies draw from to create the "files."[12] When interacting with agencies that exert major influence over the course of their lives, socioeconomically disadvantaged people bear substantial responsibility to comport themselves in ways that correspond to official dictates and norms of self-presentation in hopes of avoiding responses that will further harm their life chances.[13]

The experience of poverty is often erratic and precarious, an ongoing cascade of quotidian struggles and stresses. It is thus an unfortunate irony that people in these circumstances must also engage in forms of self-documentation and record-keeping from which better-off people are generally spared.[14] Eastcoast investigator Diego provided his perspective on welfare fraud within the context of poverty, and in particular the fundamental class disparities that characterize people's relationships with the systems that organize their lives:

> Going back to what we talked about: motive. You know, again, I, I never want to put myself in other people's shoes, but you have to, I think, see people's situations and try to attempt to understand why they do certain things. Again,

I think there's no better example than a single mother working at McDonald's. . . . You'll look at the pay stubs: person's working sixty, seventy hours a week, Monday through Saturday, at McDonald's, and they're barely scratching thirty grand a year. And then there's no one else in the household, we've verified that, and I've verified a prison match for the single father who's in prison. I know he's locked up. I know she's not getting help. She takes on another job. She works that job, she's working now, you know, from, from the moment she wakes up to the moment she goes to bed, and someone's helping with the kid. She doesn't report income . . . on face value, she violated program rules. The question is, did she do it intentionally? I don't know, man. That's, you know, I can understand the motives. She's scrappin', you know.

If I said to you, "What credit card do you have?" You say, "I have a Visa." Okay. "What are the policies for your Visa when your, when your billing cycle is on a short month on a leap year? Can you quote that to me?" No, you can't. Because you don't read your riders—why? Because you assume that a system is organized enough to treat you fairly, and you also don't have the time to do it, right? I think that applies to our clients as well. They just don't read those applications. Why? Because they're just in a state of just, panic. If it's not panic, it's a state of socioeconomic just, pressure. If it's not that, it's the mental health stuff. If it's not that, it's the substance abuse stuff. Folks come in, they're high, they're doing their application. Or they're drinking, they're a homeless guy, guy doesn't even know his last name, when he was born. It's tough.

Diego raises a crucial point: more fortunate people can "assume that a system is organized enough to treat you fairly." Failure to understand (much less memorize) the fine print of a credit card agreement, for example, is unlikely to lead to serious trouble. The poor, however, do not share this luxury. Diego describes how public assistance programs expect clients to adhere strictly to complex sets of rules and then punish them for deviations, with inadequate consideration of the circumstances surrounding potential rule violations.

Documentation of household circumstances and finances grounds applicants' official categorization as program eligible. And when fraud units challenge that categorization's legitimacy, documentary evidence becomes key in clients' incrimination or exoneration. Thus people whose lives tend to be more unstable, more stressful, and worse suited for easy documentation (and the accumulation of documentation, given precarious housing) face elevated requirements to provide it. The process of identifying, acquiring, and compiling the necessary documents can be a source of significant difficulty for these individuals and families. Agency-side errors resulting in lost or invalidated documentation—which range from commonplace to epidemic across jurisdictions[15]—compound this difficulty exponentially.

Investigatory backlogs and delays further exacerbate these issues. Fraud units routinely pursue months-old cases. In such investigations, they ask clients to respond to charges that they misrepresented circumstances that were transitory at the time and have since changed, perhaps many times over. To contravene fraud allegations pertaining to one moment in a precarious life through requisite documentation is a tall order. Recall Southwest investigator Sue's description of clients' frustrations, especially if they are no longer program participants by the time they are brought up on fraud charges: "Yeah, well, they get kind of upset. 'Well, that was like six months ago or eight months ago,' and I'm like, 'I'm sorry, we're just now getting to the investigation. We still have to question you on that part of the time frame.' Some of them get upset."

Reproducing Social Inequalities

Participation in programs like SNAP and TANF, and especially the experience of coming under investigation for welfare fraud, involves suspicion, surveillance, and scrutiny of a sort more privileged people do not usually experience. Beyond this, welfare fraud enforcement's characteristics also suggest mechanisms for the reproduction of core social inequalities. At a basic level, fraud units emblematize criminal justice–style interventions in high-profile and stigmatized social safety net programs aimed at the poor and associated with women and people of color. Within this context, these units' methods of pursuing information and constructing welfare fraud knowledge have untold potential to build upon and perpetuate social hierarchies and inequalities.

Fraud units do not generally compile information about the demographic characteristics of the people they investigate and punish; at least, not information that they are keen to share with inquiring social scientists. Fraud unit representatives acknowledge that most of those investigated and sanctioned for fraud are women, but they are generally much more reticent on the topic of race and ethnicity (about which they affirm their personal and bureaucratic neutrality). Nonetheless, how they pursue, compile, and analyze fraud information appears to bring enforcement to bear on historically disadvantaged and marginalized social groups.

SOCIAL INEQUALITY IN WELFARE SANCTIONS   Americans generally support programs designed to assist the working poor, the very young, the very old, and people with disabilities (collectively, the "deserving poor"), but there is widespread skepticism regarding the desirability of "welfare" as conventionally understood—cash benefits / TANF and, to a lesser extent, food stamps / SNAP. This discrepancy is linked to the racialization of poverty in the media, where images of the undeserving poor are consistently linked to racial/ethnic minorities: conventionally, Black Americans,[16] and more recently, Latino people, especially Latino immigrants.[17] Popular resistance to welfare spending is largely rooted in the politically constructed perception of a distinct and disproportionately minority population that deliberately avoids employment and prefers to subside on government benefits.[18]

Previous research has pointed out how efforts to deter, detect, and punish client fraud can be seen as one element of a broad-based movement toward closer policing of the lives of the urban poor.[19] Beckett and Western find a mid-1990s emergence of state-level "penal-welfare regimes" with pronounced negative relationships between welfare generosity and criminal justice harshness.[20] Between 1990 and 2000, rates of incarceration continued to climb sharply, continuing a trend that began in the late 1970s. Rates of participation in AFDC grew slowly and peaked early in the decade, beginning to fall before 1995 and falling most precipitously following the program's replacement with TANF in 1996. Over the course of the 1990s, the number of incarcerated US residents grew by more than 50 percent, while the number receiving AFDC/TANF cash assistance dropped by more than 50 percent.[21]

Available evidence indicates that contemporary welfare punishments vary across different groups of clients. Caseworkers are disproportionately likely to refer families of color for punitive TANF sanctions,[22] and states with larger percentages of racial/ethnic minorities in their welfare caseload tend to have higher rates of TANF sanctioning overall and are more likely to have disciplinary provisions built into welfare programs.[23]

Furthermore, politically conservative counties sanction TANF clients at higher rates than their more liberal counterparts, and the disparity between the likelihood of sanction for program participants in conservative counties relative to those in liberal counties grows with each month of involvement in the program.[24] TANF sanction rates for clients of color depend on local political context in ways that they do not for non-Latino Whites, with likelihoods of sanction consistently higher for Black clients than for their White counterparts and rising more sharply over time in more conservative areas.[25] Additionally, caseworkers in Florida's TANF program more often apply sanctions to clients with older children, those living in two-parent families, those who are younger, and those with lower levels of human capital (wage income and education). Sanction rates also vary by place within Florida: counties with higher poverty rates, population densities, and TANF caseloads all have elevated sanctioning rates.[26]

These findings give reason to suspect that dedicated fraud control units might demonstrate similar trends. Like other agents of formal social control, welfare fraud workers have substantial discretion in how they go about their jobs, including whom to prioritize for scrutiny and what types of charges (if any) to pursue in different cases. This discretion provides ample space for group-based stereotypes and implicit biases to factor in, shaping decision-making processes and driving outcomes.[27]

Dedicated fraud control work, though, takes place in a different bureaucratic context than caseworkers' TANF sanctioning. Like fraud charges, TANF sanctions are disciplinary and punitive interventions, levied as consequences for clients' noncompliance with program rules, including work requirements and reporting obligations.[28] While dedicated fraud investigators also discretionarily implement client punishments, their circumstances differ notably. Fraud units present a particular form of the welfare system's "marketization."[29] The broader contemporary business-style approach to welfare includes enforcing sanctions to mold welfare clients into usable workers for the low-wage labor market. Fraud units, as dedicated components of the welfare system incentivized to maximize client investigations and punishments, go further. Investigators are given targets—set numbers of investigations to complete per month or per quarter—and supervisors substantially assess their work performance in terms of completed case output. Federal financial incentives for substantiating client fraud and recovering overpayments solidify the overriding preference to invest time in cases deemed promising and deprioritize others.

Monitoring clients' rule compliance and applying sanctions is part of welfare caseworkers' jobs as "catch-all bureaucrats,"[30] and their performance assessment systems can systematically engender increased sanction rates.[31] TANF caseworkers, though, see high sanction rates as damaging to their performance assessments and accordingly express hesitation about sanctioning clients.[32] Fraud workers offer a paralleling perspective from welfare systems' dedicated enforcement wings; discussing how cases come to them, frustrated fraud workers say that caseworkers do not refer enough clients for fraud investigation, a tendency that they ascribe to caseworkers' disinclination to deal with fraud referral paperwork.

For fraud workers, enabling client punishments is not part of the job. It *is* the job. Their organizational priorities and performance assessments revolve around successfully detecting and officially substantiating clients' (intentional) rule violations; in contrast to caseworkers' reasons to hesitate about punishing, structural forces funnel fraud workers' discretion wholly toward maximizing successful charges. Straightforward bias and animus remain potential contributors to investigative tendencies for at least some fraud workers. Fraud units' policy mandate and structural position, though, suggest that gatekeepers' perceptions of comparative investigative promise can underlie between-group differences in cases' disposition, without requiring conscious or intentional discrimination.[33]

INVESTIGATIVE PROMISE IN FRAUD INVESTIGATIONS   For clients, substantiated fraud charges can result in suspensions, disqualifications, restitution orders, fines, fees, and potentially incarceration, as well as myriad indirect consequences. While all welfare clients share certain vulnerabilities to surveillance and enforcement action, people who are sanctioned for breaking rules are not a random sample of everyone who violates program policies. Clients who are hit with IPVs are those who, for various reasons, find themselves exposed to enforcement attention, and about whom, through one method or another, investigators are able to gather incriminating evidence.

Enforcement policies and practices shape this identification and labeling process, creating mechanisms for disparate impact and the reproduction of social inequalities. With limited time and resources, investigators choose strategically where to invest their labor: they prioritize promising cases and those involving higher dollar values. Both factors connote disparities in enforcement intensity across different social groups. First, perceptions of cases' likelihood of ending with substantiated charges hinge on evidentiary accessibility. Fraud investigators prioritize cases in which lots of sources of evidence are available; often this means records with state social service and law enforcement agencies. Thus people with higher levels of existing entanglement with state agencies are also better targets for fraud enforcement energies. And larger client fraud cases are usually women with children. The most likely path to accumulating the multi-thousand-dollar overpayments that investigators prize is to be the head of a household involving children; this foregrounds poor mothers in fraud investigation.

In most cases, welfare fraud allegations are small-dollar. But for clients, the stakes are high. For millions of families, this includes the risk of losing access to nutrition assistance and other forms of support they rely on to survive. Through focusing on suspensions and disqualifications, fraud control units bureaucratically instantiate welfare reform ideology, especially the objective of reducing the number of people who participate in public assistance programs. In pursuing the IPVs that permit program exclusions, fraud enforcement converts the personal into the penal, assessing and documenting people's life circumstances to justify their punishment.

REFERRALS AND EVIDENCE AVAILABILITY IN DISADVANTAGED NEIGHBOR-HOODS Putting aside explicit or implicit bias among state actors, welfare fraud enforcement's structural characteristics insinuate systematic differences in exposure to enforcement. All clients are not equally visible to fraud control authorities. There are simply more opportunities for certain clients, particularly people of color living in neighborhoods of concentrated disadvantage, to be observed and come under suspicion, and suspicion translates into referrals for investigation. The factors that contribute to case referrals correspond to major axes of social inequality.

All the organizations with outsize roles in racially/ethnically segregated neighborhoods of concentrated poverty can both report suspected fraud and provide incriminating evidence. Surveillance in disadvantaged neighborhoods creates more chances for suspicions to arise and be reported to fraud control authorities, potentially leading to formal charges.[34] When charges do eventuate, entanglement with state agencies predicts evidentiary availability. The more state agencies have tracked and documented the circumstances of someone's life, the more evidence investigators have to draw on to substantiate IPVs or criminal charges.

Fraud investigators prioritize cases that they feel they have the best chances of substantiating, and it is easier to gather evidence about people who are more thoroughly transparent to the state. In the contemporary

United States, poor, urban people of color are disproportionately entangled with state agencies engaged in various types of surveillance, including police and welfare agencies.[35] Coordination and cooperation in social control efforts across poverty management and criminal justice agencies tighten the weave of the "carceral net"[36] covering the geographic and institutional spaces occupied by the poor. This creates a wealth of evidence that can be used to initiate and pursue welfare fraud charges. Midatlantic manager Hank referred to an enforcement "tripod": local welfare offices, prosecutors' offices, and the fraud unit itself. Outcomes of successful case substantiation, and especially criminal charges, are maximized when all three legs are working synergistically. Each of the three legs has substantial footing in poor neighborhoods of color.

Evidence from this study also indicates that fraud control authorities consciously focus on neighborhoods marked by concentrated disadvantage. Recall how Southeast manager Jack described weighting perceived patterns in local areas in deciding how to allocate his unit's enforcement effort:

> Dollar amount is nice to have. We do want to try to establish large-dollar cases. But, you know, if there is an issue in a certain location with a group, I don't mind hitting that local, that area. With interviews, with making a presence there. Because it's my belief that we may deter for a little while. Now, it may come back, but maybe our presence will stop it for a little bit or slow it down for a little bit.

Jack's comments reflect the idea that groups of clients may share norms rationalizing fraud behavior and information about how to defraud welfare systems.[37] He also demonstrates how perceptions of fraud as concentrated in particular areas or among members of particular social groups can beget intensified enforcement activity and, in turn, intensified sanctioning activity. In a pattern familiar to conventional policing contexts, a rise in sanctioning can be read as concrete evidence of a given community's tendency toward rule breaking (rather than evidence of increased enforcement activity). That trend goes on to justify further concentrating control efforts. Through establishing such definitions of certain situations as fraud-riddled and dedicating enforcement resources accordingly, fraud control can create self-fulfilling prophecies,[38] as more fraud cases emerge in places where fraud units concentrate resources.[39]

Fraud control authorities also prioritize cases that they see as particularly blatant or egregious, especially if they are part of a perceived behavioral pattern. Eastcoast manager Vincent explained,

> Yeah, I mean, based on a multiple, have there been previous IPVs before. Referrals, UPVs, the duration. . . . As we apply for FNS and things like that, there is no [dollar amount] threshold. So any dollar is a taxpayer dollar, so we look at that. The difference becomes to where time comes into play and, and the biggest bang for the buck. [We're less interested] if it's a situation where there is no previous, previous infraction, there wasn't any sign, penalty warnings didn't go on, may have been a week or so overpayment. That kind of stuff. And that plays into it. So it's sort of on a case-by-case basis. But your more egregious [cases], whether they're actual bona fide fraud, where someone altered doctors' notes or someone's sending us bogus information, then of course obviously we want to look at those too.

Like focusing fraud control efforts in particular neighborhoods, this tendency implies systematic outcomes. Cases involving particularly clear evidence, such as forged documentation, make attractive enforcement targets. In addition, previous problems with the system increase the chances that future allegations will be vigorously pursued. The "suspicious" label sticks with clients and shapes their future interactions with the agency. This label can result from previous IPVs or other issues in which no determination of individual blameworthiness was made, such as an Unintentional Program Violation or simply a referral to the fraud unit. Thus attention and potential sanctions tend to accrue to clients who have been flagged as problematic, even without histories of official fraud allegations or substantiated charges.

GENDER AND MOTHERHOOD   The conventional criminal justice system predominantly processes men, but welfare fraud control focuses largely on women. Women make up almost two-thirds of adult SNAP participants and about 85 percent of adult TANF participants.[40] They also constitute the majority of people investigated and punished for program rule violations. One observer describes the moral regulation of mothers as welfare's "principal objective."[41] The present study confirms women's and mothers' visibility to enforcement authorities and consequent vulnerability to fraud punishments.

Fraud investigators seek the slightly bigger fish in a pond full of small fish. Because of their disproportionate child-rearing responsibilities, women are more likely to provide higher-dollar-value cases. With the average SNAP participant receiving about $126 per month,[42] the most likely way to rack up the larger overpayments that attract particular attention is to be the head of household in a case involving children. Generally speaking, children's presence in the home is also useful for evidentiary purposes—because of their contact with state organizations like schools and Child Protective Services, as well as other child-specific institutions such as private day care centers, kids increase the documentation that investigators can access. Because evidentiary availability influences investigators' determination of promising cases, clients with children are particularly vulnerable to scrutiny.

The prominence of "man in the home" language in fraud workers' lexicon adds to the evidence that investigations are highly gendered (and suggests heteronormativity). Across the country, fraud workers spend a lot of their time trying to place partners in women's homes. That means trying to authoritatively document that an income-earning significant other reported as living elsewhere actually lives in the program-participating household but that including their income in the eligibility determination would reduce or eliminate the family's eligibility. Household composition issues are relatively visible to program authorities and subject to substantiation through a range of different sources of information, particularly in states that heavily use fieldwork investigative techniques.

Although men make up more than a third of adult SNAP cases, fraud workers suggest that their patterns of rule violation are less visible and may present greater challenges when it comes to authoritative documentation. Man in the home cases targeting women, on the other hand, reflect the long and wide-ranging legacy of state scrutiny and policing of poor mothers' fertility and domestic lives.[43] Men can seem invisible in the welfare system,[44] including fraud investigations.

Conclusion

Punitive adversarialism's consequences flow through fraud workers' discretionary action. This discretionary action occurs within structural context. Given a criminal justice–style mandate and corresponding im-

peratives, fraud workers develop an informal criminology: they emphasize the immorality of bad behavior, depict fraud perpetrators as representatives of the undeserving poor who break rules out of greed, and
perceive welfare fraud as a crime of opportunity more often than one
of economic desperation or simple ignorance. Punishment, they argue,
functions to alter this risk-benefit calculus through discouraging opportunistic, greed-based violations of program rules and to prevent further
rule-breaking behavior through suspending or disqualifying offenders.

This occupational folk wisdom informs fraud workers' decisions
about which potential investigations to pursue; allegations that con-
form to investigators' preexisting ideas become more attractive as enforcement targets. Their thinking about punishments' purposes also reflects their criminological perspective, as they stress "making examples"
out of stereotype-confirming rule breakers and incapacitating inveterate
cheats via suspensions and disqualifications. All this demonstrates how
the image of the hyperrational, scheming, amoral welfare rule violator
permeates and influences fraud enforcement.

With limited time and resources, cases that appear to match fraud
control's conventional wisdom stand out as priorities. Outcome-driven
imperatives within fraud units also inflect decision-making: larger-
dollar-value cases and clients with bigger paper trails are prioritized. Because parents with children and people from areas of concentrated socioeconomic disadvantage have greater exposure to the pathways that
lead to both official paper trails and initial suspicion, they are especially
susceptible to aggressive fraud investigations. Such mechanisms compound long-standing structures of gender, racial/ethnic, and neighborhood inequality. In turn, corresponding differences in the rates at which
members of different groups are accused and convicted of fraud can further enflame racialized, gendered, and classed stereotypes about welfare
clients and welfare fraud incidence.

Traditionally, the pursuit and accumulation of information is not a
process we associate with the generation of inequality; however, this research shows how the availability of personal information affects state
actors' work to manage and discipline poverty. Fundamentally and thoroughly, informational exposure *is itself* a key characteristic of disadvantaged and marginal social status in the contemporary United States.
Fraud authorities expose, document, and assess the most intimate details of people's lives. In addition to residency and financial information,
these details include who clients are sleeping with, the character of their

relationships with their children, and the tenor and contents of all other intimate personal ties.

Symbolically, the results of fraud enforcement activity hold substantial implications for the ongoing construction of archetypes of public assistance and assistance fraud. They combine with misleading presentations of benefit recipients and preoccupations with fraud from other sources to create a flood of negative images. The signals that both clients and the broader public receive are substantially based on a political and media fixation on scandalous fraud incidents (real or fabricated). The outcomes of fraud control activities that focus on particular groups of clients over others threaten to combine with such messages to further entrench negative stereotypes and advance the equation of program participation with theft.

CHAPTER NINE

Conclusion

Means-tested welfare policies and practices delineate eligible and ineligible people and demarcate types and degrees of eligibility. The evaluation of disparate entities using common metrics is a hallmark of rationalization, and rule-based abstraction of this sort is central to Weberian bureaucracy.[1] It provides authority, credibility, and ostensibly neutral legitimacy. It smooths out complexities and obscures the assumptions, judgments, and preferences behind bureaucratic simplification and categorization projects.[2] Like any such process, the translation from individuals' and families' "real" circumstances into administrative categories entails costs. Applying a common metric to differing entities can lead to the loss or concealment of potentially meaningful information and variation and can also cause reactivity, in which the assessment process influences the social world it seeks to assess.[3]

Flawed informational inputs also create errors in such categorizations. In the public assistance context, these flaws can arise from several sources. Clerical errors can cause inaccuracies in agency records of eligibility-pertinent information.[4] The information about household circumstances and finances that program applicants provide may contain errors resulting from misunderstanding, forgetfulness, or mistakes. Among sources of error, however, clients' intentional acts of deception have received disproportionate political and administrative attention. Designated welfare fraud control units exemplify government's adoption of an adversarial and punitive response to this issue.

Structure, Agency, and Agencies

Asking whether one would steal a loaf of bread to feed their family as an ethical thought experiment is cliché. The general consensus is that, juxtaposed with starvation, the theft is venial. Yet we dedicate welfare fraud units to investigating and punishing just such offenses. Their punitive interventions follow from constructions of welfare clients as perfidious and rapacious, hewing closely to the social figure of the welfare queen, a political trope that agglomerated long-standing racist, sexist, and classist ideas.[5] The ideas about pathological poverty and the phenomenon of welfare fraud encapsulated in this personage drove punitive changes in public assistance during the 1980s, including the establishment of dedicated fraud control enterprises as a national standard.

Like using Linda Taylor—the original "welfare queen"—as a stand-in for all welfare clients, choosing this particular type of intervention essentially treats the unusual as typical, pointing to anecdotal (and usually exaggerated) accounts of clients' avaricious abuses as grounds for policymaking.[6] Answering the question of what limitations and conditions should accompany benefit receipt, fraud units fall on the side of robust surveillance and scrutiny. Beyond this, they represent the selection of investigations, formal charging protocols, administrative penalties, and criminal cases—in short, punitive adversarialism—to deal with program rule violations. Through their day-to-day work policing clients, designated fraud enforcement staff contribute to the "policing" of welfare programs in a broader sense, functionally treating all clients as suspects.

Fraud workers have significant agency in implementing fraud control policies, but surrounding structures funnel that agency in particular directions. Individual agents' support for close client surveillance and adversarial rule enforcement follows directly from their assigned roles within a system rife with assumptions about intentionality and individual responsibility in assessing applicants' and clients' behaviors. Giving a dedicated labor force an enforcement mandate and imperatives to establish deliberate fraud charges solidifies the likelihood that they will think and act accordingly. Responsibilities and daily tasks centered on detecting, investigating, and substantiating legal violations promote thinking punitively, talking punitively, and acting punitively. Formal and informal cooperation with conventional criminal justice agencies further entrenches such tendencies.

Fraud units demonstrate, then, how organizational structure influences workers' agency and, through that, the aggregate characteristics of the agencies they represent. Of course, assigning people to find intentional fraud means that, as a substantive outcome, the agency will produce more intentional fraud charges. This increases clients' exposure to these charges' directly penal results. Furthermore, as organizational forms that substantially predetermine the nature of agency responses, fraud units push welfare agencies—already law-saturated environments—toward the specific norms of the criminal legal system. Symbolically, this propagates distinct messaging about how government regards the people who participate in welfare programs. Fraud units count clients, the broader public, and their political and administrative superiors among the audiences for their performance of welfare fraud control. Thus a generalizable lesson of this research is that bureaucratic and organizational forms have substantive and symbolic consequences. Electing designated enforcement units as an intervention in poverty management programs is not simply a response to an existing problem; it feeds into the ongoing social construction of that problem and associated phenomena and populations.[7]

This process unfolds within bureaucratic and legal parameters established through statutes and case law. Federal legislation sets key conditions, such as requirements for states to operate fraud control units, specified punishments for fraud offenses, and provisions for cooperation and information-sharing between administrative fraud control entities and conventional criminal justice agencies. In reviewing fraud control practices, courts have ruled that criminal cases' due process protections—such as Fourth Amendment protections against unreasonable search and seizure[8] and Fifth Amendment protections against self-incrimination[9]—have limited application in welfare clients' administrative cases. Nor do indigent participants in civil and administrative adversarial legal proceedings have criminal defendants' right to public defenders.[10] Lacking a guarantee to representation as well as access to economic resources, the vast majority of welfare fraud suspects have no legal counsel. And, as in other legal contexts,[11] those fraud suspects who can retain representation may not find lawyers particularly helpful. Southeast investigator Leslie recalled,

> I've had two, two lawyers that, once I interviewed their client, they [said to the client], "You did what? No, you're going to tell her what you did." And

one lawyer actually told her client, and I quote, "I would rather pick up cans from the side of the road than get food stamps. You're on your own. You answer." I was like, "Oh, crap."

These differences in legal protections and public perceptions illustrate challenges to welfare clients' very status as citizens. Citizenship involves a set of legal rights, including the ability to own property and enjoy the fruits thereof. Those rights are attenuated for clients of means-tested public assistance programs. Welfare participants must surrender privacy rights and due process protections while also navigating manifold restrictions on their access to and use of benefits that limit otherwise standard personal property rights.[12]

Asymmetries in Power, Information, and Stakes

Like welfare clients in general, fraud suspects lack legal rights and power. Fraud investigators, on the other hand, have significant legal authority to scrutinize clients' lives and relationships for potentially incriminating information. There is a pronounced informational asymmetry between program authorities and program clients. Clients often understand rules and their own obligations poorly or not at all.[13] Yet investigators are tasked with finding evidence that clients' behaviors constituted rule violations and incentivized to assert those violations as intentional. To do so, the state empowers investigators to scour clients' personal lives.

Welfare clients tend to experience law in general, and public assistance policy specifically, as an invasive, threatening force of obscure operation and ill intent.[14] The system's enforcement-specific side penetrates clients' most intimate spaces and implicates their closest relationships. In other investigative contexts, investigators may tap into suspects' interpersonal relationships for incriminating information. Here, however, investigators do not usually pursue evidence of the kind of nefarious activity one would typically associate with a law enforcement investigation. Instead, they focus substantially on information about household circumstances and finances that is otherwise usually innocuous—and private. Southeast supervisor Helen elaborated:

My favorite part [of investigatory work]? You know what, like I tell everybody: digging in people's business is my favorite part [*laughs*]. Look: I get

paid to be nosy. […] I loved it. I tell everybody I loved it. It was never an or-
deal about it. I enjoyed my job [as an investigator]. Like I said, you're getting
paid to get into other people's business. And there isn't too much they can do
about it, because they signed the back of the application for you to be into
their business. It was one of those things: "Well, okay. Let me do my job."

These investigations reveal informational visibility as a key feature of
socioeconomic disadvantage in the contemporary United States.[15] And,
through mechanisms like welfare fraud enforcement, this visibility functions as a resource for reproducing social inequalities. Helen's comments
show how dedicated fraud control units build on welfare's long history of
privacy violations in decidedly punitive fashion, paying staff "to get into
other people's business" with the express purpose of using the resulting
information to take away welfare benefits and impose other penalties.

Asymmetry is also evident in fraud investigations' stakes. For Helen,
getting into other people's business is just part of another day at work
(and indeed, part of the workday that she relishes). For clients, investigators' use of informants and inquiries to friends, family, neighbors, land-
lords, and bosses threatens social support networks and residential and
employment stability.[16]

Fraud charges' direct consequences also appear different when viewed
from clients' perspective, rather than investigators'. Most welfare fraud is
small-dollar. In many cases, it may be relatively easy to commit; indeed,
it can be as simple as *not* listing something on a form. Investigators often portray their work as mundane and low stakes, citing the low dollar
values involved and the limitations on their authority compared to that
of conventional police. They also commonly depict the typical penalties
for substantiated fraud allegations as too lenient, even trifling, "a slap
on the wrist." Eastcoast investigator Tiffany presented this perspective:

TIFFANY: Anything handled administratively, in my opinion, is really just a
    slap on the wrist. Which is why, you know, I think the rules or the pen-
    alties are not as [*sighs*] harsh as I think they should be in some cases,
    because the majority of the population is already a struggling popula-
    tion. […]
INTERVIEWER: And you think the [suspensions, disqualifications, and repay-
    ment requirements] are not harsh enough?
TIFFANY: Ah, no. Only because, if you, let's say for most of the time when
    you're taking someone to a hearing, majority of the time it's gonna be a

one, a first-time offense. And with the penalties being you're disqualified for a year, okay, but with the overpayment amount. . . . Pretty much, if you are head of household, you're a mom with two kids, you committed Intentional Program Violations, so we remove the mom from the case, but the mom will still get benefits for those two children. And basically then they'll just reduce the overpayment from the food stamp account. So really there's no paying back money . . . it's pretty much, "Oh, we'll just reduce your benefits. You lied to us, you provided false information, we are just gonna reduce your benefits." And I don't know. Personally, I feel like . . . the penalties are not harsh enough to make people not want to do it.

From Tiffany's perspective as a rule enforcement agent, the consequences of substantiated charges are often inadequate. For clients, though, the stakes are high. What may seem banal, even trivial, to investigators can be vital to clients attempting to patch together resources to keep themselves and their families afloat. Since the War on Poverty, means-tested benefits' real economic value has fallen, but they remain crucial to millions of poor families. SNAP is especially important to poor Americans' subsistence formulae; as cash welfare has largely evaporated in the post-PRWORA era,[17] SNAP has filled some of the gap, helping monthly averages of between forty and fifty million Americans meet their nutritional needs in recent years.[18]

The potential repercussions of a mistake or an omission on an eligibility form deviate dramatically from the compromising action's surface inconsequentiality. Administrative, noncriminal charges are still significant,[19] especially when they implicate families' basic survival resources. Even when intentional fraud allegations are not substantiated, merely the status of having been suspected of violating rules can increase clients' likelihoods of facing future fraud charges and having those charges pursued aggressively. If administrative charges are substantiated, clients can be suspended or disqualified from programs they rely on and required to pay fines, fees, and restitution they can ill afford. And criminal charges, of course, significantly compound fraud investigations' harms to clients.

Fraud Control, Retrenchment, and Punitiveness in Public Assistance

The administrative system, as symbol and ritual, thus serves as legitimizer of elite objectives, as reassurance against threats, and sometimes as catalyst of symbiotic ties between adversaries. It should not be surprising that we find these larger social functions of the administrative system mirrored inside each of the agencies as well, in the gathering and choice of premises upon which decisions are made. — Murray Edelman, *The Symbolic Uses of Politics*, p. 68

Penalties for substantiated fraud cases look much different depending on whether one takes the perspective of an enforcement agent or a client. When viewed from a systemic perspective, they reflect broader objectives: shaping welfare programs' public image and participation climate and ultimately reducing their size.

Dedicated fraud control units are the enforcement arm of a system of public assistance that has moved steadily toward austerity and responsibilization. Their proliferation over the last four decades demonstrates the influence of a cost-control mentality that focuses on limiting social spending through shrinking welfare rolls. Anti-fraud rhetoric was central to broader welfare reform initiatives, and the creation of dedicated fraud units was an emblematic aspect of policy changes that stressed the importance of personal responsibility for life outcomes and of aggressively targeting perceived social loafers.[20] Today's fraud control units are bureaucratic entities organized around the goal of continuing to advance the ideological agenda of welfare reform in the wake of major changes to public assistance policy.

Different fraud units and different investigators assess various sources of evidence differently, but all pursue a common substantive goal: moving people off SNAP and TANF. This is fundamentally represented in the focus on—and incentivization of—establishing IPVs. Fraud control units' activities are oriented around these charges, which allow the application of punitive sanctions of suspension and disqualification. As Tiffany succinctly summarized, "Our goal is actually to get, you know, someone disqualified from the program and get the overpayment."

Symbolically, investigative units' activities advance images of poor people as devious and untrustworthy and thoroughgoing surveillance as an appropriate response. In implementing these measures, they build bridges between criminal justice agencies and welfare agencies and incorporate the former's functions into the latter, dissolving the boundary between two nominally different functions of the modern state. Welfare scholars have incisively critiqued the integration of social control functions into US public assistance programs, especially the stigmatized programs of ADC/AFDC/TANF and Food Stamps/SNAP.[21] Austin Sarat memorably recorded a welfare client's distillation of his legal consciousness: "the law is all over."[22] Recalling his days as a caseworker, before he moved into fraud control, Southeast supervisor Antoine described the agency side of this experience:

> When I was an eligibility worker and had a caseload, I used to always tell my clients at the end of the interview, "If you have a toothache, you call a dentist. Something's wrong with your hair, go to your hairdresser. If something concerns your household, you call me." I say, "And remember that. Because I have to make sure that everything you have on here [*taps desk, as if indicating an application form*] is correct." And I would always tell it to them in a joking manner, but they understood that I wasn't trying to be the Big Brother or the bearer of the stick, but to understand that, you know, this is your responsibility to report this information accurately. And if you don't report it to me and something happens, then we have a problem. It's just the way that you present it to them.

Dedicated fraud units build on the legacy of suspicion, scrutiny, and surveillance in public assistance, adding to that long tradition in a decidedly punitive fashion. These boundary-straddling actors are not quite agents of public assistance and not quite agents of law enforcement. They are intersectional legal-bureaucratic agents who draw from and collapse both worlds. Like Antoine describing his past life as a caseworker, they make claims upon and have access to the most intimate aspects of clients' personal lives. But in contrast to caseworkers, fraud workers' sole objectives are policing and punishing rule violations.

For the poor, fraud control activities convert the personal into the penal. Outside of some especially egregious cases, federal jurisprudence has generally upheld the constitutionality of close oversight and management of people who participate in public assistance programs.[23] If a person or family is struggling and seeks assistance, the application they sign permits investigative staff to collect information relevant to the eligibility determination, potentially touching all aspects of their personal and interpersonal lives. In conducting these operations, dedicated welfare fraud units provide a definitive instantiation of the overlap and in-terpenetration of policing and poverty management.

Intensified surveillance and punishment systems change programs' climates. Punitive adversarialism blurs the distinction between deter-ring fraud behavior and deterring program participation via "adminis-trative exclusion."[24] Fraud workers often speak about such climate shifts in terms of reducing clients' likelihood of attempted or successful fraud perpetration. But many also express broader opinions that program par-ticipation is too easy, too comfortable, and too often taken for granted. The threat of fraud investigation and sanction helps authorities discour-age specific rule-violating behaviors and also pushes people to limit their overall claims on public programs. Thus punishment systems function to change people's behavior in desired directions, both away from of-ficially proscribed actions and toward broader individual responsibility and self-reliance.[25]

As they have throughout their histories,[26] policing and welfare co-evolved in the late twentieth and early twenty-first centuries.[27] Invoking broken windows theory, both police departments and welfare agencies enhanced their efforts to identify, catch, and punish comparatively mi-nor infractions.[28] In the conventional criminal justice system, these en-hanced surveillance and individual accountability measures escalated detentions, arrests, charges, and criminal sanctions, contributing to mass incarceration[29] and mass correctional supervision.[30] Paralleling mea-sures in public assistance similarly strengthened mechanisms for holding people accountable for modest transgressions, making programs more punitive and providing avenues to disqualify their participants.

Policy Implications

As federal courts have confirmed,[31] government has a legitimate interest in overseeing its programs and monitoring how resources are used. The designated fraud unit model is one avenue for pursuing this interest. It is not, however, the only possible policy choice.

Some amount of rule breaking is likely inevitable in forms of public assistance for the poor based on categorical eligibility. A broad-based guaranteed minimum income policy, on the other hand, would preclude many of the infractions that fraud units investigate, as well as potentially offering significant reductions in costs associated with administering current safety net programs. In the absence of such fundamental changes to US social policy, however, incremental changes could help make program integrity measures fairer and more efficient.

The focus on investigating individual clients, and especially on substantiating their rule violations as intentional, is a narrow way of looking at problems in public programs. To be sure, investigations of clients deemed suspicious are not the only program integrity efforts that public assistance authorities undertake. But government substantially emphasizes such investigations. This emphasis manifests in investigatory authority devolved from the federal level to mandated state-level fraud control units. Financial incentives encouraging these units to focus on intentional client fraud evince it further.

Yet prioritizing the pursuit and punishment of individual clients among potential program integrity activities demonstrates an emotional reaction and symbolic response to perceived wrongdoing among members of a stigmatized group. Thinking about welfare program integrity issues dispassionately, as public administration problems, there is no obvious reason to focus on individual clients' actions over other areas of program waste or abuse. Even an enforcement-minded figure like Southeast manager Jack indicates awareness of the inefficiencies such incentive structures impose. His unit, he said, could be "making money" if they were provided similar incentives to focus on investigating agency-side errors.

The current emphasis on client surveillance and policing, though, does seem an effective avenue to the specific goal of shrinking the size of program populations. Client suspensions and disqualifications advance this goal directly, while fraud control–associated changes in the climate of program participation advance it indirectly. Although fraud control interventions are not generally explicitly presented as methods of reducing programs' overall participation numbers, the specifics of fraud control practice reveal this as a central and desired outcome.

Within the category of client-focused investigations, the current referral system for launching fraud cases connotes significant disparities in different clients' likelihood of becoming the subject of investigations and charges. These irregularities derive from variations in clients' levels of informational exposure, and potentially their perceived levels of baseline "suspiciousness" as well. A randomized audit approach—such as that used in FNS's required SNAP quality control review—could help correct for such differences. There is less potential for bias to affect investigation originations and generate between-group disparities in outcomes if cases are selected for inspection on the basis of random draw rather than reported suspicions. A policy shift toward random audits would also hew more closely to government oversight methods in other state–individual financial interactions, such as taxation.

Relying on random audits would nevertheless entail problems of its own. Some caseworkers would doubtless continue to have suspicions about certain clients, and it would be difficult for enforcement authorities to deny requests for inspection from these and other stakeholders. And, although fraud investigators invest time in preliminarily reviewing many case referrals that go nowhere under the current system, a randomized audit approach would likely increase the share of fruitless case inspections. Finally, processes of selecting cases for review would likely include risk-assessment algorithms, which have their own implications for reproducing social inequalities.[32]

Investigations under the current system do not appear to provide good, concrete return on investment. Restitution from destitute people is akin to the proverbial blood from a stone. The investigation process is costly. And so is sanctioning; beyond the expenses of conducting adversarial proceedings and imposing punishments, over the long term, welfare fraud investigations threaten to produce cumulative disadvantage spirals, moving people farther from financial independence. Disciplinary records with assistance agencies constitute grounds for future scrutiny, increasing chances of repeated exposure to sanctions. Investigations tapping people's social networks sow distrust and damage social ties, removing nongovernmental sources of support while injecting stigma.[33] Program suspensions and disqualifications foreclose legitimate means of accessing resources, increasing people's likelihood of turning to illegitimate means;[34] criminal records resulting from these behaviors (or fraud investigations themselves) impede employment opportunities and otherwise harm life chances. All these effects engender instability and uncertainty and exacerbate problems and stressors in poor people's lives. These worsened circumstances, in turn, complicate efforts to advance toward self-sufficiency and increase demand on street-level services like police, ambulances, and emergency rooms.

Strictly in fiscal terms, efforts to counteract corporate and professional fraud in the social safety net offer much more promise for the government's bottom line. The return on investment of client investigation in programs such as SNAP is dubious,[35] and by far the largest dollar-value frauds in social welfare systems are systematic schemes perpetrated by professionals and businesses, especially health care organizations and medical service providers in publicly supported health care programs.[36] Oversight of these actors through entities like the Department of Health and Human Services' Office of Inspector General offers far greater return on enforcement investment and constitutes a more rational way of policing welfare.

Acknowledgments

My first thanks go out to all the fraud control workers and other assistance agency representatives across the country who assisted me with this research, particularly those who facilitated my visits to their offices and took the time to share their thoughts and experiences with me. To protect their confidentiality, I cannot name them here, but they all have my sincere gratitude. I am also grateful for the hospitality and generosity shown to me by new friends throughout the country as I traveled to complete this research. My thanks go out especially to Jesse and his family, Andrew, and Misha and Sergey, all of whom welcomed me into their homes. Additionally, I am indebted to the airport taxi coordinator, cab driver, and motel manager who helped me retrieve the wallet I left in the cab from the airport on the first night of a multicity data collection trip; regretfully, I cannot thank them by name, but they saved my bacon.

This book began at the Northwestern University Department of Sociology, a truly remarkable place. Along with the rest of the Northwestern Sociology community, I thank my committee of John Hagan, Bob Nelson, Jeremy Freese, and Laura Beth Nielsen for their individual and collective contributions to the project's origination and early development. I wrote most of the first draft of what would become *Policing Welfare* at the American Bar Foundation, an exceptional intellectual second home for my years in Chicago; thanks to Bob Nelson and Ajay Mehrotra for accommodating me during their respective directorships.

At Purdue, Sociology Department heads Ken Ferraro and Linda Renzulli enthusiastically supported the project and provided everything I needed to complete it. Ken, Bert Useem, and Dan Winchester offered valuable feedback on early chapter drafts, and Shawn Bauldry helped me think through many of the book's ideas and arguments with characteristic thoughtfulness and insight.

I am particularly beholden to Monica Bell, Ben Fleury-Steiner, Kaaryn Gustafson, Reuben Miller, Bob Nelson, Laura Beth Nielsen, and John Robinson for their immense contributions to the manuscript's revision through their participation in a book workshop in May 2018 and separate conversations about the research. The final product reflects input from each of them and is stronger for it. Special thanks to Kaaryn; *Cheating Welfare* helped inspire this project, and I have returned to my extensively dog-eared copy countless times throughout it. Thanks also to Purdue's College of Liberal Arts, which awarded the grant supporting the book workshop.

A host of other friends, colleagues, and mentors offered advice, ideas, and encouragement along the way. This list includes Nate Baker, Jean Beaman, Hana Brown, Pryce Davis, Ronit Dinovitzer, Rachel Einwohner, Patrick Emery, Scott Feld, Kelley Fong, Jen Foray, Cybelle Fox, Juliette Galonnier, Phil Goodman, John Halushka, Kelly Hannah-Moffat, Beth Hoffmann, Marcus Hunter, Jennifer Jones, Danielle Kane, Brian Kelly, Sarah Lageson, Ron Levi, Mona Lynch, Freda Lynn, Tom Maher, Paula Maurutto, David McElhattan, Trent Mize, Shaun Ossei-Owusu, Pierre Pénet, David Peterson, Cassidy Puckett, Margarita Rayzberg, Dan Rees Lewis, David Reingold, Justin Rex, Jeremy Reynolds, Dorothy Roberts, Christie Sennott, Jack Spencer, Swati Srivastava, Kevin Stainback, Robin Stryker, Patti Thomas, Chris Uggen, Celeste Watkins-Hayes, Rhaisa Williams, and Marina Zaloznaya. Any omissions are unintentional; please forgive them.

Chuck Myers and the rest of the team at the University of Chicago Press have my gratitude for seeing promise in the project and expertly shepherding the book through the publication process. Two anonymous readers for the Press provided incisive and enormously helpful reviews, for which I am very grateful. Thanks also to Callie Zaborenko for able research assistance and Letta Page for her help polishing the manuscript.

Parts of this book draw on articles published in *American Sociological Review*, *Law & Society Review*, *Punishment & Society*, and *Social Justice*. Thanks to those journals' editors, reviewers, and staff for helping the project's development and for permission to use elements of those articles here. I have also benefited from feedback to talks at the University of Iowa Department of Sociology, the Penal Boundaries Workshop at the University of Toronto Centre for Criminology and Sociolegal Studies, and sessions at the annual meetings of the American Sociological Association and the Law and Society Association. I appreciate these opportunities to share my work and participants' engagement with the research.

Reaching further back, thanks to Neil Browne and Don Callen at Bowling Green State University, who inspired me to become a professor, and Bob Garot, who inspired me to become a sociologist.

Finally, thanks to my family for their love and backing. My mom, Sue; my sister, Biz; and my late father, Mike, have been behind me every step of the way. My uncles Bill and Dave shared insights about working in social services. Allison McKay continues to be an unfailing beacon of solace, support, and motivation.

Appendix

Pseudonym	State	Race/Ethnicity	Age	Position
Adriana	Northeast	White	Early 40s	Coordinator
Andrew	Eastcoast	White	Early 30s	Analyst
Antoine	Southeast	Black	Mid 50s	Supervisor
Ashley	Southwest	White	Mid 30s	Investigator
Billy	Eastcoast	White	Mid 20s	Analyst
Brian	Midatlantic	White	Late 30s	Manager
Carly	Southwest	White	Early 30s	Supervisor
Caroline	Eastcoast	White	Mid 40s	Manager
Danielle	Southeast	White	Late 40s	Investigator
Diego	Eastcoast	Latino	Late 30s	Investigator
Dusty	Southwest	White	Late 20s	Investigator
Edward	Eastcoast	White	Mid 50s	Administrator
Frank	Midatlantic	White	Late 50s	Administrator
George	Eastcoast	White	Early 60s	Administrator
Geraldine	Southeast	Black	Late 40s	Investigator
Hank	Midatlantic	White	Mid 40s	Manager
Helen	Southeast	Black	Early 40s	Supervisor
Jack	Southeast	White	Late 40s	Manager
Keith	Southwest	White	Late 20s	Coordinator
Ken	Northeast	White	Late 40s	Administrator
Leslie	Southeast	White	Late 30s	Investigator
Luis	Eastcoast	Latino	Early 50s	Manager
Mary Anne	Eastcoast	White	Early 50s	Supervisor
Morgan	Northeast	White	Mid 30s	Coordinator
Oscar	Southwest	White	Early 60s	Manager
Patricia	Eastcoast	White	Mid 50s	Investigator
Penelope	Midatlantic	White	Late 40s	Administrator
Peter	Southeast	White	Late 50s	Supervisor
Ramona	Southwest	White	Early 50s	Investigator
Robert	Eastcoast	White	Mid 60s	Administrator
Roger	Northeast	White	Early 60s	Administrator
Rosemary	Southeast	White	Early 50s	Supervisor
Sandra	Northeast	White	Mid 50s	Manager
Stephen	Eastcoast	Black	Mid 40s	Manager

(*continued*)

Pseudonym	State	Race/Ethnicity	Age	Position
Sue	Southwest	White	Mid 40s	Investigator
Tabitha	Northeast	White	Mid 40s	Investigator
Tiffany	Eastcoast	White	Mid 20s	Investigator
Todd	Southwest	White	Late 40s	Supervisor
Veronica	Northeast	White	Early 60s	Administrator
Vincent	Eastcoast	White	Late 40s	Manager
Wanda	Eastcoast	White	Late 40s	Manager
Zosia	Eastcoast	White	Early 50s	Manager

Notes

Chapter One

1. Throughout the book, ellipses (. . .) within interviewee quotes indicate the removal of some of the interviewee's words for parsimony and clarity. Ellipses within brackets ([. . .]) indicate removal of words from both the interviewee and the interviewer.

2. Katz ([1989] 2013); Stone (1984).

3. Horder (2015).

4. P.L. 99–198, § 1526.

5. See Gustafson (2009; 2011; 2013); Simon (2007).

6. See Kagan (2001).

7. Kagan (2001, 159).

8. 397 U.S. 254 (1970).

9. See Porter, Welch, and Mitchell (2019).

10. Kagan (2001, 175). See also Herd and Moynihan (2018).

11. Chunn and Gavigan (2004); see also Foucault ([1977] 1979); Rose (2001); Stuart (2016).

12. Gustafson (2011, 9).

13. See Sarat (1990).

14. Gustafson (2009; 2011; 2013); Natapoff (2015).

15. See Woolford and Nelund (2013).

16. I. Kohler-Hausmann (2018).

17. O'Regan (2010, 424). Like fines and fees in the conventional criminal justice system, welfare fraud investigations constitute a mechanism by which legal authorities extract resources from the citizenry. See Blessett and Box (2016); Harris (2016); Harvard Law Review Editors (2015).

18. Center on Budget and Policy Priorities (2018, 7).

19. Miller and Alexander (2016, 307); see also Berrey, Hoffman, and Nielsen

(2012, 20) on plaintiffs' and defendants' profoundly different stakes in employment discrimination litigation.

20. Edin and Shaefer (2015); Tach and Edin (2017).

21. Food and Nutrition Service (2017, 2).

22. Headworth (2020b).

23. Headworth (2019).

24. Gring-Pemble (2003); see also Haltom and McCann (2004).

25. Cline and Aussenberg (2018, 8–11).

26. Cline and Aussenberg (2018, 11).

27. Understood comprehensively, "welfare" also includes a multitude of other programs and policies; see Gottschalk (2000); Howard (1997; 2007); Mettler (2011); Tahk (2014; 2018).

28. Gilens (1999); Gordon (1994, ch. 1); Haney (2004); Hancock (2004); Katz ([1989] 2013); Neubeck and Cazenave (2001); Ocen (2012); Piven and Cloward ([1971] 1993); Roberts ([1997] 1999, 18).

29. See Maynard-Moody and Musheno (2003).

30. Eubanks (2018).

31. Brodkin and Majmundar (2010); Sheely (2013).

32. P.L. 99–198, § 1526.

33. See Headworth (2020a).

34. L. Edelman (1992); Lageson, Vuolo, and Uggen (2015).

35. Brodkin (1997); Lipsky ([1980] 2010); Maynard-Moody and Musheno (2003); Soss, Fording, and Schram (2011a, ch. 10); Watkins-Hayes (2009b).

36. Gordon (1994, 298).

37. Bridges (2017); Gilliom (2001); Gilman (2008); Gustafson (2009, 701–7); Slobogin (2003).

38. Headworth and Ossei-Owusu (2017).

39. Epp, Maynard-Moody, and Haider-Markel (2014).

40. Lara-Millán (2014).

41. Lara-Millán and Van Cleve (2017).

42. Gustafson (2011); Hancock (2004); J. Kohler-Hausmann (2017).

43. Soss, Fording, and Schram (2008; 2011a).

44. Monnat (2010); Schram et al. (2009); Soss, Fording, and Schram (2011b). See also Keiser, Mueser, and Choi (2004), who find that people of color are sanctioned more than Whites within local areas but that non-Whites' disproportionate residence in areas with lower sanction rates leads to overall lower sanction rates.

45. Headworth and Ríos (2020); Schram et al. (2009).

46. Stone (1984, 35).

47. Piven and Cloward ([1971] 1993, 23).

48. Piven and Cloward ([1971] 1993, 22).

49. Stone (1984); Woodbridge (2001).

50. Gordon (1994, 45–47).

51. Pope (2018).

52. Fox (2012); Gordon (1994); Quadagno (1994).

53. Meyer (2000); Rothstein (2017).

54. J. Kohler-Hausmann (2015, 760); Levin (2019, 40–41).

55. Hacker, Mettler, and Soss (2007); Piven and Cloward ([1971] 1993); Schneider and Ingram (1993).

56. Bobo, Kluegel, and Smith (1997); Brodkin (1986); M. Brown (1999); Chunn and Gavigan (2004); Fraser and Gordon (1994); Gans (1995); Gilens (1999); Gustafson (2011); Hancock (2004); Katz ([1989] 2013); J. Kohler-Hausmann (2017, ch. 4); Neubeck and Cazenave (2001); Quadagno (1994); Reyna et al. (2005).

57. Hinton (2016, 105); see also Bridges (2017).

58. J. Kohler-Hausmann (2017).

59. Gardiner and Lyman (1984); J. Kohler-Hausmann (2015, 761); Matt and Cook (1993).

60. Levin (2019, 154).

61. Levin (2019, 155).

62. Brodkin (1993); Gustafson (2011); Levin (2019).

63. Edsall (1984, 17).

64. P.L. 99–198, § 1526.

65. Edin and Shaefer (2015); Mink (1998); Tach and Edin (2017); Watkins-Hayes (2009b, 6).

66. Mink (1998, 104).

67. Mink (1998, 108–9).

68. Brodkin (1986); Brodkin and Lipsky (1983); Lipsky ([1980] 2010, 225–26).

69. Soss, Fording, and Schram (2011a, 121–22).

70. Center on Budget and Policy Priorities (2018, 2).

71. Blank and Blum (1997, 36); Center on Budget and Policy Priorities (2018, 7).

72. Edin and Shaefer (2015, 9); Tahk (2014; 2018, 876).

73. Peck (2001).

74. Edin and Shaefer (2015, 9).

75. Hinton (2016); J. Kohler-Hausmann (2017); Roberts ([1997] 1999; 2012); Wacquant (2009).

76. Garland (1985).

77. Brodkin (1986); Edin and Shaefer (2015); Gilliom (2001); Gustafson (2011); Soss, Fording, and Schram (2011a).

78. Beckett and Herbert (2009); I. Kohler-Hausmann (2018); Stuart (2016).

79. Garland (2001); Western (2006).

80. Phelps (2013; 2017).

81. Beckett and Western (2001); R. Miller (2014); Stuart (2016); Wacquant (2001; 2009). See also Garland (2017); Morgan and Orloff (2017).

82. Edin and Lein (1997); Gilliom (2001).

83. Marx (2016).

84. Browning (2018); Eubanks (2018).

85. Headworth (2019).

86. E.g., M. Brown (1999); Chunn and Gavigan (2004); Gans (1995); Goldberg (2007); Gordon (1990); Katz ([1989] 2013); Mink (1998); Mink and Solinger (2003); Piven and Cloward ([1971] 1993); Teles (1996); Ward (2005).

87. E.g., Edin and Lein (1997); Edin and Shaefer (2015).

88. E.g., Watkins-Hayes (2009a; 2009b).

89. Beckett and Western (2001); Garland (1985); Wacquant (2001; 2009).

90. Gilliom (2001); Gustafson (2009; 2011); J. Kohler-Hausmann (2007; 2015); Schram et al. (2009); Soss, Fording, and Schram (2011a).

91. They concentrate particularly on SNAP, which has grown substantially over recent years, filling some of the vacuum left by "cash" welfare's retrenchment.

92. See Gustafson (2009).

93. R. Miller (2014, 307).

94. Guam and the US Virgin Islands have their own fraud control systems (Cline and Aussenberg 2018, 10) but were excluded from the study due to these territories' distinct political characteristics.

95. These are state-level factors that previous research indicates may influence punitiveness in welfare programs. See Beckett and Western (2001); Soss, Fording, and Schram (2011a). I follow Beckett and Western (2001) in using incarceration rate as a measure of penal punitiveness. On "sampling for range," see Barker (2009); Becker (1998); Small (2009); Weiss (1994).

96. Berrey, Nelson, and Nielsen (2017); Ewick and Silbey (1998); Gilliom (2001); Gustafson (2011); McCann (1994).

97. One investigator and one administrator in Eastcoast were unable to travel to agency headquarters and were interviewed via phone.

98. Midatlantic permitted interviews with only a handful of higher-ranking agency representatives.

99. See Maynard-Moody and Musheno (2003); Watkins-Hayes (2009a; 2009b).

100. See Pugh (2013); Small (2009); Yin (2014).

101. See Winchester and Green (2019).

102. Sandelowski (2008, 875).

103. Zussman (2004, 362).

104. Gustafson (2009; 2011).

105. Pound (1910).

106. Headworth (2020b).

107. See Duneier (1999, 343–44).

108. See, e.g., Miron-Shatz, Stone, and Kahneman (2009).

109. See Jerolmack and Khan (2014).

110. Pugh (2013).

111. Brodkin (2013, 8).

112. For other studies of street-level bureaucrats' implementation of welfare policies, see Brodkin (1997); Lipsky ([1980] 2010); Riccucci (2005a; 2005b); Soss, Fording, and Schram (2011a); Watkins-Hayes (2009a; 2009b).

113. Gilliom (2001); Gustafson (2011).

114. Soss, Fording, and Schram (2011a).

115. Beckett and Western (2001); Garland (1985); Wacquant (2009).

116. Esping-Andersen (1990, 64).

117. Hinton (2016); J. Kohler-Hausmann (2017); Wacquant (2009).

118. Pound (1910).

119. Lipsky ([1980] 2010).

Chapter Two

1. See Hinton (2016); Marion (1994).

2. L. Miller (2016).

3. Kogan (2017); Lipsky ([1980] 2010); Maynard-Moody and Musheno (2003).

4. Pound (1910).

5. Gottschalk (2000); Hacker (2002).

6. Food and Nutrition Service (2016a).

7. R. Miller (2014); Soss, Fording, and Schram (2008).

8. Kornbluh (2007); Piven and Cloward (1977).

9. Hacker, Mettler, and Soss (2007); Piven and Cloward ([1971] 1993); Schneider and Ingram (1993).

10. Hancock (2004).

11. P.L. 94–505, Title II.

12. P.L. 95–452.

13. 36 FR 3869; 45 CFR 235.110.

14. Gardiner and Lyman (1984, 6).

15. P.L. 95–113, Title XIII, § 11 (e)(3), § 11 (e)(9)(B).

16. P.L. 95–113, Title XIII, § 6 (b)(1).

17. P.L. 95–113, Title XIII, § 15(b), § 15 (c).

18. P.L. 95–113, Title XIII, § 16 (a). This figure was later reduced to 50 percent. See P.L. 106–580, § 16(a)(7).

19. P.L. 99–198, § 1526.

20. Gustafson (2009, 659); J. Kohler-Hausmann (2015, 6; 2017, 172); Levin (2019, 154–55).

21. Wisconsin is the only state that divides SNAP and TANF administration between two agencies.

22. P.L. 104–193, § 402(a)(6).

23. P.L. 104–193, § 409(a)(4).

24. See Kogan (2017, 634).

25. Such fraud-specific second-order devolution decisions operate along-side broader decisions to cede welfare policy control to local jurisdictions. Soss, Fording, and Schram (2008) find that these more general second-order devolution decisions are more likely in states that have elected to adopt more stringent TANF rules; those with larger and more geographically concentrated Black populations; and those that spend more on their correctional systems.

26. Adair and Simmons (1988); Moore and Gates (1986).

27. Bostick et al. (1994); Brodkin (1993); Katz ([1989] 2013, ch. 4).

28. See Tani (2016) on the roles of the national government and federalist dynamics in the development of the US welfare system.

29. Food and Nutrition Service (2016b); Office of Family Assistance (2015).

30. Center on Budget and Policy Priorities (2015, 2).

31. Center on Budget and Policy Priorities (2015, 2).

32. Food and Nutrition Service (2015c, 11).

33. Allard (2009, 4).

34. Allard (2009, 4).

35. Schott and Floyd (2017, 7).

36. Clark (2016).

37. See, e.g., Harden (2012).

38. Lipsky ([1980] 2010, 225–26).

39. See Headworth and Ríos (2020).

40. See Food and Nutrition Service (2016c).

41. Brodkin (1986, 51).

42. P.L. 95–113, Title XIII, §16 (d)(1).

43. See Gabor et al. (2003, 52).

44. Provine et al. (2016, 3).

45. See L. Miller (2016).

46. J. Kohler-Hausmann (2017, 171–72).

47. Author's personal correspondence with Hawaii fraud control representative.

48. Engel (2016); Haltom and McCann (2004).

49. Haltom and McCann (2004, ch. 2).

50. Gring-Pemble (2003); Hancock (2004).

51. Haltom and McCann (2004, 63).

52. Haskins and Margolis (2014).

53. Dunleavy and Hood (1994); Hood (1995); Lane (2000).

54. Weber ([1922] 1978, 24–25).

55. Dunleavy et al. (2006).

56. Lipsky ([1980] 2010); Riccucci (2005a; 2005b); Watkins-Hayes (2009b).

57. Kogan (2017).

58. Pound (1910).

59. See, e.g., Scott (1998).

60. Gring-Pemble (2003); Hancock (2004).

61. See also L. Edelman (1990; 1992).

62. L. Miller (2016).

63. See Daston (1992); Daston and Galison (1992; 2007); Porter (1995); Tuchman (1972).

64. Weber ([1922] 1978, 978–80; [1947] 2012, 340).

65. Albrow (1992); Sutton (1991).

66. Michels ([1915] 1966); Mills ([1956] 2000).

67. M. Edelman (1964, 6).

68. See also Soss and Schram (2007).

69. Roscigno (2011, 362).

Chapter Three

1. Watkins-Hayes (2009b).

2. Headworth and Ríos (2020).

3. See Miller et al. (2015) on racial repression as a mill.

4. See also Bruhn, Nylander, and Lindberg (2016); Heimer (2001); Ulsperger and Knotterus (2009).

5. Prottas (1979).

6. Clients can use SNAP benefits to purchase "junk" food like candy and soda, as well as "luxury" food such as steak and shellfish. The relevant rules are federal; despite high-profile introductions of demonstrative state legislation such as Missouri's H.B. 813, states cannot change them (Delaney 2013; Ferdman 2015). FNS sometimes waives restrictions on hot and ready-to-eat food after natural disasters. Other nutrition assistance programs, such as the Special Supplemental Nutrition Program for Women, Infants, and Children (WIC), place more restrictions on product eligibility.

7. The state-level fraud control units on which this study focuses are not the only bureaucratic entities tasked with this objective. There are also county and local-level fraud control units within public assistance systems. Some states rely heavily on these relatively decentralized enforcement bodies. Some conventional criminal justice agencies also contain dedicated welfare fraud enforcement staff (see, e.g., Gustafson 2009).

8. Bollerman et al. (2016); Jesilow, Pontell, and Geis (1993); Sparrow (2000; 2008a).

9. Skolnick (1966, 27).

10. Brodkin (1997); Kogan (2017); Lipsky ([1980] 2010); Maynard-Moody

and Musheno (2003); Soss, Fording, and Schram (2011a, ch. 10); Watkins-Hayes (2009b).

11. Edin and Lein (1997, 41–45); Edin and Shaefer (2015, ch. 4); Gilliom (2001, 6).

12. Edin and Lein (1997, 144–45); Gilliom (2001, 88); Gustafson (2011, 154).

13. Gustafson (2011, 151–52).

14. Gustafson (2011, 110–12); Levine (2013, ch. 2); see also Herd and Moynihan (2018).

15. Gustafson (2011, 124, 129).

16. Edin and Lein (1997); Edin and Shaefer (2015).

17. Gustafson (2011, 139).

18. See Headworth (2020a).

19. Given the extent to which the number of referrals fraud units receive generally overwhelms their capacities to vigorously pursue them, as well as the nature of the pertinent incentive structures, fraud units have the luxury (from their perspective) of concentrating their efforts on those referrals seen as likely to produce the strongest cases. In terms of disparate impact of enforcement energies across different social groups and the reproduction of social inequalities, most important are the systematic factors shaping which cases get referred to fraud units and how their characteristics drive perceptions of their likelihood to produce successful outcomes. Chapter 8 explores these factors.

20. See Headworth (2020a).

21. Merton (1948).

22. See Brodkin and Majmundar (2010); Herd and Moynihan (2018).

23. Katz ([1989] 2013).

24. Sparrow (2008b, 53).

25. McCubbins and Schwartz (1984).

26. Joh (2014; 2016).

27. Investigators do not describe out-and-out identity misrepresentation as common but perceive it as more likely in individual–agency interactions that do not foreground direct face-to-face contact.

28. Moskos (2008, 65).

29. Headworth (2019).

30. See Headworth (2019) for details on how fraud investigators appropriate clients' social ties for enforcement purposes.

31. Van Cleve (2016, 166).

32. Gilens (1999); Gring-Pemble (2003); Hancock (2004); Katz ([1989] 2013); Schram (2006).

33. Many factors complicate welfare workers' relationships to clients, including strong views about politics and inequality and personal histories of socioeconomic disadvantage and professional marginalization. See Gilliom (2001); Schram et al. (2009); Soss, Fording, and Schram (2011a, ch. 10); Watkins-Hayes (2009a; 2009b, ch. 4).

34. Fraud workers see information that they actively solicit from knowledge-able informants as somewhat more reliable. See Headworth (2019).

35. Center on Budget and Policy Priorities (2014).

36. Food and Nutrition Service (2015a).

37. DiPrete and Eirich (2006); Merton (1968; 1995).

38. Sparrow (2008b, 56).

39. Sparrow (2008b, 188).

40. Cebula and Feige (2011).

41. Slack et al. (2017).

42. Desmond (2016); Edin and Lein (1997); Edin and Shaefer (2015).

43. Lipsky ([1980] 2010).

44. Leo (2008).

45. See Headworth (2019).

46. Eubanks (2018).

47. See also Eubanks (2018, 50).

48. Hasenfeld (1992); Soss, Fording, and Schram (2011b).

49. Halushka (2017).

50. 397 U.S. 254 (1970).

51. Headworth and Ossei-Owusu (2017).

52. Davis (2007); Moskos (2008, 50).

53. See Galanter (1974).

54. See Ewick and Silbey (1998, 71–73).

Chapter Four

1. Watkins-Hayes (2009b).

2. Gustafson (2009); J. Kohler-Hausmann (2017).

3. This punishment–provision hybridity parallels the rise of therapeutic and welfare logics in criminal justice systems. See Hannah-Moffat and Maurutto (2012); R. Miller (2014); Stuart (2016).

4. Morgan and Orloff (2017, 3).

5. Gustafson (2011, 18).

6. Bridges (2017); Katz (1995); Polsky (1991).

7. See Cook (1989).

8. Gilliom (2001); Gustafson (2009; 2011); Haney (2004); Neubeck and Caze-nave (2001); Piven and Cloward ([1971] 1993).

9. Welfare clients' privacy rights are subject to multiple forms of legal circum-scription. Courts have repeatedly ruled that Fourth Amendment protections against unreasonable search and seizure do not apply in the cases of welfare clients (or applicants) in the same way they would to other citizens. Key decisions include *Wyman v. James* (1971), which declared announced home visits by social

workers as a mandatory condition of program participation to be constitutional, and *Sanchez v. County of San Diego* (2006), which similarly upheld the constitutionality of mandatory home visits for assistance applicants. (As a US Supreme Court decision, *Wyman v. James* set nationwide precedent; *Sanchez v. County of San Diego*, on the other hand, is a decision from the Ninth Circuit, which has jurisdiction in nine western states.) See Bridges (2017); Gustafson (2009); Headworth and Ossei-Owusu (2017); Slobogin (2003). While Ashley reports needing consent for her home inspections, investigators say that they usually obtain consent, limiting this requirement's functional importance; Ashley recounts gaining consent to search around 80 percent of the time.

10. See, e.g., Leo (2008).

11. Headworth (2019).

12. See chapter 5 for more discussion of career transitions from conventional policing to welfare fraud enforcement.

13. Simon (2007).

14. Gustafson (2009); Hinton (2016).

15. Food and Nutrition Service (1996).

16. 81 FR 122:41288–41289.

17. P.L. 97–98, 95 Stat. 1213–1358. See also Gustafson (2011, 54).

18. Food and Nutrition Service (1998).

19. Soss and Weaver (2017, 577–78).

20. See Soss (1999).

21. Brayne (2014).

22. Lerman and Weaver (2014).

23. Brayne (2014).

24. This charging discretion has become increasingly concentrated in prosecutors' offices in recent years (Davis 2007; Stuntz 2001).

25. Shapiro (1987).

26. P.L. 96–249, 94 Stat. 357–370.

27. On criminalizing public assistance clients, see especially Gustafson (2009). For studies in other contexts, see, for example, Ferguson (2000), Rios (2006; 2011), and Theriot (2009) on criminalization of youth and Engel and Silver (2001), Lamb and Weinberger (1998; 2005), and Teplin (1984) on criminalization of mental illness.

28. Brown, Novack, and Frank (2009); Moskos (2008); Piliavin and Briar (1964).

29. Davis (2007); Stuntz (2001); Vogel (2007).

30. Beckett and Murakawa (2012); Desmond and Valdez (2013); Galanter (1991); Velloso (2013).

31. R. Miller (2014); Stuart (2016); Wacquant (2009).

32. Hagan (2010); Headworth (2014); Headworth and Hagan (2016).

33. Using a different state for this illustration permits a level of detail that could functionally identify an anonymized case study state.

34. HFSOIG (2013, 6).

35. HFSOIG (2006, 24).

36. HFSOIG (2005, 27).

37. HFSOIG (2003, 18).

38. Feinberg (1984; 1988).

39. Duff and Green (2005, 4).

40. Harcourt (1999).

41. Hirsch and Morris (2010).

42. Conklin (1977); Headworth and Hagan (2016).

43. State statutes (and allegations' specifics) determine what type of charges will be brought if a criminal case is pursued. Some states have statutes specifically criminalizing public assistance fraud, usually providing dollar thresholds for felonious fraud. In other cases, criminal prosecutions may be pursued under broader laws pertaining to fraud, theft, or perjury. One respondent explained his state's welfare fraud statute, which includes different gradations and sanction structures for frauds of different dollar amounts: "We need to establish three elements of welfare fraud . . . attempt, success, and intent, which is interpreted as 'failure to disclose a material fact intentionally.' We need to prove each of those three elements separately to establish a criminal case."

44. See Benson and Cullen (1998).

45. Gustafson (2009).

46. During criminal sentencing under uniform sentencing guidelines, downward departures are situations in which judges use their assessments of the particulars of a case as the basis for handing down shorter sentences. See Johnson, Ulmer, and Kramer (2008); Kramer and Ulmer (2002).

47. Depending on jurisdiction, this formal threshold for criminal prosecution may be as low as a few hundred dollars in alleged overpayment.

48. Merry (1998).

49. Balko (2014).

50. Blessett and Box (2016).

51. Harris (2016).

52. Garland (2017).

53. Foucault ([1977] 1979); Garland (1985); Simon (1993).

54. Beckett and Western (2001); Garland (2001); J. Kohler-Hausmann (2017); Wacquant (2009).

55. See Simon (2007).

Chapter Five

1. Seim (2017).

2. Watkins-Hayes (2009b); see also Soss, Fording, and Schram (2011a).

3. See Winchester and Green (2019).

4. Watkins-Hayes (2009b, 15).

5. Occupational trajectories into fraud control vary substantially between states. Fraud workers are more likely to have backgrounds in conventional law enforcement in states where they are commissioned as peace officers.

6. According to fraud workers, punitive adversarialism in welfare can beget similar defensive reactions among clients (Headworth 2020b).

7. Goffman (1974).

8. Boltanski and Thévenot (1999; 2006); Swidler (2001).

9. Winchester and Green (2019).

10. Adair and Simmons (1988); Moore and Gates (1986).

11. Hagan (2010).

12. Policy-wise, the zero-sum depiction is roughly accurate for TANF's block grant–based funding, for which the federal contribution has been flat at $16.5 billion annually since 1996. Under this system, the federal government contributes a set amount, to which the states are required to add their own matching funds; thus money that goes out to one family really can be money that is therefore no longer available for another. The zero-sum depiction does not really hold for SNAP. The federal government subsidizes the entire cost of SNAP benefits, splitting administrative costs with the states, and policy dictates that all households that qualify can receive benefits. Thus in no immediate sense does money that goes out to ineligible recipients thereby become unavailable for legitimate qualifiers.

13. See Espeland and Sauder (2016); Espeland and Stevens (2008); March and Simon (1958); Porter (1995).

14. See Cohen and Dromi (2018).

15. Winchester and Green (2019).

16. Maynard-Moody and Musheno (2003).

17. Morgan and Orloff (2017, 3).

Chapter Six

1. These restricted benefit funds continue a legacy of delimited or system-bound forms of provision for the poor with limited fluidity and fungibility (Zelizer 1994, ch. 4). Related examples include the feudal system, sharecropping, and company stores (Simmel [1900] 2011, 308–11).

2. The 2020 movement against racial injustice in policing highlighted police departments' budgets.

3. See Headworth and Ríos (2020) and Walsh, Dando, and Ormerod (2018) for details on how fraud unit gatekeepers make decisions about case referrals' dispositions.

4. See Blessett and Box (2016); Harris (2016); Harvard Law Review Editors (2015).

5. See, e.g., Illinois Department of Healthcare and Family Services Office of Inspector General (2018, 25).

6. Edin and Lein (1997); Edin and Shaefer (2015).

7. Food and Nutrition Service (2017).

8. Food and Nutrition Service (2017, 24).

9. These calculations are more feasible at the state level; Gustafson (2011, 184), for instance, found that in 2008, California spent $34 million on investigations to identify (let alone recover) $19.6 million in TANF overpayments.

10. Gustafson (2011, 184–85).

11. Bernstein and Isackson (2014); Manning (1977, 130–31).

12. Gardiner and Lyman (1984).

13. Brodkin (1986).

14. Brodkin and Majmundar (2010); Sheely (2013).

15. Friedrichs (2010); Shapiro (1990).

16. Benson, Madensen, and Eck (2009).

17. Buell (2013, 50); Mann (1985).

18. Fombrun (1996); Fombrun, Gardberg, and Barnett (2000); Power (2004; 2007; 2014); Power et al. (2009).

19. Fraser and Gordon (1994).

20. Chunn and Gavigan (2006).

21. Lara-Millán and Van Cleve (2017).

22. Both of these aspirations correspond to objectives pursued in conventional law enforcement agencies' community policing initiatives. See Skogan and Hartnett (1997).

23. See Headworth (2019); Headworth and Ríos (2020).

24. Brodkin (1993); Gustafson (2011, 70); Schneider and Ingram (1993).

25. Gustafson (2011, 3); Hughes (2019).

26. Espeland and Sauder (2016); Sparrow (2008b, 124).

27. Tilly (2006).

28. Hood (2011).

29. See Cohen and Dromi (2018).

30. Bourdieu (1994, 12).

31. Weber ([1919] 1946, 78).

32. Bourdieu (1994, 3).

33. Bourdieu (1994, 6).

34. Bourdieu (1994, 6–7).

Chapter Seven

1. Gilens (1999); Gordon (1990); Hancock (2004); Neubeck and Cazenave (2001); Hirschmann and Liebert (2001).

2. See also Cook (1989).

3. While race and ethnicity are formally rule irrelevant, immigration status is not: undocumented immigrants and many other noncitizen adults are categorically ineligible for SNAP. See Headworth and Ríos (2020) for a mixed-method analysis of how race/ethnicity and English proficiency interact in shaping fraud unit gatekeepers' responses to case referrals.

4. Women make up almost two-thirds of adult SNAP participants and about 85 percent of adult TANF participants (Falk 2014; Gray and Eslami 2014).

5. Epp (2009).

6. Van Cleve (2016, 53).

7. Weber ([1922] 1978, 975).

8. Bonilla-Silva (2003).

9. Fording, Soss, and Schram (2011); Lara-Millán and Van Cleve (2017).

10. Gilens (1999); Gring-Pemble (2003).

11. See Peck (2001).

12. Esping-Andersen (1990).

13. Korteweg (2003, 446).

14. See, e.g., Gilliom (2001); Gordon (1990; 1994); Gring-Pemble (2003); Mink and Solinger (2003); Skocpol (1992).

15. Mink (1998); Stone (1984, 12).

16. Korteweg (2003).

17. Mink (1998).

18. 2 Thess. 3:10. Peter did not note Lenin's use of this aphorism.

19. Houser et al. (2014); Roberts ([1997] 1999).

20. J. Kohler-Hausmann (2015).

21. J. Kohler-Hausmann (2007).

22. Watkins-Hayes (2009a).

23. See Sutton (1991).

Chapter Eight

1. Edin and Lein (1997); Gilliom (2001); Sarat (1990).

2. Gustafson (2011, 151).

3. Meyer and Rowan (1977).

4. Lipsky ([1980] 2010).

5. The presumption of future guilt contradicts foundational principles of the US legal system.

6. Regev-Messalem (2014).

7. Scott (1985).

8. Gilliom (2001).

9. Gustafson (2011, 166–67).

10. Halushka (2020, 241).

11. Prottas (1979).

12. Weber ([1922] 1978, 957).

13. Miller and Alexander (2016, 311).

14. This reflects a broader trend of imposing heightened expectations and responsibilities on members of society's most marginalized groups. See Miller and Stuart (2017, 542).

15. Eubanks (2018, 50, 53).

16. Gustafson (2011); Hancock (2004); J. Kohler-Hausmann (2017); Ocen (2012); Roberts (2012; 1492).

17. Amundson and Zajicek (2017, 395–96); J. Brown (2016); Chavez ([2008] 2013); Garand, Xu, and Davis (2017); Headworth and Ríos (2020); Massey (2007, 146).

18. Gilens (1999); Hussey and Pearson-Merkowitz (2013).

19. Wacquant (2009); Gustafson (2009; 2011); Beckett and Herbert (2009); Desmond and Valdez (2013).

20. Beckett and Western (2001).

21. Soss, Fording, and Schram (2011a, 112–13).

22. Fording, Soss, and Schram (2007); Schram et al. (2009).

23. Soss, Fording, and Schram (2011a, 126, 170). In general, Whites have more punitive criminal justice attitudes and lower levels of support for public welfare programs, compared to their racial/ethnic minority counterparts (Barkan and Cohn 2005; Gilens 1999).

24. Soss, Fording, and Schram (2011a, 166).

25. Soss, Fording, and Schram (2011a, 166).

26. Soss, Fording, and Schram (2011a, 158–59). This research also found that men (who constitute a small minority of TANF clients) were more likely to be sanctioned than women.

27. Epp, Maynard-Moody, and Haider-Markel (2014).

28. Soss, Fording, and Schram (2011a, 153).

29. Soss, Fording, and Schram (2011a, 176).

30. Watkins-Hayes (2009b).

31. Soss, Fording, and Schram (2011a, ch. 9).

32. Soss, Fording, and Schram (2011a, 223).

33. See also Bonilla-Silva (2003); Epp, Maynard-Moody, and Haider-Markel (2014); Headworth and Ríos (2020).

34. This echoes the greater likelihood of child abuse being detected and formally alleged in more system-involved families (Roberts 2002, 32).

35. See, e.g., Goffman (2014).

36. Foucault ([1977] 1979).

37. See Headworth (2020b).

38. Merton (1948).

39. This parallels conventional criminal justice, where the concentration of police activity in poor and minority neighborhoods tends to result in disproportionate numbers of poor and minority people stopped, arrested, processed, and punished (Moskos 2008, 157).

40. Falk (2014); Gray and Eslami (2014).

41. Mink (1998, 105).

42. Center on Budget and Policy Priorities (2018, 7).

43. Bridges (2011; 2017); Roberts ([1997] 1999; 2002; 2012).

44. Gustafson (2011, 74).

Chapter Nine

1. Weber ([1922] 1978, 978–80).

2. March and Simon (1958); Porter (1995).

3. Espeland and Sauder (2007; 2016); Espeland and Stevens (1998). See also Headworth (2020b).

4. Eubanks (2018, 50).

5. Hancock (2004); J. Kohler-Hausmann (2015).

6. Gring-Pemble (2003); Haltom and McCann (2004). For more on Linda Taylor, see Levin (2019).

7. See MacKenzie (2008).

8. Gustafson (2009, 701–7); *Sanchez v. County of San Diego* (2006).

9. *Rivera-Padilla v. Commonwealth of Virginia* (2009).

10. Davis (2013); Desmond (2016, 303); Headworth and Ossei-Owusu (2017); Lidman (2006). See also *Gideon v. Wainwright* (1963).

11. Berrey, Nelson, and Nielsen (2017).

12. See also Bridges (2017).

13. Gustafson (2009).

14. DeParle (2005); Gilliom (2001); Gustafson (2011); Sarat (1990).

15. See also Eubanks (2018).

16. Headworth (2019).

17. Edin and Shaefer (2015).

18. Food and Nutrition Service (2017, 2).

19. See Reiter and Coutin (2017).

20. J. Kohler-Hausmann (2007; 2015).

21. Gilliom (2001); Piven and Cloward ([1971] 1993); Soss, Fording, and Schram (2011a); Wacquant (2009).

22. Sarat (1990).

23. Roberts ([1997] 1999, 227).

24. Brodkin and Majmundar (2010); Sheely (2013). See also Herd and Moynihan (2018).

25. See also Stuart (2016, 13).

26. Garland (1985; 2017).

27. Beckett and Western (2001); Gustafson (2009); Hinton (2016); J. Kohler-Hausmann (2017); Wacquant (2009).

28. Harcourt (2001); I. Kohler-Hausmann (2018).

29. Garland (2001); Western (2006).

30. Phelps (2017).

31. See, e.g., *Wyman v. James* (1971); *Sanchez v. County of San Diego* (2006).

32. Eubanks (2018).

33. Headworth (2019).

34. Merton (1938).

35. Matt and Cook (1993).

36. Bollerman et al. (2016); Jesilow, Pontell, and Geis (1993); Sparrow (2000; 2008a).

References

Adair, John J., and Rex Simmons. 1988. "From Voucher Auditing to Junkyard Dogs: The Evolution of Federal Inspectors General." *Public Budgeting & Finance* 8 (2): 91–100.

Albrow, Martin. 1992. "Sine Ira et Studio—or Do Organizations Have Feelings?" *Organization Studies* 13 (3): 313–29.

Allard, Scott W. 2009. *Out of Reach: Place, Poverty, and the New American Welfare State*. New Haven, CT: Yale University Press.

Amundson, Kalynn, and Anna Zajicek. 2017. "A Case Study of State-Level Policymakers' Discursive Co-constructions of Welfare Drug Testing Policy and Gender, Race, and Class." *Sociological Inquiry* 88 (3): 383–409.

Balko, Radley. 2014. "How Municipalities in St. Louis County, Mo., Profit from Poverty." *Washington Post*, September 3.

Barkan, Steven E., and Steven F. Cohn. 2005. "Why Whites Favor Spending More Money to Fight Crime: The Role of Racial Prejudice." *Social Problems* 52 (2): 300–14.

Barker, Vanessa. 2009. *The Politics of Imprisonment: How the Democratic Process Shapes the Way America Punishes Offenders*. New York: Oxford University Press.

Becker, Howard S. 1998. *Tricks of the Trade: How to Think about Your Research While You're Doing It*. Chicago: University of Chicago Press.

Beckett, Katherine, and Steve Herbert. 2009. *Banished: The New Social Control in Urban America*. New York: Oxford University Press.

Beckett, Katherine, and Naomi Murakawa. 2012. "Mapping the Shadow Carceral State: Toward an Institutionally Capacious Approach to Punishment." *Theoretical Criminology* 16 (2): 221–44.

Beckett, Katherine, and Bruce Western. 2001. "Governing Social Marginality: Welfare, Incarceration, and the Transformation of State Policy." *Punishment & Society* 3 (1): 43–59.

Benson, Michael, Tamara D. Madensen, and John E. Eck. 2009. "White-Collar Crime from an Opportunity Perspective." In *The Criminology of White-Collar Crime*, edited by Sally S. Simpson and David Weisburd, 175–93. New York: Springer.

Benson, Michael L., and Francis T. Cullen. 1998. *Combating Corporate Crime: Local Prosecutors at Work*. Boston, MA: Northeastern University Press.

Bernstein, David, and Noah Isackson. 2014. "The Truth about Chicago's Crime Rates, Parts 1 and 2." *Chicago Magazine*, April 7 and May 19, 2014. http://www.chicagomag.com/Chicago-Magazine/May-2014/Chicago-crime-rates/.

Berrey, Ellen, Steve G. Hoffman, and Laura Beth Nielsen. 2012. "Situated Justice: A Contextual Analysis of Fairness and Inequality in Employment Discrimination Litigation." *Law & Society Review* 46 (1): 1–36.

Berrey, Ellen, Robert L. Nelson, and Laura Beth Nielsen. 2017. *Rights on Trial: How Workplace Discrimination Law Perpetuates Inequality*. Chicago: University of Chicago Press.

Blank, Susan W., and Barbara B. Blum. 1997. "A Brief History of Work Expectations for Welfare Mothers." *The Future of Children* 7 (1): 28–38.

Blessett, Brandi, and Richard C. Box. 2016. "Sharecropper Finance: Using the Justice System as a Public Revenue Source." *Public Integrity* 18 (2): 113–26.

Bobo, Lawrence, James R. Kluegel, and Ryan A. Smith. 1997. "Laissez-Faire Racism: The Crystallization of a Kinder, Gentler Anti-Black Ideology." In *Racial Attitudes in the 1990s: Continuity and Change*, edited by Steven A. Tuch and Jack K. Martin, 15–42. Westport, CT: Praeger.

Bollerman, Kerry, Alexander Egbert, Michael Fazio, and Bobby Graves. 2016. "Health Care Fraud." *American Criminal Law Review* 53:1393–458.

Boltanski, Luc, and Laurent Thévenot. 1999. "The Sociology of Critical Capacity." *European Journal of Social Theory* 2 (3): 359–77.

———. 2006. *On Justification: Economies of Worth*. Princeton, NJ: Princeton University Press.

Bonilla-Silva, Eduardo. 2003. *Racism without Racists: Color-Blind Racism and the Persistence of Racial Inequality in the United States*. Lanham, MD: Rowman & Littlefield.

Bostick, Leah K., Kevin Golladay, Nancy Watts, and Alan Levine. 1994. "State Verification and Eligibility Verification Systems (IEVS): Summary of Literature." Washington, DC: US Department of Health and Human Services.

Bourdieu, Pierre. 1994. "Rethinking the State: Genesis and Structure of the Bureaucratic Field." *Sociological Theory* 12 (1): 1–18.

Brayne, Sarah. 2014. "Surveillance and System Avoidance: Criminal Justice Contact and Institutional Attachment." *American Sociological Review* 79 (3): 367–91.

Bridges, Khiara M. 2011. *Reproducing Race: An Ethnography of Pregnancy as a Site of Racialization*. Berkeley: University of California Press.

———. 2017. *The Poverty of Privacy Rights*. Stanford, CA: Stanford University Press.

Brodkin, Evelyn Z. 1986. *The False Promise of Administrative Reform: Implementing Quality Control in Welfare*. Philadelphia, PA: Temple University Press.

———. 1993. "The Making of an Enemy: How Welfare Policies Construct the Poor." *Law & Social Inquiry* 18 (4): 647–70.

———. 1997. "Inside the Welfare Contract: Discretion and Accountability in State Welfare Administration." *Social Service Review* 71 (1): 1–33.

———. 2013. "Work and the Welfare State." In *Work and the Welfare State: Street-Level Organizations and Workfare Politics*, edited by Evelyn Z. Brodkin and Gregory Marston, 3–16. Washington, DC: Georgetown University Press.

Brodkin, Evelyn Z., and Michael Lipsky. 1983. "Quality Control in AFDC as an Administrative Strategy." *Social Service Review* 57 (1): 1–34.

Brodkin, Evelyn Z., and Malay Majmundar. 2010. "Administrative Exclusion: Organizations and the Hidden Costs of Welfare Claiming." *Journal of Public Administration Research and Theory* 20:827–48.

Brown, Jessica Autumn. 2016. "The New 'Southern Strategy': Immigration, Race, and 'Welfare Dependency' in Contemporary US Republican Political Discourse." *Geopolitics, History, and International Relations* 8 (2): 22–41.

Brown, Michael K. 1999. *Race, Money, and the American Welfare State*. Ithaca, NY: Cornell University Press.

Brown, Robert A., Kenneth J. Novack, and James Frank. 2009. "Identifying Variation in Police Officer Behavior between Juveniles and Adults." *Journal of Criminal Justice* 37:200–208.

Browning, Kellen. 2018. "Sacramento Welfare Investigators Track Drivers to Find Fraud. Privacy Group Raises Red Flags." *Sacramento Bee*, August 10. https://www.sacbee.com/news/local/article216093470.html.

Bruhn, Anders, Per-Åke Nylander, and Odd Lindberg. 2016. "Swedish 'Prison Exceptionalism' in Decline: Trends toward Distantiation and Objectification of the Other." In *Punishing the Other: The Social Production of Immorality Revisited*, edited by Anna Eriksson, 101–23. New York: Routledge.

Buell, Samuel W. 2013. "Is the White Collar Offender Privileged?" *Duke Law Journal* 63:1–54.

Cebula, Richard, and Edgar L. Feige. 2011. "America's Underground Economy: Measuring the Size, Growth and Determinants of Income Tax Evasion in the U.S." University of Wisconsin: Unpublished manuscript.

Center on Budget and Policy Priorities. 2014. "A Quick Guide to SNAP Eligibility and Benefits." Washington, DC: Center on Budget and Policy Priorities.

———. 2015. "Policy Basics: An Introduction to TANF." Washington, DC: Center on Budget and Policy Priorities.

———. 2018. "Chart Book: SNAP Helps Struggling Families Put Food on the

Table." Washington, DC: Center on Budget and Policy Priorities. https://www.cbpp.org/sites/default/files/atoms/files/3-13-12fa-chartbook.pdf.

Chavez, Leo R. (2008) 2013. *The Latino Threat: Constructing Immigrants, Citizens, and the Nation.* Stanford, CA: Stanford University Press.

Chunn, Dorothy E., and Shelley A. M. Gavigan. 2004. "Welfare Law, Welfare Fraud, and the Moral Regulation of the 'Never Deserving' Poor." *Social & Legal Studies* 13 (2): 219–43.

———. 2006. "From Welfare Fraud to Welfare as Fraud: The Criminalization of Poverty." In *Criminalizing Women,* edited by Gillian Balfour and Elizabeth Comack, 217–35. Black Point, Canada: Fernwood.

Clark, Krissy. 2016. "'Oh My God—We're on Welfare?!' The Strange Story of What 'Welfare' Has Become since the 1996 Reforms." *Slate,* June 2.

Cline, Daniel R., and Randy Alison Aussenberg. 2018. *Errors and Fraud in the Supplemental Nutrition Assistance Program.* Washington, DC: Congressional Research Service.

Cohen, Andrew C., and Shai M. Dromi. 2018. "Advertising Morality: Maintaining Moral Worth in a Stigmatized Profession." *Theory and Society* 47 (2): 175–206.

Conklin, John. 1977. *Illegal but Not Criminal: Business Crime in America.* New York: Prentice Hall.

Cook, Dee. 1989. *Rich Law, Poor Law: Different Response to Tax and Supplementary Benefit Fraud.* London: Open University Press.

Daston, Lorraine. 1992. "Objectivity and the Escape from Perspective." *Social Studies of Science* 22 (4): 597–618.

Daston, Lorraine, and Peter Galison. 1992. "The Image of Objectivity." *Representations* 40:81–128.

———. 2007. *Objectivity.* Cambridge, MA: MIT Press.

Davis, Angela J. 2007. *Arbitrary Justice: The Power of the American Prosecutor.* New York: Oxford University Press.

Davis, Martha F. 2013. "Participation, Equality, and the Civil Right to Counsel: Lessons from Domestic and International Law." *Yale Law Journal* 122:2260–81.

Delaney, Arthur. 2013. "How Food Stamp Resentment Feeds Crabby Conservatism." *Huffington Post,* July 1. http://www.huffingtonpost.com/2013/07/01/food-stamps-resentment_n_3518821.html.

DeParle, Jason. 2005. *American Dream: Three Women, Ten Kids, and a Nation's Drive to End Welfare.* New York: Penguin.

Desmond, Matthew. 2016. *Evicted: Poverty and Profit in the American City.* New York: Crown Publishers.

Desmond, Matthew, and Nicol Valdez. 2013. "Unpolicing the Urban Poor: Consequences of Third-Party Policing for Inner-City Women." *American Sociological Review* 78 (1): 117–41.

DiPrete, Thomas A., and Gregory M. Eirich. 2006. "Cumulative Advantage as a Mechanism for Inequality: A Review of Theoretical and Empirical Developments." *Annual Review of Sociology* 32:271–97.

Duff, R.A., and Stuart P. Green. 2005. *Defining Crimes: Essays on the Special Part of the Criminal Law*. New York: Oxford University Press.

Duneier, Mitchell. 1999. *Sidewalk*. New York: Farrar, Straus and Giroux.

Dunleavy, Patrick, and Christopher Hood. 1994. "From Old Public Administration to New Public Management." *Public Money & Management* 14 (3): 9–16.

Dunleavy, Patrick, Helen Margetts, Simon Bastow, and Jane Tinkler. 2006. "New Public Management Is Dead—Long Live Digital-Era Governance." *Journal of Public Administration Research and Theory* 16 (3): 467–94.

Edelman, Lauren B. 1990. "Legal Environments and Organizational Governance: The Expansion of Due Process in the American Workplace." *American Journal of Sociology* 1990 (95): 1401–40.

———. 1992. "Legal Ambiguity and Symbolic Structures: Organizational Mediation of Civil Rights Law." *American Journal of Sociology* 97 (6): 1531–76.

Edelman, Murray. 1964. *The Symbolic Uses of Politics*. Urbana: University of Illinois Press.

Edin, Kathryn, and Laura Lein. 1997. *Making Ends Meet: How Single Mothers Survive Welfare and Low-Wage Work*. New York: Russell Sage Foundation.

Edin, Kathryn J., and H. Luke Shaefer. 2015. *$2.00 a Day: Living on Almost Nothing in America*. New York: Houghton Mifflin Harcourt.

Edsall, Thomas Byrne. 1984. *The New Politics of Inequality*. New York: W. W. Norton.

Engel, David M. 2016. *The Myth of the Litigious Society: Why We Don't Sue*. Chicago: University of Chicago Press.

Engel, Robin Shepard, and Eric Silver. 2001. "Policing Mentally Disordered Suspects: A Reexamination of the Criminalization Hypothesis." *Criminology* 39 (2): 225–52.

Epp, Charles R. 2009. *Making Rights Real: Activists, Bureaucrats, and the Creation of the Legalistic State*. Chicago: University of Chicago Press.

Epp, Charles R., Steven Maynard-Moody, and Donald Haider-Markel. 2014. *Pulled Over: How Police Stops Define Race and Citizenship*. Chicago: University of Chicago Press.

Espeland, Wendy, and Mitchell Stevens. 2008. "A Sociology of Quantification." *European Journal of Sociology* 49 (3): 401–36.

Espeland, Wendy Nelson, and Michael Sauder. 2007. "Rankings and Reactivity: How Public Measures Recreate Social Worlds." *American Journal of Sociology* 113:1–40.

———. 2016. *Engines of Anxiety: Academic Rankings, Reputation, and Accountability*. New York: Russell Sage Foundation.

Espeland, Wendy Nelson, and Mitchell Stevens. 1998. "Commensuration as a Social Process." *Annual Review of Sociology* 24:313–43.

Esping-Andersen, Gøsta. 1990. *The Three Worlds of Welfare Capitalism*. Princeton, NJ: Princeton University Press.

Eubanks, Virginia. 2018. *Automating Inequality: How High-Tech Tools Profile, Police, and Punish the Poor*. New York: St. Martin's Press.

Ewick, Patricia, and Susan S. Silbey. 1998. *The Common Place of Law: Stories from Everyday Life*. Chicago: University of Chicago Press.

Falk, Gene. 2014. "Temporary Assistance for Needy Families (TANF): Eligibility and Benefit Amounts in State TANF Cash Assistance Programs." Washington, DC: Congressional Research Service.

Feinberg, Joel. 1984. *Harm to Others*. New York: Oxford University Press.

———. 1988. *Offense to Others*. New York: Oxford University Press.

Ferdman, Roberto A. 2015. "Missouri Republicans Are Trying to Ban Food Stamp Recipients from Buying Steak and Seafood." *Washington Post*, April 3. https://www.washingtonpost.com/news/wonk/wp/2015/04/03/missouri-republicans-are-trying-to-ban-food-stamp-recipients-from-buying-steak-and-seafood/.

Ferguson, Ann Arnett. 2000. *Bad Boys: Public Schools in the Making of Black Masculinity*. Ann Arbor: University of Michigan Press.

Fombrun, Charles. 1996. *Reputation*. New York: John Wiley & Sons.

Fombrun, Charles J., Naomi A. Gardberg, and Michael L. Barnett. 2000. "Opportunity Platforms and Safety Nets: Corporate Citizenship and Reputational Risk." *Business and Society Review* 105 (1): 85–106.

Food and Nutrition Service. 1996. "Evaluation of Food Retailer Compliance Management Demonstrations in EBT-Ready States and Related Initiatives." Washington, DC: United States Department of Agriculture.

———. 1998. "Cumulative PRWORA Q's and A's on Food Stamp Fraud, Disqualifications, and Recipient Claims." Washington, DC: United States Department of Agriculture.

———. 2015a. "Broad-Based Categorical Eligibility." Washington, DC: United States Department of Agriculture.

———. 2015b. "Supplemental Nutrition Assistance Program: Payment Error Rates FY 2014." Washington, DC: United States Department of Agriculture.

———. 2015c. "Supplemental Nutrition Assistance Program State Activity Report: Fiscal Year 2014." Washington, DC: United States Department of Agriculture.

———. 2016a. "2016 SNAP Retail Management Year End Summary." Washington, DC: United States Department of Agriculture.

———. 2016b. "Supplemental Nutrition Assistance Program Participation and Costs, 1969–2015." Washington, DC: United States Department of Agriculture.

——. 2016c. "Supplemental Nutrition Assistance Program Quality Control Review Handbook (FNS Handbook 310)." Washington, DC: United States Department of Agriculture.

——. 2017. "Supplemental Nutrition Assistance Program State Activity Report, Fiscal Year 2016." Washington, DC: United States Department of Agriculture.

Fording, Richard C., Joe Soss, and Sanford F. Schram. 2007. "Devolution, Discretion, and the Effect of Local Political Values on TANF Sanctioning." *Social Service Review* 81 (2): 285–316.

——. 2011. "Race and the Local Politics of Punishment in the New World of Welfare." *American Journal of Sociology* 116 (5): 1610–57.

Foucault, Michel. (1977) 1979. *Discipline and Punish: The Birth of the Prison.* New York: Vintage Books.

Fox, Cybelle. 2012. *Three Worlds of Relief: Race, Immigration, and the American Welfare State from the Progressive Era to the New Deal.* Princeton, NJ: Princeton University Press.

Fraser, Nancy, and Linda Gordon. 1994. "A Genealogy of Dependency: Tracing a Keyword of the U.S. Welfare State." *Signs* 19 (2): 309–36.

Friedrichs, David O. 2010. *Trusted Criminals: White Collar Crime in Contemporary Society.* Belmont, CA: Wadsworth.

Gabor, Vivian, Brooke Layne Hardison, Christopher Botsko, and Susan Bartlett. 2003. "Food Stamp Program Access Study: Local Office Policies and Practices." Washington, DC: Economic Research Service.

Galanter, Marc. 1974. "Why the 'Haves' Come Out Ahead: Speculations on the Limits of Legal Change." *Law & Society Review* 9 (1): 95–160.

——. 1991. "Punishment: Civil Style: Punishment Outside the Criminal Law in the Contemporary United States." *Israel Law Review* 25 (3–4): 759–78.

Gans, Herbert J. 1995. *The War against the Poor: The Underclass and Antipoverty Policy.* New York: Basic Books.

Garand, James C., Ping Xu, and Belinda C. Davis. 2017. "Immigration Attitudes and Support for the Welfare State in the American Mass Public." *American Journal of Political Science* 61 (1): 146–62.

Gardiner, John A., and Theodore R. Lyman. 1984. *The Fraud Control Game: State Responses to Fraud and Abuse in AFDC and Medicaid Programs.* Bloomington: Indiana University Press.

Garland, David. 1985. *Punishment and Welfare: A History of Penal Strategies.* Aldershot, UK: Gower.

——. 2001. *The Culture of Control: Crime and Social Order in Contemporary Society.* Chicago: University of Chicago Press.

——. 2017. "Punishment and Welfare: Social Problems and Social Structures." In *The Oxford Handbook of Criminology*, edited by Alison Liebling, Shadd Maruna, and Lesley McAra, 77–97. New York: Oxford University Press.

Gilens, Martin. 1999. *Why Americans Hate Welfare: Race, Media, and the Politics of Antipoverty Policy*. Chicago: University of Chicago Press.

Gilliom, John. 2001. *Overseers of the Poor: Surveillance, Resistance, and the Limits of Privacy*. Chicago: University of Chicago Press.

Gilman, Michele E. 2008. "Welfare, Privacy, and Feminism." *University of Baltimore Law Forum* 39 (1): 1–25.

Goffman, Alice. 2014. *On the Run: Fugitive Life in an American City*. Chicago: University of Chicago Press.

Goffman, Erving. 1961. *Asylums: Essays on the Social Situation of Mental Patients and Other Inmates*. New York: Anchor Books.

———. 1974. *Frame Analysis: An Essay on the Organization of Experience*. Cambridge, MA: Harvard University Press.

Goldberg, Chad Alan. 2007. *Citizens and Paupers: Relief, Rights, and Race, from the Freedman's Bureau to Workfare*. Chicago: University of Chicago Press.

Gordon, Linda (Ed.). 1990. *Women, the State, and Welfare*. Madison: University of Wisconsin Press.

———. 1994. *Pitied but Not Entitled: Single Mothers and the History of Welfare*. New York: Free Press.

Gottschalk, Marie. 2000. *The Shadow Welfare State: Labor, Business, and the Politics of Health Care in the United States*. Ithaca, NY: Cornell University Press.

———. 2006. *The Prison and the Gallows: The Politics of Mass Incarceration in America*. New York: Cambridge University Press.

Gray, Kelsey Farson, and Esa Eslami. 2014. "Characteristics of Supplemental Nutrition Assistance Program Households: Fiscal Year 2012." Washington, DC: USDA FNS Office of Policy Support.

Gring-Pemble, Lisa M. 2003. *Grim Fairy Tales: The Rhetorical Construction of American Welfare Policy*. Westport, CT: Praeger.

Gustafson, Kaaryn S. 2009. "The Criminalization of Poverty." *Journal of Criminal Law & Criminology* 99 (3): 643–716.

———. 2011. *Cheating Welfare: Public Assistance and the Criminalization of Poverty*. New York: New York University Press.

———. 2013. "Degradation Ceremonies and the Criminalization of Low-Income Women." *UC Irvine Law Review* 3:297–358.

Hacker, Jacob S. 2002. *The Divided Welfare State: The Battle over Public and Private Social Benefits in the United States*. New York: Cambridge University Press.

Hacker, Jacob S., Suzanne Mettler, and Joe Soss. 2007. "The New Politics of Inequality: A Policy-Centered Perspective." In *Remaking America: Democracy and Public Policy in an Age of Inequality*, edited by Joe Soss, Jacob S. Hacker, and Suzanne Mettler, 3–23. New York: Russell Sage Foundation.

Hagan, John. 2010. *Who Are the Criminals? The Politics of Crime Policy from Roosevelt to the Age of Reagan*. Princeton, NJ: Princeton University Press.

Haltom, William, and Michael McCann. 2004. *Distorting the Law: Politics, Media, and the Litigation Crisis*. Chicago: University of Chicago Press.

Halushka, John M. 2017. "Managing Rehabilitation: Negotiating Performance Accountability at the Frontlines of Reentry Service Provision." *Punishment & Society* 19 (4): 482–502.

———. 2020. "The Runaround: Punishment, Welfare, and Poverty Survival after Prison." *Social Problems* 67:233–50.

Hancock, Ange-Marie. 2004. *The Politics of Disgust: The Public Identity of the Welfare Queen*. New York: New York University Press.

Haney, Lynne. 2004. "Introduction: Gender, Welfare, and States of Punishment." *Social Politics* 11 (3): 333–62.

Hannah-Moffat, Kelly, and Paula Maurutto. 2012. "Shifting and Targeted Forms of Penal Governance: Bail, Punishment, and Specialized Courts." *Theoretical Criminology* 16 (2): 201–19.

Harcourt, Bernard E. 1999. "The Collapse of the Harm Principle." *Journal of Criminal Law & Criminology* 90:109–94.

———. 2001. *Illusion of Order: The False Promise of Broken Windows Policing*. Cambridge, MA: Harvard University Press.

Harden, Gil H. 2012. "Analysis of FNS' Supplemental Nutrition Assistance Program Fraud Prevention and Detection Efforts." Washington, DC: USDA Office of Inspector General.

Harris, Alexes. 2016. *A Pound of Flesh: Monetary Sanctions as Punishment for the Poor*. New York: Russell Sage Foundation.

Harvard Law Review Editors. 2015. "Policing and Profit." *Harvard Law Review* 128 (6): 1723–46.

Hasenfeld, Yeheskel. 1992. "Theoretical Approaches to Human Service Organizations." In *Human Services as Complex Organizations*, edited by Yeheskel Hasenfeld, 24–44. Newbury Park, CA: SAGE.

Haskins, Ron, and Greg Margolis. 2014. *Show Me the Evidence: Obama's Fight for Rigor and Results in Social Policy*. Washington, DC: Brookings Institution Press.

Headworth, Spencer. 2014. "Class, Crime, and Social Control in the Contemporary United States." In *The Routledge Handbook of Poverty in the United States*, edited by Stephen Nathan Haymes, María Vidal De Haymes, and Reuben Jonathan Miller, 367–77. New York: Routledge.

———. 2019. "Getting to Know You: Welfare Fraud Investigation and the Appropriation of Social Ties." *American Sociological Review* 84 (1): 171–96.

———. 2020a. "Broke People, Broken Rules: Explaining Welfare Fraud Investigators' Attributions." *Punishment & Society*. June 10. Online first. https://doi.org/10.1177/1462474520928131.

———. 2020b. "The Power of Second-Order Legal Consciousness: Authorities' Perceptions of 'Street Policy' and Welfare Fraud Enforcement." *Law & Society Review* 54 (2): 320–53.

Headworth, Spencer, and John Hagan. 2016. "White-Collar Crimes of the Financial Crisis." In *The Oxford Handbook of White-Collar Crime*, edited by Shanna R. Van Slyke, Michael L. Benson, and Francis T. Cullen, 275–93. New York: Oxford University Press.

Headworth, Spencer, and Shaun Ossei-Owusu. 2017. "The Accused Poor." *Social Justice* 44 (2/3): 55–82.

Headworth, Spencer, and Viridiana Ríos. 2020. "Listening to Snitches: Race/Ethnicity, English Proficiency, and Access to State Agencies' Enforcement Systems." Unpublished manuscript.

Heimer, Carol A. 2001. "Case and Biographies: An Essay on Routinization and the Nature of Comparison." *Annual Review of Sociology* 27:47–76.

Herd, Pamela, and Donald P. Moynihan. 2018. *Administrative Burden: Policymaking by Other Means*. New York: Russell Sage Foundation.

Hinton, Elizabeth. 2016. *From the War on Poverty to the War on Crime: The Making of Mass Incarceration in America*. Cambridge, MA: Harvard University Press.

Hirsch, Paul M., and Mary-Hunter Morris. 2010. "Immoral but Not Illegal: Monies vs. Mores amidst the Mortgage Meltdown." *Strategic Organization* 8 (1): 60–75.

Hirschmann, Nancy J., and Ulrike Liebert, eds. 2001. *Women and Welfare: Theory and Practice in the United States and Europe*. New Brunswick, NJ: Rutgers University Press.

Hood, Christopher. 1995. "The 'New Public Management' in the 1980s: Variations on a Theme." *Accounting, Organizations and Society* 20 (2): 93–109.

———. 2011. *The Blame Game: Spin, Bureaucracy, and Self-Preservation in Government*. Princeton, NJ: Princeton University Press.

Horder, Jeremy. 2015. "Excusing Information-Provision Crimes in the Bureaucratic State." *Current Legal Problems* 68 (1): 197–227.

Houser, Linda, Sanford F. Schram, Joe Soss, and Richard C. Fording. 2014. "Babies as Barriers: Welfare Policy Discourse in an Era of Neoliberalism." In *The Routledge Handbook of Poverty in the United States*, edited by Stephen Nathan Haymes, María Vidal De Haymes, and Reuben Jonathan Miller, 143–60. New York: Routledge.

Howard, Christopher. 1997. *The Hidden Welfare State: Tax Expenditures and Social Policy in the United States*. Princeton, NJ: Princeton University Press.

———. 2007. *The Welfare State Nobody Knows: Debunking Myths about U.S. Social Policy*. Princeton, NJ: Princeton University Press.

Hughes, Cayce C. 2019. "From the Long Arm of the State to Eyes on the Street:

How Poor African American Mothers Navigate Surveillance in the Social Safety Net." *Journal of Contemporary Ethnography* 48 (3): 339–76.

Hussey, Laura S., and Shanna Pearson-Merkowitz. 2013. "The Changing Role of Race in Social Welfare Attitude Formation: Partisan Divides over Undocumented Immigrants and Social Welfare Policy." *Political Research Quarterly* 66 (3): 572–84.

Illinois Department of Healthcare and Family Services Office of Inspector General. 2003. "2002 Annual Report." Springfield, IL.

———. 2005. "2004 Annual Report." Springfield, IL.

———. 2006. "2005 Annual Report." Springfield, IL.

———. 2013. "2012 Annual Report." Springfield, IL.

Jerolmack, Colin, and Shamus Khan. 2014. "Talk Is Cheap: Ethnography and the Attitudinal Fallacy." *Sociological Methods & Research* 43 (2): 178–209.

Jesilow, Paul, Henry N. Pontell, and Gilbert Geis. 1993. *Prescription for Profit: How Doctors Defraud Medicaid.* Berkeley: University of California Press.

Joh, Elizabeth E. 2014. "Policing by Numbers: Big Data and the Fourth Amendment." *Washington Law Review* 89:35–68.

———. 2016. "The New Surveillance Discretion: Automated Suspicion, Big Data, and Policing." *Harvard Law and Policy Review* 10:15–42.

Johnson, Brian D., Jeffery T. Ulmer, and John H. Kramer. 2008. "The Social Context of Guidelines Circumvention: The Case of Federal District Courts." *Criminology* 46 (3): 737–83.

Kagan, Robert A. 2001. *Adversarial Legalism: The American Way of Law.* Cambridge, MA: Harvard University Press.

Katz, Michael B. (1989) 2013. *The Undeserving Poor: America's Enduring Confrontation with Poverty.* New York: Oxford University Press.

———. 1995. *Improving Poor People: The Welfare State, the "Underclass," and Urban Schools as History.* Princeton, NJ: Princeton University Press.

Keiser, Lael R., Peter R. Mueser, and Seung-Whan Choi. 2004. "Race, Bureaucratic Discretion, and the Implementation of Welfare Reform." *American Journal of Political Science* 48 (2): 314–27.

Kogan, Vladimir. 2017. "Administrative Centralization and Bureaucratic Responsiveness: Evidence from the Food Stamp Program." *Journal of Public Administration Research and Theory* 27 (4): 629–46.

Kohler-Hausmann, Issa. 2018. *Misdemeanorland: Criminal Courts and Social Control in an Age of Broken Windows Policing.* Princeton, NJ: Princeton University Press.

Kohler-Hausmann, Julilly. 2007. "'The Crime of Survival': Fraud Prosecutions, Community Surveillance and the Original 'Welfare Queen.'" *Journal of Social History* 41 (2): 329–54.

———. 2015. "Welfare Crises, Penal Solutions, and the Origins of the 'Welfare Queen'." *Journal of Urban History* 41 (5): 756–71.

——. 2017. *Getting Tough: Welfare and Imprisonment in 1970s America*. Princeton, NJ: Princeton University Press.

Kornbluh, Felicia Ann. 2007. *The Battle for Welfare Rights: Politics and Poverty in Modern America*. Philadelphia: University of Pennsylvania Press.

Korteweg, Anna C. 2003. "Welfare Reform and the Subject of the Working Mother: 'Get a Job, a Better Job, and then a Career.'" *Theory and Society* 32 (4): 445–80.

Kramer, John H., and Jeffery T. Ulmer. 2002. "Downward Departures for Serious Violent Offenders: Local Court 'Corrections' to Pennsylvania's Sentencing Guidelines." *Criminology* 40 (4): 897–932.

Lageson, Sarah, Mike Vuolo, and Christopher Uggen. 2015. "Legal Ambiguity in Managerial Assessments of Criminal Records." *Law & Social Inquiry* 40 (1): 175–204.

Lamb, H. Richard, and Linda E. Weinberger. 1998. "Persons with Severe Mental Illness in Jails and Prisons: A Review." *Psychiatric Services* 49 (1): 483–92.

——. 2005. "The Shift of Psychiatric Inpatient Care from Hospitals to Jails and Prisons." *Journal of the American Academy of Psychiatry and Law* 33 (4): 529–34.

Lane, Jan-Erik. 2000. *New Public Management*. New York: Routledge.

Lara-Millán, Armando. 2014. "Public Emergency Room Overcrowding in the Era of Mass Imprisonment." *American Sociological Review* 79 (5): 866-87.

Lara-Millán, Armando, and Nicole Gonzalez Van Cleve. 2017. "Interorganizational Utility of Welfare Stigma in the Criminal Justice System." *Criminology* 55 (1): 59–84.

Leo, Richard A. 2008. *Police Interrogation and American Justice*. Cambridge, MA: Harvard University Press.

Lerman, Amy E., and Vesla M. Weaver. 2014. *Arresting Citizenship: The Democratic Consequences of American Crime Control*. Chicago: University of Chicago Press.

Levin, Josh. 2019. *The Queen: The Forgotten Life Behind an American Myth*. New York: Little, Brown.

Levine, Judith A. 2013. *Ain't No Trust: How Bosses, Boyfriends, and Bureaucrats Fail Low-Income Mothers and Why It Matters*. Berkeley: University of California Press.

Lidman, Raven. 2006. "Civil Gideon as a Human Right: Is the U.S. Going to Join Step with the Rest of the Developed World?" *Temple Political and Civil Rights Law Review* 15 (3): 769–800.

Lipsky, Michael. (1980) 2010. *Street-Level Bureaucracy: Dilemmas of the Individual in Public Services*. New York: Russell Sage Foundation.

MacKenzie, Donald. 2008. *An Engine, Not a Camera: How Financial Models Shape the Markets*. Cambridge, MA: MIT Press.

Mann, Kenneth. 1985. *Defending White-Collar Crime: A Portrait of Attorneys at Work*. New Haven, CT: Yale University Press.

Manning, Peter K. 1977. *Police Work: The Social Organization of Policing*. Cambridge, MA: MIT Press.

March, James G., and Herbert A. Simon. 1958. *Organizations*. New York: Wiley.

Marion, Nancy E. 1994. *A History of Federal Crime Control Initiatives, 1960–1993*. Westport, CT: Praeger.

Marx, Gary T. 2016. *Windows into the Soul: Surveillance and Society in an Age of High Technology*. Chicago: University of Chicago Press.

Massey, Douglas S. 2007. *Categorically Unequal: The American Stratification System*. New York: Russell Sage Foundation.

Matt, Georg E., and Thomas D. Cook. 1993. "The War on Fraud and Error in the Food Stamp Program: An Evaluation of Its Effects in the Carter and Reagan Administrations." *Evaluation Review* 17 (1): 4–26.

Maynard-Moody, Steven, and Michael Musheno. 2003. *Cops, Teachers, Counselors: Stories from the Front Lines of Public Service*. Ann Arbor: University of Michigan Press.

McCann, Michael. 1994. *Rights at Work: Pay Equity Reform and the Politics of Legal Mobilization*. Chicago: University of Chicago Press.

McCubbins, Mathew D., and Thomas Schwartz. 1984. "Congressional Oversight Overlooked: Police Patrols versus Fire Alarms." *American Journal of Political Science* 28 (1): 165–79.

Merry, Sally Engle. 1998. "The Criminalization of Everyday Life." In *Everyday Practices and Trouble Cases*, edited by Austin Sarat, Marianne Constable, David Engel, Valerie Hans, and Susan Lawrence, 14–39. Evanston, IL: Northwestern University Press.

Merton, Robert K. 1938. "Social Structure and Anomie." *American Sociological Review* 3 (5): 672–82.

——. 1948. "The Self-Fulfilling Prophecy." *Antioch Review* 8 (2): 193–210.

——. 1968. "The Matthew Effect in Science." *Science* 159 (3810): 56–63.

——. 1995. "The Thomas Theorem and the Matthew Effect." *Social Forces* 74 (2): 379–424.

Mettler, Suzanne. 2011. *The Submerged State: How Invisible Government Policies Undermine American Democracy*. Chicago: University of Chicago Press.

Meyer, John, and Brian Rowan. 1977. "Institutionalized Organizations: Formal Structure as Myth and Ceremony." *American Journal of Sociology* 83 (2): 340–63.

Meyer, Stephen Grant. 2000. *As Long as They Don't Move Next Door: Segregation and Racial Conflict in American Neighborhoods*. Lanham, MD: Rowman & Littlefield.

Michels, Robert. (1915) 1966. *Political Parties: A Sociological Study of the Oligarchical Tendencies of Modern Democracy*. New York: Free Press.

Miller, Lisa L. 2016. *The Myth of Mob Rule: Violent Crime and Democratic Politics*. New York: Oxford University Press.

Miller, Reuben Jonathan. 2014. "Devolving the Carceral State: Race, Prisoner Reentry, and the Micro-politics of Urban Poverty Management." *Punishment & Society* 16 (3): 305–35.

Miller, Reuben Jonathan, and Amanda Alexander. 2016. "The Price of Carceral Citizenship: Punishment, Surveillance, and Social Welfare Policy in an Age of Carceral Expansion." *Michigan Journal of Race and Law* 21:291–314.

Miller, Reuben Jonathan, Janice Williams Miller, Jelena Zeleskov Djoric, and Desmond Patton. 2015. "Baldwin's Mill: Race, Punishment, and the Pedagogy of Repression, 1965–2015." *Humanity & Society* 39 (4): 456–75.

Miller, Reuben Jonathan, and Forrest Stuart. 2017. "Carceral Citizenship: Race, Rights, and Responsibility in the Age of Mass Supervision." *Theoretical Criminology* 21 (4): 532–48.

Mills, C. Wright. (1956) 2000. *The Power Elite*. New York: Oxford University Press.

Mink, Gwendolyn. 1998. *Welfare's End*. Ithaca, NY: Cornell University Press.

Mink, Gwendolyn, and Rickie Solinger (Eds.). 2003. *Welfare: A Documentary History of U.S. Policy and Politics*. New York: New York University Press.

Miron-Shatz, Talya, Arthur Stone, and Daniel Kahneman. 2009. "Memories of Yesterday's Emotions: Does the Valence of Experience Affect the Memory-Experience Gap?" *Emotion* 9 (6): 885–91.

Monnat, Shannon M. 2010. "The Color of Welfare Sanctioning: Exploring the Individual and Contextual Roles of Race on TANF Case Closures and Benefit Reductions." *Sociological Quarterly* 51 (4): 678–707.

Moore, Mark H., and Margaret Jane Gates. 1986. *Inspectors-General: Junkyard Dogs or Man's Best Friend?* New York: Russell Sage Foundation.

Morgan, Kimberly J., and Ann Shola Orloff. 2017. "Introduction: The Many Hands of the State." In *The Many Hands of the State: Theorizing Political Authority and Social Control*, edited by Kimberly J. Morgan and Ann Shola Orloff, 1–32. New York: Cambridge University Press.

Moskos, Peter. 2008. *Cop in the Hood: My Year Policing Baltimore's Eastern District*. Princeton, NJ: Princeton University Press.

Natapoff, Alexandra. 2015. "Gideon's Servants and the Criminalization of Poverty." *Ohio State Journal of Criminal Law* 12:445–64.

Neubeck, Kenneth J., and Noel A. Cazenave. 2001. *Welfare Racism: Playing the Race Card Against America's Poor*. New York: Routledge.

Ocen, Priscilla A. 2012. "The New Racially Restrictive Covenant: Race, Welfare, and the Policing of Black Women in Subsidized Housing." *UCLA Law Review* 59:1540–82.

Office of Family Assistance. 2015. "TANF Caseload Data 2014." Washington,

DC: US Department of Health and Human Services, Administration for Children and Families.

———. 2018. "Annual Report: Fiscal Year 2017." Springfield, IL.

O'Regan, Philip. 2010. "'A Dense Mass of Petty Accountability': Accounting in the Service of Cultural Imperialism during the Irish Famine." *Accounting, Organizations and Society* 35 (4): 416–30.

Peck, Jamie. 2001. *Workfare States*. New York: Guilford Press.

Phelps, Michelle S. 2013. "The Paradox of Probation: Community Supervision in the Age of Mass Incarceration." *Law & Policy* 35 (1–2): 51–80.

———. 2017. "Mass Probation: Toward a More Robust Theory of State Variation in Punishment." *Punishment & Society* 19 (1): 53–73.

Piliavin, Irving, and Scott Briar. 1964. "Police Encounters with Juveniles." *American Journal of Sociology* 70 (2): 206–14.

Piven, Frances Fox, and Richard A. Cloward. (1971) 1993. *Regulating the Poor: The Functions of Public Welfare*. New York: Vintage Books.

———. 1977. *Poor People's Movements: Why They Succeed, How They Fail*. New York: Vintage Books.

Polsky, Andrew J. 1991. *The Rise of the Therapeutic State*. Princeton, NJ: Princeton University Press.

Pope, Andrew. 2018. "Making Motherhood a Felony: African American Women's Welfare Rights Activism in New Orleans and the End of Suitable Home Laws, 1959–1962." *Journal of American History* 105 (2): 291–310.

Porter, Robert, Vicki Welch, and Fiona Mitchell. 2019. "Adversarialism in Informal, Collaborative, and 'Soft' Inquisitorial Settings: Lawyers Roles in Child Welfare Legal Environments." *Journal of Social Welfare and Family Law* 41 (4): 425–44.

Porter, Theodore M. 1995. *Trust in Numbers: The Pursuit of Objectivity in Science and Public Life*. Princeton, NJ: Princeton University Press.

Pound, Roscoe. 1910. "Law in Books and Law in Action." *American Law Review* 44:12–36.

Power, Michael. 2004. "The Risk Management of Everything." *Journal of Risk Finance* 5 (3): 58–65.

———. 2007. *Organized Uncertainty: Designing a World of Risk Management*. New York: Oxford University Press.

———. 2014. "Risk, Social Theories, and Organizations." In *The Oxford Handbook of Sociology, Social Theory, and Organization Studies: Contemporary Currents*, edited by Paul Adler, Paul Du Gay, Glenn Morgan, and Mike Reed, 370–92. New York: Oxford University Press.

Power, Michael, Tobias Scheytt, Kim Soin, and Kerstin Sahlin. 2009. "Reputational Risk as a Logic of Organizing in Late Modernity." *Organization Studies* 30 (2–3): 301–24.

Prottas, Jeffrey Manditch. 1979. *People Processing: The Street-Level Bureaucrat in Public Service Bureaucracies.* Lexington, MA: Lexington Books.

Provine, Doris Marie, Monica W. Varsanyi, Paul G. Lewis, and Scott H. Decker. 2016. *Policing Immigrants: Local Law Enforcement on the Front Lines.* Chicago: University of Chicago Press.

Pugh, Allison J. 2013. "What Good Are Interviews for Thinking about Culture? Demystifying Interpretive Analysis." *American Journal of Cultural Sociology* 1 (1): 42–68.

Quadagno, Jill S. 1994. *The Color of Welfare: How Racism Undermined the War on Poverty.* New York: Oxford University Press.

Regev-Messalem, Shiri. 2014. "Trapped in Resistance: Collective Struggle through Welfare Fraud in Israel." *Law & Society Review* 48 (4): 741–72.

Reiter, Keramet, and Susan Bibler Coutin. 2017. "Crossing Borders and Criminalizing Identity: The Disintegrated Subjects of Administrative Sanctions." *Law & Society Review* 51 (3): 567–601.

Reyna, Christine, P. J. Henry, William Korfmacher, and Amanda Tucker. 2005. "Examining the Principles in Principled Conservatism: The Role of Responsibility Stereotypes as Cues for Deservingness in Racial Policy Decisions." *Journal of Personality and Social Psychology* 90 (1): 109–28.

Riccucci, Norma M. 2005a. *How Management Matters: Street-Level Bureaucrats and Welfare Reform.* Washington, DC: Georgetown University Press.

———. 2005b. "Street-Level Bureaucrats and Intrastate Variation in the Implementation of Temporary Assistance for Needy Families Policies." *Journal of Public Administration Research and Theory* 15 (1): 89–111.

Rios, Victor M. 2006. "The Hyper-criminalization of Black and Latino Male Youth in the Era of Mass Incarceration." *Souls* 8 (2): 40–54.

———. 2011. *Punished: Policing the Lives of Black and Latino Boys.* New York: New York University Press.

Roberts, Dorothy. (1997) 1999. *Killing the Black Body: Race, Reproduction, and the Meaning of Liberty.* New York: Vintage Books.

———. 2002. *Shattered Bonds: The Color of Child Welfare.* New York: Basic Books.

———. 2012. "Prison, Foster Care, and the Systematic Punishment of Black Mothers." *UCLA Law Review* 59:1474–500.

Roscigno, Vincent J. 2011. "Power, Revisited." *Social Forces* 90 (2): 349–74.

Rose, Nikolas. 2001. "The Politics of Life Itself." *Theory, Culture & Society* 18 (6): 1–30.

Rothstein, Richard. 2017. *The Color of Law: A Forgotten History of How Our Government Segregated America.* New York: W. W. Norton.

Sandelowski, Margarete. 2008. "Theoretical Saturation." In *The Sage Encyclopedia of Qualitative Methods*, edited by Lisa M. Given, 875–76. Thousand Oaks, CA: SAGE.

Sarat, Austin. 1990. "'. . . The Law Is All Over': Power, Resistance, and the Legal Consciousness of the Welfare Poor." *Yale Journal of Law & the Humanities* 2 (2): 343–79.

Schneider, Anne, and Helen Ingram. 1993. "Social Construction of Target Populations: Implications for Politics and Policy." *American Political Science Review* 87 (2): 334–47.

Schott, Liz, and Ife Floyd. 2017. "How States Use Funds under the TANF Block Grant." Washington, DC: Center on Budget and Policy Priorities.

Schram, Sanford. 2006. *Welfare Discipline: Discourse, Governance, and Globalization.* Philadelphia, PA: Temple University Press.

Schram, Sanford F., Joe Soss, Richard C. Fording, and Linda Houser. 2009. "Deciding to Discipline: Race, Choice, and Punishment at the Frontlines of Welfare Reform." *American Sociological Review* 74 (3): 398–422.

Scott, James C. 1985. *Weapons of the Weak: Everyday Forms of Peasant Resistance.* New Haven: Yale University Press.

———. 1998. *Seeing like a State: How Certain Schemes to Improve the Human Condition Have Failed.* New Haven: Yale University Press.

Seim, Josh. 2017. "The Ambulance: Toward a Labor Theory of Poverty Governance." *American Journal of Sociology* 82 (3): 451–75.

Shapiro, Susan P. 1987. "The Social Control of Impersonal Trust." *American Journal of Sociology* 93 (3): 623–58.

———. 1990. "Collaring the Crime, Not the Criminal: Reconsidering the Concept of White-Collar Crime." *American Sociological Review* 55:346–65.

Sheely, Amanda. 2013. "Second-Order Devolution and Administrative Exclusion in the Temporary Assistance for Needy Families Program." *Policy Studies Journal* 41 (1): 54–69.

Simmel, Georg. (1900) 2011. *The Philosophy of Money.* New York: Routledge.

Simon, Jonathan. 1993. *Poor Discipline: Parole and the Social Control of the Underclass 1890–1990.* Chicago: University of Chicago Press.

———. 2007. *Governing through Crime: How the War on Crime Transformed American Democracy and Created a Culture of Fear.* New York: Oxford University Press.

Skocpol, Theda. 1992. *Protecting Soldiers and Mothers: The Political Origins of Social Policy in the United States.* Cambridge, MA: Harvard University Press.

Skogan, Wesley G., and Susan M. Hartnett. 1997. *Community Policing, Chicago Style.* New York: Oxford University Press.

Skolnick, Jerome H. 1966. *Justice without Trial: Law Enforcement in Democratic Society.* New York: Macmillan.

Slack, Tim, Michael R. Cope, Leif Jensen, and Ann R. Tickamyer. 2017. "Social Embeddedness, Formal Labor Supply, and Participation in Informal Work." *International Journal of Sociology and Social Policy* 37 (3/4): 248–64.

Slobogin, Christopher. 2003. "The Poverty Exception to the Fourth Amendment." *Florida Law Review* 55:391–412.

Small, Mario. 2009. "'How Many Cases Do I Need?': On Science and the Logic of Case Selection in Field-Based Research." *Ethnography* 10 (1): 5–38.

Soss, Joe. 1999. "Lessons of Welfare: Policy Design, Political Learning, and Political Action." *American Political Science Review* 93 (2): 363–80.

———. 2017. "Food Stamp Fables: The *New York Times*' Front-Page Attack on Food Stamps over the Weekend Peddled Harmful Myths and Outright Lies." *Jacobin*, January 16. https://www.jacobinmag.com/2017/01/food-stamps-snap-welfare-soda-new-york-times/.

Soss, Joe, Richard C. Fording, and Sanford F. Schram. 2008. "The Color of Devolution: Race, Federalism, and the Politics of Social Control." *American Journal of Political Science* 52 (3): 536–53.

———. 2011a. *Disciplining the Poor: Neoliberal Paternalism and the Persistent Power of Race*. Chicago: University of Chicago Press.

———. 2011b. "The Organization of Discipline: From Performance Management to Perversity and Punishment." *Journal of Public Administration Research and Theory* 21 (suppl. 2): i203–i32.

Soss, Joe, and Sanford F. Schram. 2007. "A Public Transformed? Welfare Reform as Policy Feedback." *American Political Science Review* 101 (1): 111–27.

Soss, Joe, and Vesla Weaver. 2017. "Police Are Our Government: Politics, Political Science, and the Policing of Race-Class Subjugated Communities." *Annual Review of Political Science* 20:565–91.

Sparrow, Malcom K. 2000. *License to Steal: How Fraud Bleeds America's Health Care System (Updated Edition)*. Boulder, CO: Westview Press.

———. 2008a. "Fraud in the U.S. Health Care System: Exposing the Vulnerabilities of Automated Payment Systems." *Social Research* 75 (4): 1151–80.

———. 2008b. *The Character of Harms: Operational Challenges in Control* New York: Cambridge University Press.

Stone, Deborah A. 1984. *The Disabled State*. Philadelphia, PA: Temple University Press.

Stuart, Forrest. 2016. *Down, Out, and Under Arrest: Policing and Everyday Life in Skid Row*. Chicago: University of Chicago Press.

Stuntz, William J. 2001. "The Pathological Politics of Criminal Law." *Michigan Law Review* 100 (3): 505–600.

Sutton, Robert I. 1991. "Maintaining Norms about Expressed Emotions: The Case of Bill Collectors." *Administrative Science Quarterly* 36 (2): 245–68.

Swidler, Ann. 2001. *Talk of Love: How Culture Matters*. Chicago: University of Chicago Press.

Tach, Laura, and Kathryn Edin. 2017. "The Social Safety Net after Welfare Reform: Recent Developments and Consequences for Household Dynamics." *Annual Review of Sociology* 43:541–61.

Tahk, Susannah Camic. 2014. "The Tax War on Poverty." *Arizona Law Review* 56 (3): 791–851.

———. 2018. "The New Welfare Rights." *Brooklyn Law Review* 83 (3): 875–931.

Tani, Karen M. 2016. *States of Dependency: Welfare, Rights, and American Governance, 1935–1972.* New York: Cambridge University Press.

Teles, Steven Michael. 1996. *Whose Welfare? AFDC and Elite Politics.* Lawrence: University Press of Kansas.

Teplin, Linda A. 1984. "Criminalizing Mental Disorder: The Comparative Arrest Rate of the Mentally Ill." *American Psychologist* 39 (7): 794–803.

Theriot, Matthew T. 2009. "School Resource Officers and the Criminalization of Student Behavior." *Journal of Criminal Justice* 37:280–87.

Tilly, Charles. 2006. *Credit and Blame.* Princeton, NJ: Princeton University Press.

Tuchman, Gaye. 1972. "Objectivity as Strategic Ritual: An Examination of Newsmen's Notions of Objectivity." *American Journal of Sociology* 77 (4): 660–79.

Ulsperger, Jason S., and J. David Knotterus. 2009. "Illusions of Affection: Bureaucratic Ritualization's Relation to Emotional Abuse and Neglect in Nursing Homes." *Humanity & Society* 33:238–57.

Van Cleve, Nicole Gonzalez. 2016. *Crook County: Racism and Injustice in America's Largest Criminal Court.* Stanford, CA: Stanford University Press.

Velloso, João Gustavo Vieira. 2013. "Beyond Criminocentric Dogmatism: Mapping Institutional Forms of Punishment in Contemporary Societies." *Punishment & Society* 15 (2): 166–86.

Vogel, Mary E. 2007. *Coercion to Compromise: Plea Bargaining, the Courts, and the Making of Political Authority.* New York: Oxford University Press.

Wacquant, Loïc. 2001. "The Penalisation of Poverty and the Rise of Neoliberalism." *European Journal on Criminal Policy and Research* 9:401–12.

———. 2009. *Punishing the Poor: The Neoliberal Government of Social Insecurity.* Durham, NC: Duke University Press.

Walsh, David, Coral J. Dando, and Thomas C. Ormerod. 2018. "Triage Decision-Making by Welfare Fraud Investigators." *Journal of Applied Research in Memory and Cognition* 7 (1): 82–91.

Ward, Deborah E. 2005. *The White Welfare State: The Racialization of U.S. Welfare Policy.* Ann Arbor: University of Michigan Press.

Watkins-Hayes, Celeste. 2009a. "Race-ing the Bootstrap Climb: Black and Latino Bureaucrats in Post-reform Welfare Offices." *Social Problems* 56 (2): 285–310.

———. 2009b. *The New Welfare Bureaucrats: Entanglements of Race, Class, and Policy Reform.* Chicago: University of Chicago Press.

Weber, Max. (1919) 1946. "Politics as a Vocation." In *From Max Weber: Essays in Sociology,* edited by H. H. Gerth and C. Wright Mills, 77–128. New York: Oxford University Press.

———. (1922) 1978. *Economy and Society: An Outline of Interpretive Sociology.* Berkeley: University of California Press.

———. (1947) 2012. *The Theory of Social and Economic Organization.* Mansfield Center, CT: Martino.

Weiss, Robert S. 1994. *Learning from Strangers: The Art and Method of Qualitative Interview Studies.* New York: Free Press.

Western, Bruce. 2006. *Punishment and Inequality in America.* New York: Russell Sage Foundation.

Winchester, Daniel and Kyle Green. 2019. "Talking Your Self into It: How and When Accounts Shape Motivation for Action." *Sociological Theory* 37 (3): 257–81.

Woodbridge, Linda. 2001. *Vagrancy, Homelessness, and English Renaissance Literature.* Urbana: University of Illinois Press.

Woolford, Andrew, and Amanda Nelund. 2013. "The Responsibilities of the Poor: Performing Neoliberal Citizenship within the Bureaucratic Field." *Social Service Review* 87 (2): 292–318.

Yin, Robert K. 2014. *Case Study Research*, 5th ed. Thousand Oaks, CA: SAGE.

Zelizer, Viviana A. 1994. *The Social Meaning of Money.* New York: Basic Books.

Zussman, Robert. 2004. "People in Places." *Qualitative Sociology* 27 (4): 351–63.

Bills, Cases, and Statutes Cited

36 FR 3869.

45 CFR 235.110.

81 FR 122.

H.B. 813, 2017 Regular Session (Missouri 2017).

P.L. 94–505. "HEW Inspector General Act."

P.L. 95–113, Title XIII. "Food Stamp Act of 1977."

P.L. 95–452. "Inspector General Act of 1978."

P.L. 97–98, 95 Stat. 1213–1358.

P.L. 96–249, 94 Stat. 357–370.

P.L. 99–198, 99 Stat. "Food Security Act of 1985."

P.L. 104–193. "Personal Responsibility and Work Opportunity Act of 1996."

P.L. 106–580. "Food Stamp Act of 1977, as Amended through P.L. 106–580."

Gideon v. Wainwright, 372 U.S. 335 (1963)

Goldberg v. Kelly, 397 U.S. 254 (1970)

Wyman v. James, 400 U.S. 309 (1971)

Sanchez v. County of San Diego, 464 F.3d 916 (9th Cir. 2006)

Rivera-Padilla v. Commonwealth of Virginia (Court of Appeals of Virginia, 2009).

Index

Printed in the USA
CPSIA information can be obtained
at www.ICGtesting.com
LVHW051533170923
758449LV00007B/127